The Form of the Ancient Greek Letter

# A STUDY IN GREEK EPISTOLOGRAPHY

A DISSERTATION
Submitted to the Faculty of Letters of the Catholic University of America in Partial Fulfilment of the Requirements for the Degree of

DOCTOR OF PHILOSOPHY

By
THE REV. FRANCIS XAVIER J. EXLER, O. PRAEM., M. A.
OF ST. NORBERT'S PRIORY
WEST DEPERE, WIS.

*Wipf and Stock Publishers*
EUGENE, OREGON

Wipf and Stock Publishers
199 West 8th Avenue, Suite 3
Eugene, Oregon 97401

A Study in Greek Epistolography
The Form of the Ancient Greek Letter
By Exler, Francis Xavier J.
ISBN: 1-59244-215-3
Publication date: April, 2003
Previously published by Catholic University of America, January, 1923 .

ADMODUM REVERENDO DOMINO

BERNARDO HENRICO PENNINGS

CANONICORUM REGULARIUM ORDINIS PRAEMONSTRATENSIS PRIORI
COLLEGII SANCTI NORBERTI FUNDATORI AC PRAESIDI
HAS PRIMITIAS

D D D

AUCTOR

# TABLE OF CONTENTS

# BIBLIOGRAPHY

(Selected)

## Collections of Papyri.


| | |
|---|---|
| Archiv | Archiv für Papyrusforschung, Wilcken, U., Leipzig I 1901; II 1902; III 1903; IV 1907; V 1915; VI fascicles. |
| B. G. U. | Aegyptische Urkunden aus den Kgl. Museen zu Berlin, Griechische Urkunden. Berlin I - IV 1892 - 1905. |
| C. P. H. | Corpus Papyrorum Hermopolitanorum, Wessely C. Leipzig I 1905. |
| C. P. R. | Corpus Papyrorum Raineri, Wessely C., Veinna I 1895. |
| P. Amh. | The Amherst Papyri, Grenfell B. P., Hunt A. S. I (only lit.), II London 1901. |
| P. B. M. | Greek Papyri in the British Museum, Kenyon F., I 1893; II 1898; Kenyon F., Bell H., III 1907 London. (IV. V, late papyri) |
| P. Eleph. | Elephantine Papyri mit Beiträge von W. Schubart und W. Spiegelberg, Berlin 1907, von Rubenshon, O. |
| P. Fay. | Fayum Towns and their Papyri, Grenfell B. P., Hunt A. S., London 1900. |
| P. Flor. | Pap'ri Greco-Egizii, Papiri Fiorentini, Milan, I Vitelli G., II Comparetti D., III Vitelli G., 1905— |
| P. Gen. | Les Papyrus de Genève, Nicole Jules, I 1 1896, I 2 1900, Genève; Collection Papyrologique de Genève, 1909 Genève. |
| P. Giss. | Griechische Papyri zu Giesssen, I Korneman E., Egger O., Meyer P. M., Leipzig 1910. |
| P. Gizeh | Ptolemaic Papyri in the Gizeh Museum, in Archiv I pp. 57-65. |
| P. Good. | Greek Papyri from the Cairo Museum (Decennial Publications) Goodspeed E. J., Chicago 1902. also: Papyri from Karanis in Class. Phil. III (1902) 1-67. |
| P. Grenf. | Greek Papyri, series I Grenfell B. P. 1896; series II Grenfell B. P.. Hunt A. S., 1897 Oxford. |
| P. Hamb. | Griechische Papyrusurkunden der Hamburgschen Stadtbibliothek, Meyer P. M., Leipzig-Berlin I 1 1911; I 2 1913. |
| P. Hib. | The Hibeh Papyri, Grenfell B. P., Hunt A. S., I London 1906. |
| P. Iand. | Papyri Iandanae, Kalbfleisch, I Schäfer E., 1912; II Eisner L. 1913; III Spohn L., 1913; IV Spiess G., 1914. Leipzig. |
| P. Leipz. | Griechische Urkunden der Papyrussammlung zu Leipzig, Mitteis L., Wilcken U., I 1906 Leipzig. |
| P. Leid. | Papyri Graeci Musei Antiquarii Publici Lugduni-Batavi, Leemans C., Leyden I 1843; II 1885. |
| P. Lille | Papyrus Grecs de Lille, Jouquet P., Lesquier J., e.a.; Paris I 1907-8; II 1912. |
| P. Meyer | Griechische Texte aus Aegypten, Meyer P. M., Berlin 1916. |

P. Oxy. The Oxyrhynchus Papyri, Grenfell B. P., Hunt A. S., London. I 1898; II 1899; III 1903; IV 1904; V 1908; VI 1908; VII 1910; VIII 1911; IX 1912; X 1914; XI 1915; XII 1916; XIII 1919; XIV 1920: XV 1922. (V. XI, XIII, XV only literary texts).

P. P. The Flinders Petrie Papyri, (in Royal Irish Academy, Cunningham Memoirs VIII, IX, XI) Mahaffy J. P. I 1891; II 1893-4; Mahaffy J. P., Smyly G. J., III 1905. Dublin.

P. Rein. Papyrus Grecs et Démotiques, Reinach Th., e.a. Paris 1905.

P. Ryl. Catalogue of the Greek Papyri in the Rylands Library, Manchester I (only literary), II Johnson J de M., Martin V., Hunt A. S., Manchester 1915.

P. S. I. Papiri Greci e Latini della Societa Italiana, Vitelli e.a. I-VI.

P. Strassb. Griechische Papyri der Kgl. Universitätsbibliothek zu Strassburg Preisigke F., Leipzig 1912 (1906).

P. Hawara P. Hawara in Archiv

P. Tebt. The Tebtunis Papyri, Grenfell B. P., HuntA. S., Smyly J. G., Goodspeed E. J., London I 1902; II 1907.

Ostraka Griechische Ostraka, Wilcken U., Leipzig–Berlin I and II 1899.

Witk. Epistulae Privatae Graecae, Witkowski S., Leipzig 1911[2].

Wessely C. Palaeographie und Papyruskunde I—XIX Leipzig 1901-1920.

---

## Works on Papyri

Calderini Ar., Lettere Private dell' Egitto greco-romano. Bibl. in S. A. M.

S. A. M. Studi della scuola papirologica de Milano I 1915; II 1917; III 1920.

Gradenwitz O. Einführung in die Papyruskunde, Leipzig 1900.

Kenyon F., Palaeography of Greek Papyri, Oxford 1899.

Lietzmann H., Griechische Papyri, Bonn 1910.

Mayser E., Grammatik der griechischen Papyri aus der Ptolemäerzeit, Leipzig 1906.

Milligan G., Selections from the Greek Papyri, Cambridge 1910.

Mitteis L., Wilcken U., Grundzüge und Chrestomathie der Papyruskunde, Leipzig I 1, 2; II 1, 2; 1912.

Meyer P. M., Die Libelli aus den Decianischen Christenverfolgung. Anhang. 2 d. Abh. Kgl. Preuss. Akad. d. Wiss. 1910 p. 439.

Preisigke F., Sammelbuch griechischer Urkunden aus Aegypten.

Schubert W., Einführung in die Papyruskunde, Berlin 1918.

---

General collections of ancient letters (exclusive of papyri).

Hercher, R., Epistolographi Graeci, Paris 1873.

Orelli J. C., Collection Epistularum Graecarum, Leipzig 1815.

Westermann A., De Epistolarum Scriptoribus Graecis, Leipzig 1851-8.

Lightfoot J. B., The Apostolic Fathers (J. R. Harmer) London 1891.

Migne, Patrologia Graeca, Paris 1857—1866.

---

## Special Works.


Albert P., Le genre epistolaire chez les anciens, Paris (1869) 1896.

Bähr J., Epistolographie, in Ersch-Grüber Encyclopaedie.

Bentley R. A., Dissertation upon the Epistles of Phalaris with an answer to the Objections of Ch. Boyle, London 1699; Leipzig 1823; reprinted in the Bohne Library by W. Wagner 1874.

Brinkmann A., Der älteste Briefsteller, in Rh. Mus. 64 (1909) 310 seqq.

Deissmann A., Epistolary Literature, in Encyclopedia Biblica. II col. 1323 seqq.

Deissmann A., Licht vom Osten, Tübingen 1909 (Engl. Light from the Ancient East, London (1910) 1911.)

Deissmann A., Bible Studien, Marburg 1895 (Engl. Bible Studies[2] 1903).

Dziatzko C., Der Brief, in Pauly-Wissowa Realencyclopaedie II 836 seqq., Stuttgart 1899.

Gerhardt G. A., Untersuchungen zur Geschichte des Griechischen Briefes, in Philologus 64 (1905) 27 seqq.

Hercher R., Zu dem Griechischen Epistolographen, in Hermes 4 (1870).

Horn R. C. Life and Letters in the Papyri, in Class. Journal 17 (1922) 487 seqq.

Huit Ch., Les Epistolographes Grecs, in Revue des Études Grecques 2 (1889) 149 seqq.

Lafoscade L., De Epistulis aliisque titulis imperatorum magistratuumque Romanorum quas usque ad Constantinum Graece scriptas lapides papyrive servaverunt. Diss. Paris 1902.

Martin V., Essai sur les lettres de St. Basil le grand, Rennes 1865.

Peter H., Der Brief in der römischen Literatur, Leipzig 1901.

Preisigke F., Familienbriefe aus alter Zeit, in Preuss. Jahrb. 108 (1902) 88 seqq.

Rabe H., Aus Rhetoren-handschriften: Griechische Briefsteller, in Rh. Mus. 64 (1909) 284 seqq.

Roberts W., History of Letter-writing from the earliest period to the Fifth Century, London (1843) 1848.

Seeck O., Der Antike Brief, in Deutsche Rundsch. 133 (1907).

Wehofer Th. W., Untersuchungen zur altchristlichen Epistolographie, in Wien Akad. Phil. Hist. Kl. 143 (1900).

Wenger L., Der Eid in den griechischen Papyrusurkunden, in Zeitschrift der Savigny Stiftung f. Rechtsg. Rom. Abt. 23 (1902) 158 seqq.

Ziemann F., De Epistularum Graecarum Formulis Sollemnibus Quaestiones Selectae, in Diss. Phil. Hal. 18 (1911) 253 seqq. Cp. Berl. Philol. Woch. 32 (1912) 321 seqq. (Haas).


---

## Handbooks and General Reference Works


Bardenhewer O., Geschichte der altkirchlichen Literatur, Freiburg 1913[2].

Bardenhewer O., Patrologie, Engl. transl. by Shahan Th., St. Louis 1908.

Batiffol P., La Littérature Grecque, Paris 1897[2], 1908[4].

Birt, Th., Das Antike Buchwesen, Berlin 1882.

Ceillier R., Histoire générale des Auteurs Sacrés Ecclésiastiques., Paris (1729—1763) 1858—1865.
Croiset M., Histoire de la Littérature Grecque, Paris (1901) 1910[3].
Egger E., Memoires de la Littérature Ancienne, Paris 1862.
Fabricius J. A. Bibliotheca Graeca, Hamburg 1708 I 2 ch. 10.
Jordan H., Geschichte der altchristlichen Literatur, Leipzig 1911.
Norden E., Das Antike Kunstprosa, Leipzig (1896) 1909.
Susemihl F., Geschichte der griechischen Literatur in der Alexanderzeit II 579 seqq. Leipzig 1892.
Wendland P., Die urchristlichen Literaturformen, Tübingen 1912.
Wessely C., Patrologia Orientalis IV 2, 135 seqq.

# PREFACE

During the last fifty years the sands and the cemeteries of Egypt have given up a precious treasure of papyrus documents of a greatly varied nature. Among these documents were found many letters, both private and official, as well as other documents which exhibited an epistolary form. These letters cover a period extending from the beginning of the third century before Christ far into the Christian era.

In the past years this epistolary material has been studied from various angles by scholars both in Europe and in America. The result of their combined efforts has been that we have now a much clearer idea of social and official life in Egypt during the Ptolemaic and the Roman periods. In the field of philology also much was gained by a study of these documents.

It must be borne in mind that at the present stage of things we must proceed warily, and not draw conclusions too hastily from this material. On account of the vastness of these documents we are truly warranted in basing upon them conclusions of real probability. Yet we must not lose sight of the fact that these documents cover an extended period; that they are confined to a relatively small part of the Greek world; and especially, that they have all been preserved by accidental circumstances without a view to their value, whilst a far greater number of documents of at least equal value have perished. Although the number of the papyri recovered from Egypt is very large, it constitutes but a small fraction of what was actually written. On the strength of the documents we have we are justified in forming conclusions. But future discoveries may yield supplementary matter, or bring to light new material, which may compel us to revise, either completely or in part, the conclusions we have so far reached.

It was our intention in the beginning, to investigate the origin of the Greek letter-form. This study we intended to base exclusively on an examination of the papyri. After all that has been written, we are still in doubt as to how much is fact, how much rhetorical fiction, in the literary letters that have come down to us. If the origin of the Greek epistolary form was to be ascertained, only such material could be used as is of undoubted authenticity. It was soon found, however, that the material at hand does not warrant any conclusions concerning the origin of the Greek epistolary form. There is a remarkable similiarity in the letter-forms throughout the Ptolemaic and the Roman periods. In fact, apart from a certain pompousness in the later Roman documents, there is no radical difference between the letter-form exhibited by documents dated in the third century before Christ, and that found in the letters of the third century of the Christian era. If there has been no external influence shaping these forms, we must assume that there has been a long period of development before the third century B. C.,—if the same rate of progress then obtained as is manifested during the subsequent six hundred years. Unfortunately our papyri do not take us back, at least in the field of epistolography, before the third century B. C.; that is, the earliest among them belong to a period more than one hundred years after the golden age of Greece. This aim, therefore, had to be abandoned.

Until the historical development of the Greek epistolary forms has been established, there is, in our opinion, little use in studying the origin of the grammatical phrases employed in epistolary expressions. There is the same lack of historical evidence as in the case of the letter-form itself. In the earliest letters we have practically the same grammatical formulas as are in use in the latest letters of the Roman period. There would be too much danger of a "post factum" explanation. Such an explanation might be quite suitable, and form an acceptable hypothesis; but it would lack historical proof. Just as the papyri found during the last fifty years have proved beyond doubt that the well-known salutatory phrases in Latin letters are but renderings of the salutations in vogue among the Greeks, so also future discoveries may prove that both the form and the grammar of Greek epistolary phrases have been influenced by external agents, such for instance as the rich epistolary literature of the oriental empires.

When we found it to be futile, at this time, to investigate the origin of the Greek letter-form, we decided to employ the material we had collected to illustrate the history of the Greek letter-form during the Ptolemaic and the Roman periods. Part of this work has already been done by Ferdinand Ziemann in a dissertation submitted to the Faculty of the University of Halle, Saxony, in 1911. But since that time several important collections of papyri have been published, notably eight volumes of the Oxyrhynchus Papyri (VIII - XV inclusive); the Rylands Papyri, containing many letters of the Ptolemaic period; the second volume of the Lille Papyri; the six volumes of the papyri published by the Societa Italiana; the Hamburg Papyri; the Florence Papyri; the Giessen Papyri; the Meyer Papyri; etc., so that it was thought worth while to undertake the task, for the purpose of ascertaining if any new light could be shed on the matter.

It has been our aim to present in full the evidence on which the conclusions are based. Accordingly numerous texts have been quoted in full, that they may speak for themselves. The basis for arrangement has been similarity in form and chronological sequence. On account of the many slight variations in the texts, at times only the chronological order could be observed. Where the texts are so numerous that it is not possible to quote all, only references have been given, it being understood that not all similar texts are referred to, but only a sufficient number to show the relative frequency of their occurrence. Such comments as are necessary have been added at the end of each section or chapter.

The material we have gathered has been classified under four heads: The Opening Formulas; The Closing Formulas; The Date Formulas; Conventional Phrases. Each chapter is preceded by a brief statement of its internal arrangement. We have premised as an Introduction a brief survey of Greek Epistolography. At the end will be found a summary of those conclusions which seem warranted by the material at hand. The Bibliography contains a list of the principal collections of Papyri, with the abbreviations in general use among scholars; also a selected list of works more or less related to the subject.

In this dissertation we have limited ourselves to the period between the third century B. C. and the third century A. D. The earliest epistolary papyri now extant date from the second quarter of the third century B. C. The end of the reign of Diocletian forms a convenient "terminus ad quem." The traces of what is considered characteristic of the Byzantine period are found during the generation which preceded the transfer of the imperial government from Rome to Constantinople.

# INTRODUCTION

The discovery in Egypt of large quantities of ancient papyri has given the scholar new material for learned research. For in these papyri is contained much valuable information about social customs and conditions in ancient times; about philosophy and art; about language and literature. Much may be learned about the mechanics of language, the history of grammar, the development of speech. For the study of epistolography, also, they prove useful, since they supply a large number of authentic letters.

That writing was well known among the ancient oriental nations, need not be stressed here. The excavations in Crete have brought to light that in the Minoan kingdom the art of writing was practised. And as the Minoan civilization is supposed to be reflected in the Mycenean civilization which we find depicted in the Homeric poems, it would seem a probable inference that the Homeric Greeks were not unacquainted with the art. In fact Homer himself says as much in Iliad VI 169:

*γράψας ἐν πίνακι πτυκτῷ θυμοφθόρα πολλά.*

The letter may be defined as a "written conversation." This definition is rather generally accepted. According to Cicero, the purpose of the letter is "ut certiores faceremus absentes."[1] Huit calls it a "long-distance conversation, a connective between persons separated in space, yet united in affections or in community of interests."[2] Deissmann also defines the letter by the function it serves. "The function of the letter is to maintain intercourse, in writing, between persons who are separated by distance."[3] Hermann Jordan defines the letter as "in itself the simplest written form of communication with one person or with one more or less definite group of persons."[4] In its simplest form the letter is essentially intimate, individual, personal, intended exclusively for the eyes of the person or persons to whom it is addressed. It

[1]Ad Fam. II 4.
[2]Les Epistolographes Grecs, in Revue des Études Grecques 2 (1889) 149-163.
[3]Epistolary Literature, in Encyclopedia Biblica II.
[4]Geschichte der altchristlichen Litteratur 123.

is of an ephemeral character; called forth by the need of the moment, it has no purpose of existence, when this need has been attended to. In no essential particular does it differ from a spoken conversation. It concerns only the writer and his correspondent; as far as others are concerned, it is supposed to be secret and sacred.[5]

As a rule, a letter, once it has been read, has no further interest. Consequently the vast majority of such letters are destroyed. Their loss would not be regretted, were it not for the fact that they may have a scientific or a literary value quite independent of their epistolary nature. At times a special importance attaches to letters which makes their preservation worth while. Thus official or commercial letters are often kept for future reference. Occasionally letters are kept on account of their contents or their form. Of the great number of letters written relatively few are of this kind.

The letter is called a written conversation. Practically anything can be the subject of a conversation; and if such a conversation were committed to writing, it would quite properly form a letter. The letter, unrestricted as it is by the conventions of other forms of literature, at one time found great favor with a certain class of writers—the sophists—, especially because it offered them an opportunity for displaying their learning. Thus epistolography came into being as a branch of literature.

It is not easy to determine when a letter is, and when it is not, literature. Scholars have divided letters into "literary" and "non-literary" letters, meaning by the former "fictitious" and by the latter "real" letters. This distinction does not seem to hold, unless the terms are modified. For "literary" letters may be of such poor workmanship as to be undeserving of being ranked as literature; whereas "non-literary" letters may be literary gems. It seems better to distinguish letters as "real" and "unreal," with the understanding that neither kind is necessarily literature.

A letter may have been destined for one definite person or group of persons. In such a case it is a real letter and is not destined, directly or indirectly, for the public at large. It will be, what every real letter ought to be, a frank intercourse between distant persons. Such letters may be devoid of literary merit, as for instance a large number of the letters found among the

[5]Epistolary Literature, in Encyclopedia Biblica II.

Oxyrhynchus papyri—though these have great value for the linguist, the philologist, and others,— or they may have a distinct literary value, such as the letters of Cicero or of St. Basil. This polished form of letter is as genuine a letter as the unpolished specimen. The difference lies in the fact that the latter is written by one unskilled in the literary art, whereas the former is the product of a litterateur. It is not impossible that the latter, aware of his literary skill and of the value of his writing, does not forget that his correspondence, though destined for a private person only, may fall into the hands of others. In so much as this possibility influences his writing, his letters lose the character of the real letter, and approach that of the unreal or "literary" letter.

The "literary" letter may be defined as an essay in the form of a real letter, not necessarily addressed to any definite individual or group of individuals, and destined, at least indirectly, and ultimately for the world at large. It may be of three principal kinds: a real letter, in which the possibility of its becoming public has influenced the writing; a fictitious letter, in every respect of form and content a real letter, but addressed to a purely imaginary being, the real addressee being the public at large; and a treatise, which has some of the external forms of the letter, such as the salutation and the signature, but as to contents is in reality a didactic composition.

The epistolary treatise has little in common with the letter. Like the epistolary sermon, it serves a didactic purpose, and is often drawn out at great length. Though length as such does not affect the nature of a letter, too great length would establish a presumption against any work being properly classified under epistolography.

The real letter is by far the most common. Only persons possessing literary skill are able to produce the unreal or "literary" letter. The transition from the real letter to this form of literature is gradual, so that in many cases it is not easy to draw a line of demarcation. Some writers call the "literary" letter "epistle" to distinguish it from the real letter. What is of importance in the latter, such as address or signature, becomes in the epistle ornamental detail added merely to maintain the illusion of this particular literary form. A real letter differs from an epistle, as nature differs from art.[6]

[6]Deissmann, l. c.

The main difference between the epistle and the polished real or "non-literary" letter is that the latter is private, whereas the former is intended primarily for publicity.[7] It is difficult, if not impossible, to determine in each case whether a certain document belongs to the class of polished real letters or to that of epistles. There is of course a wide range of intermediary forms. Some of the epistles in the New Testament are evidently real letters, for instance St. Paul's epistle to Philemon. Perhaps most of the epistles of St. Paul come under this head. Yet much of what is called letter, especially in the Apostolic and the Patristic age, would be more properly classified as treatise, whether theological or homiletic.

However much one feels inclined to divide the history of epistolography into pre-Christian and Christian, such a division must be rejected, because it lacks an historic basis, and is therefore unsatisfactory. The birth of Christ does not mark a radical change in letter-writing as such. The pagan letter continued its course, developing or degenerating, as literature in general was affected in such manner; and the Christian letter is simply a new use to which an old instrument was put, following its own course of development, and reaching its greatest perfection in the fourth century. A general division into Pagan and Christian letter seems to have the advantage of being both logical and historical.

Of the great mass of ancient letters only a relatively small number have come down to us. The Aldus Brothers of Venice published 1600 Greek letters attributed to sixty different authors. Most of these letters, with many additions, have been reprinted in Hercher's Epistolographi Graeci. The Patristic letters are very numerous; they have been published in Migne's Patrologia Graeca. The various collections of papyri, published during the last twenty-five years, contain many private and official letters.

The origin of letter-writing is unknown. In ancient times the invention of this art was attributed to Atossa, daughter of Cyrus and wife of Cambyses. It is possible that this queen contributed something towards the development of the epistolary art. The earliest reference in Greek literature to the art of letter-writing is in Homer, Iliad VI 169. Whether the writing of letters was a common art in Homer's day may perhaps be open to doubt. There is no proof for it, remarks W. Roberts.[8] To which may

[7]Deissmann, l. c.
[8]History of Letter-writing, London 1843.

be replied that there is no proof against it either. The argument from silence about the non-existence of anything is not convincing. It is not at all inconceivable that the advanced Homeric civilization was acquainted with an art which was practised at the time in neighboring countries.

Time has been more generous concerning a later period of Greek literary history. Up to 1881 only about 150 papyri were known in Europe. Since then numerous papyri have been found by the Fellahs while digging among the ancient cities of the Fayoum and other places in Egypt. These papyri were acquired by archduke Rainer of Austria, and, later, by various universities and learned societies in Europe. Messrs. Grenfell and Hunt were fortunate enough to discover valuable papyri at Oxyrhynchus, which have since been published as the Oxyrhynchus Papyri, the latest volume appearing only last year (volume XV). This collection, one of the most extensive and valuable of all, and edited in an excellent manner, contains numerous letters belonging to the last three centuries before Christ, and many of the first centuries A. D., until late into the Byzantine period. These papyri-letters have revolutionized the study of epistolography.

After the Peloponnesian wars, and especially when Macedonia held the hegemony over Greece, the Greek mind turned away from politics, and began to devote more time to intellectual pursuits. Sophistic and rhetoric flourished, and pervaded every branch of literature. At this time the letter became the literary fashion, and, rapidly losing its real character, developed into a distinct branch of literature. It became customary to collect the letters of great men, especially if these men had founded schools of philosophy. Undoubtedly there were many authentic collections in existence at the time; and it is not impossible that among the forgeries which now parade under the names of the men of that day traces may be found of these genuine collections.

The development of the real letter into the fictitious or purely literary letter must be attributed to the sophists. With the death of Aristotle the creative spirit seemed to have departed from Greece. Henceforth its literature is learned, is scientific, but lacks inspiration. The form, not the contents, matters. To teach this nicety of form, this fluency of expression, the sophists introduced the letter into their schools. They taught their pupils to write letters which would resemble those written by the great men of Greece, imitating their style as closely as possible. Some writers gained great proficiency in this art, so that it became difficult to distinguish the genuine from the imitation. Even nowadays there is dispute among scholars as to the authenticity of some of these collections.

At this time also, according to Huit,[9] philosophers began to write to friends and disciples, sending in letter-form explanations of their teachings. The letter lent itself well to didactic purposes, being less formal than a treatise, less learned than a dialogue. In this function it enjoyed great vogue. Being a comparatively easy form of literary effort, it has remained a popular form of literature to this day. In the imitations of the real letter lies the origin of the letter as a purely literary product. It flourished as long as pagan literature. When pagan literature gradually died out, the pagan letter also disappeared.

When the Church was founded, and received the charge of teaching all nations, oral teaching was the first means employed. But when an apostle had visited a place, and had established there a Christian community, he naturally desired to maintain contact with it for its direction and further instruction. To do this he had quite obviously recourse to an existing means of communication—the letter. It is clear that the apostolic letter or epistle is not an artificial creation, but a natural development. Preoccupied with their great task, these first evangelists did not seek to clothe their letters in the artistic form with which we are familiar in a later age. Their purpose was to instruct; hence their letters are didactic. They had to admonish, to reprimand, to warn, and their letters became moral sermons. As overseers of the newly founded Church they had the direction of the scattered communities; and quite naturally their letters became pastoral epistles. Though many of these epistles do not read like letters, yet their proper place is under epistolography. Nor are they devoid of literary merit. As Deissmann remarks: "Though not a man of letters, yet his (St. Paul's) writings incorporated in the New Testament have exercised a literary influence that is incalculable."[10]

The practice of writing letters and epistles was not confined to the Apostles. The churches also commended themselves to

[9]Huit l. c.
[10]Deissmann l. c.

each other, and also their brethren who visited each other, as appears from Acts XVIII and I Cor. XVI 3. The extant scriptural epistolography is but a small part of what had actually been written. The churches of Rome, Philippi, Smyrna, and other places bear witness a long time after the Apostles had gone that this mode of communication had not ceased. The correspondence of St. Ignatius Martyr shows how active he was in this regard. Irenaeus knew of a still more extended correspondence of St. Polycarp.[11]

We may mention here also the official epistolography of the early Church, which consisted of episcopal and synodal letters. Even in our day bishops send out letters of instruction or direction to the faithful of their dioceses. In Alexandria the patriarch sent out annually after Epiphany a letter to the churches within his jurisdiction, in which he announced the date of Easter and the beginning of Lent. This custom was doubtless observed in many other churches. These letters were called "Festal Letters."

After the edict of Milan in 312-313, the Church entered upon another period of strife, this time against disturbers from within. For the next two centuries or more the Christological heresies demand her full attention. Able men, in great numbers, rose in her defense. These men developed, again quite naturally, the treatise clothed in letter-form.

It is impossible, within this brief space, to give even a synopsis of the extant correspondence of this period. One needs but recall the great names of Athanasius, of the two Cyrils, of the three Cappadocians, and of John surnamed Chrysostom, all scholars, all saints, all men filled with a consuming desire to safeguard the Church against the virus of heresy, and all interpreting this desire in golden words. It is of these men that Egger said: "The collections of their letters count among the consolations of a man of taste amidst the ruins of a great literature, which Christianity reanimated without, however, repairing all its losses."[12]

In the real letters of these great men we find reflected souls of surpassing beauty. In them we can read the story of their tremendous and varied activity. The letters of St. Gregory Nazianzen especially are artistic jewels. "Quite laconic, short, replete with 'thoughts' and 'points,' written with a painstaking industry that is evident, they are often meant for an audience beyond the

[11]Batiffol, P., La Littérature Grecque, Paris 1897.
[12]Memoires de la littérature ancienne l. c.

immediate recipient."[13] Of St. John Chrysostom's large correspondence 238 letters are extant. Most of them are quite brief. Nearly all of them date from his second exile. Many are mere answers to correspondents; most are consolatory in tone. His seventeen letters to the widow and deaconess Olympias are especially deserving of note. They are numerous, long, exceptionally cordial and frank, never weary of expatiating on the utility of sorrow and trial.[14] All of these letters are couched in such language as only St. John Chrysostom knew how to use. Yet this rich and valuable correspondence is unknown to, even unsuspected by, many scholars who pride themselves on their familiarity with the great writers of ancient days.

From this brief survey it appears that Greek Epistolography is not undeserving of our attention. Most of the ancient pagan letters were considered spurious. With the aid of the recently-discovered papyri letters we may yet be able to determine in how far this opinion is justified. The various Τύποι ἐπιστολικοί reprinted by Hercher in his Epistolographi Graeci have been discussed by many scholars, more recently by A. Brinkman in Rh. Mus. 64 (1909) 310. He places the prototype of these letter-books between the second century B. C. and the middle of the first century A. D. basing his conclusions mostly upon similarity in phraseology between the *τύποι* and the papyri letters. Here again a fresh consideration of the new material may tell us more exactly what phraseology prevailed in the papyri at the various periods, and thus enable us to arrive at safer conclusions regarding the other extant letters. Finally, the Patristic letters, so eminently worthy of our attention—even from a purely literary point of view—can be studied with greater profit, when we have more definite knowledge of the development of the letter-form during the centuries that preceded. It is hoped that the following pages will contribute a little to this end.

[13]Bardenhewer, Patrologie (Shahan) St. Louis 1908.
[14]Bardenhewer l. c.

# I. THE OPENING FORMULAS

The texts from which we quote the opening formulas treat of a great variety of matters. For the sake of convenience we have grouped them under four heads: Familiar Letters; Business Letters; Petitions and Applications; Official Letters. This division is based upon the contents of the documents. It is obvious that this arrangement is somewhat arbitrary. For familiar letters may treat of business; and a strategus may write to a fellow-strategus about official business in such a manner that his letter is classified more properly among familiar letters than among official communications. This division, therefore, is observed only in a general way, as a convenient means of roughly classifying the multiplicity of documents with which we have to deal. Since our main concern is with the letter-form, in particular cases we have grouped the documents according to similarity of form rather than according to the nature of the contents.

Under the head: Familiar Letters, we have arranged the communications between relatives and friends; also other letters which in their expressions betray a certain degree of familiarity. Under Business Letters have been collected all documents that treat of commercial affairs, including contracts, receipts, leases, and acknowledgments of indebtedness, which have been drawn up in epistolary form. Under the third head we have placed petitions addressed to officials, as well as complaints and other documents couched in similar forms. The last division comprises official letters which were written or received by official persons.

The basic type of the opening phrase in the Greek letter is expressed by the formula: A— to B— *χαίρειν*. "A" stands for the writer or addressant, "B" for the addressee. Almost every possible variation of this type occurs, the principal variant being: To B— from A—, usually without the addition of the salutation. It will be observed that the formula: A— to B— *χαίρειν*, occurs quite frequently in familiar letters, business letters, and official communications. The formula To B— from A—, is usually employed in petitions, complaints. and applications.

In the texts quoted the spelling has been given as found in the original. The accents, however, have been written as if the spelling were correct. The collections of papyri in which the texts are found are denoted by the abbreviations commonly employed by scholars. A list of these abbreviations is given in the bibliography. Following the number of the papyrus quoted is the number of the page on which the document is found.

---

## *A. TEXTS*

### 1. FAMILIAR LETTERS

A— to B— *χαίρειν.*

B. C. 265 (about) P. Hib. 68 (208)

Κρίτων Πλουτάρχωι χαίρειν.

B. C. 264-3 P. Hib. 64 (210)

Πάρις Πλουτάρχωι χαίρειν.

B. C. 261-0 P. S. I. IV 433 (158)

Εὐέμπολος Ζήνωνι χαίρειν.

also: B. C. 257. 330 (67); B. C. 256. 345 (80); B. C. 255. 347 (82); B. C. 251. 364 (95); B. C. 250. 375 (104); B. C. 241. 392 (121); B. C. 3dc. 415 (141); 417 (142); 444 (170);

B. C. 245 P. Hib. 54 (200)

Δημοφῶν Πτολεμαίωι χαίρειν.

B. C. 258-7 P. S. I. IV. 329 (67)

'Αμύντας Ζήνωνι χαίρειν.

also: P. S. I. V. B. C. 257. 500 (81); 502 (83); VI. B. C. 253. 569 (18); B. C. 248. 577 (25); B. C. 3dc. 590 (35);

B. C. 3dc. P. Good. I. 3 (7)

Πτολεμαῖος 'Αχιλλεῖ χαίρειν.

B. C. 2dc. P. Good. I. 4 ( 8)

Πολυκράτης Φιλοξένωι χαίρειν.

B. C. Ptol. P. P. II. 29 (78)

'Αλκαῖος Σωσιφάνει χαίρειν.

B. C. 2dc. P. Par. 58

Πτολεμαῖος 'Ιππάλωι χαίριν.

B. C. 2dc. P. Amh. II 40 (48)

'Ηπιόδωρος τῶι λεσώνει καὶ τοῖς ἱερεῦσι τοῦ Σοκνοπαίου χαίρειν.

A. D. 1stc. P. Oxy. II 296 (296)

'Ηρακλείδης 'Ασκλατᾶι χαίρειν.

A. D. 1stc. P. Fay. 109 (260)

Πισᾶις 'Ηρακλήῳ χαίρειν.

A. D. 2dc. P. Fay. 124 (280)

Θεογίτων 'Απολλωνίῳ χαίρειν.

A. D. 2dc. P. Tebt. II 415 (291); also: A. D. 117-38 P. Oxy X 1203 (245)

'Ηρακλᾶς 'Ιπ—— χαίρειν.

A. D. 2d—3dc. P. Oxy XII 1483 (242); also: P. Oxy VII 1067 (221); IX 1215 (259); 1216 (259);
Δῖος Ζωίλωι χαίρειν.
A. D. 3dc. P. Tebt. II 421 (298)
Ἀπίων Διδύμῳ χαίρειν.
A. D. 3dc. P. Oxy. XII 1576 (280)
Ὡρίων Δίῳ χαίρειν.
also: P. Oxy XIV 1669 (125)
Ὡρείων Σερήνῳ χαίρειν.
A. D. 3dc. (middle) P. Ryl. 239 (388)
Ὡρίων Εὐπόρῳ χαίρειν.

---

A— to B— (τῷ πατρί, ἀδελφῷ, κτέ) χαίρειν.

B. C. 260 P. P. 112 (4) c.
Διοσκουρίδης Διοφάνει τῶι πατρὶ χαίρειν.
B. C. 257-6 P. S. I. IV. 331 (68)
Ἐφάρμοστος τῶι ἀδελφῶι χαίρειν.
B. C. 250 P. P. II 42 (139); also P. P. III 42 (113).
Φιλωνίδης τῶι πατρὶ χαίρειν.
B. C. 245 P. Lille 17 (87)
———— Ἀριστάρχηι τῶι υἱῶι καὶ Μικκάληι τῆι θυγατρὶ χαίρειν.
B. C. 240 P. P. I 30 (80) 2; also P. P. II 11 (27).
Πολυκράτης τῶι πατρὶ χαίρειν.
B. C. 3dc. P. Lille 26 (116)
Ἀπολλώνιος τῶι πατρὶ χαίρειν.
B. C. 223-22 P. Eleph. 13 (47)
Ἄνδρων Μίλωνι τἀδελφῶι χαίρειν.
B. C. 172 P. B. M. I. 42 (29)
Ἰσίας Ἡφαιστίωνι τῶι ἀδελφῶι (greeting not expressed)
B. C. 168 P. Vat. A.
Διονύσιος Ἡφαιστίωνι τῶι ἀδελφῶι χαίρειν.
B. C. 162 P. Par. 32
Λυσίμαχος Πτολεμαίωι καὶ ταῖς διδύμαις καὶ Ἀπολλωνίωι τοῖς ἀδελφοῖς χαίρειν.
B. C. 160 P. Par. 59. also: B. C. 154, P. Par. 60; B. C. 153 P. Par. 44.
Ἀπολλώνιος Πτολεμαίωι τῶι πατρεὶ χαίρειν.
B. C. 153 P. Par. 45, 46, 47, 48.
Ἀπολλώνιος Ἀπολλωνίωι τῷ ἀδελφῶι χαίρειν.
B. C. 114 P. Tebt. 19 (89)
Πολέμων Μεγχεῖ τῶι ἀδελφῶι χαίρειν.
B. C. 2dc. P. Grenf. I 43 (74)
Μένων Ἑρμοκράτει τἀδελφῶι χαίρειν.
B. C. 1stc. P. Tebt. II 284 (43)
Λυσίμαχος Τααρμιῦσι τῆι ἀδελφῆι χαίρειν.

B. C. 1stc. P. Hawara (Archiv 76)
Παμμένης Ἀλκίμωι τῶι ἀδελφῶι χαίρειν.
A. D. 1stc. P. Oxy. XIV 1756 (180)
Σαραπίων Διονυσίωι τῶι πατρὶ χαίρειν.
A. D. 1stc. P. Oxy. VIII 1153 (254)
Ἀπολλώνιος Ἀπολλωνίωι τῶι υἱῶι χαίρειν.
A. D. 1stc. P. Oxy. VIII 1154 (256)
Θέων Σαραποῦτι τῇ ἀδελφῇ χαίρειν.
A. D. 30 P. Oxy. X 1291 (243)
Ζωΐς Ἰσχυρίωνι τῶι ἀδελφῶι χαίρειν.
A. D. 54 P. Oxy. II 297 (297)
Ἀμμώνιος Ἀμμωνίωι τῶι πατρὶ χαίρειν.
A. D. 100 P. Fay. 123 (279)
Ἁρποκρατίων Βελλήνωι Σαβείνωι τῶι ἀδελφῶι χαίρειν.
A. D. 100 P. Fay. 119 (275); also P. Fay 113 (268); 114 (269).
Λούκιος Βελλῆνος Γέμελλος Σαβίνωι τῷ οιείῶι χαίρειν.
A. D. 2dc. P. Giss. III 71 (60)
Τιθοητίων Ἀπολλωνίωι τῶι ἀδελφῶι χαίρειν.
A. D. 2dc. P. Giss. III 78 (68); also: P. Oxy. XII 1488 (245), 1581 (282).
Ἀλινὴ Τετῆτι τῆι μητρὶ χαίρειν.
A. D. 2dc. P. Oxy. III 531 (268)
Κορνήλιος Ἱέρακι τῷ γλυκυτάτωι υἱῷ χαίρειν.
A. D. 2dc. B. G. U. II 615 (267)
Ἀμμωνοῦς τῷ γλυκυτάτῳ πατρὶ χαίρειν.
A. D. 2dc. P. Flor. III 332 (67)
Εὐδαιμονὶς Ἀπολλωνίωι τῶι υἱῶι χαίρειν.
A. D. 2dc. P. Amh. II 131 (160); also: 132, 133, 134, 135;
Σαραπίων Σελήνηι τῆι ἀδελφῆι χαίρειν.
A. D. 2dc. P. Tebt. II 411 (286)
Παυλεῖνος Ἥρωνι τῶι υἱῶι χαίρειν.
A. D. 2dc.-3d. B. G. U. II 450 (109)
Ὀρσενοῦπις Νείλωι τῶι ἀδελφῶι χαίρειν.
A. D. 2dc-3d P. Oxy. I 117 (182)
Χαιρέας Διονυσίωι τῶι κυρίωι ἀδελφῶι χαίρειν.
also: A. D. 2dc. late P. Tebt. II 412 (287); A. D. 2d-3dc P. Oxy. VI 928 (293); B. G. U. I 164 (175); II 417 (78). P. Oxy. I 119 (185); P. Hamb. I 54 (194); P. Fay. 124 (283).
A. D. 3dc. early P. Oxy. XII 1586 (283)
Ἁρποκρατίων Ἡραΐδι τῆι ἀδελφῆι χαίρειν.
A. D. 3dc. P. Oxy. VII 1064 (218)
Διογένης Διδυμᾶτι τῶι ἀδελφῶι χαίρειν.
A. D. 3dc. P. Oxy. VI 936 (303)
Παυσανίας Ἰουλίῳ Ἀλεξάνδρωι τῶι πατρὶ χαίρειν.
A. D. 3dc. P. Ryl. 240 (389)
Ὡρίων Ἡρωνείνῳ τῷ ἀδελφῷ χαίρειν.

also: A. D. 253 P. Flor. II 180 (139); A. D. 259 P. Flor. II 186 (145); A. D. 256 P. Flor. II 192 (158); 208 (174); 187;

A. D. 3dc. P. Tebt. II 422 (299); also 416 (292)
Αὐρήλιος Σύρος Αὐρηλίῳ Ἀκουτᾶτι τῷ ἀδελφῷ χαίρειν.

A. D. 3dc. P. Amh. II 136 (165)
Ἀπίων Ὡρίωνι τῶι υἱῶι χαίρειν.
also: B. G. U. III 822 (137); P. Fay. 128 (285); B. G. U. IV 1080 (125); P. Oxy. IX 1219 (262); XIV 1666 (121); 1670 (126); 1674 (132)

A. D. 3dc. P. Oxy. XIV 1768 (184)
Ἡράκλειος Θέωνι καὶ Σαραπιάδι τοῖς γλυκυτάτοις τέκνοις χαίρειν.

A. D. 3dc. P. Oxy. I 118 (184)
Σάρας καὶ Εὐδαίμων Διογένει τῷ υἱῷ χαίρειν.
also: A. D. 3d-4thc. P. S. I. IV 305 (38); A. D. 4thc. P. Oxy. XII 1491 (248)

---

A— to B— πολλὰ χαίρειν.

B. C. 118 P. Tebt. I 12 (75) b; B. C. 99 P. Leid. K. (52)
Μεγχῆς Ἀμμωνίωι τῶι ἀδελφῶι πολλὰ χαίρειν.

A. D. 1stc. B. G. U. I 38 (53)
Σερῆνος Ἀπολιναρίῳ τῷ πατρεὶ πολλὰ χαίρειν.

A. D. 2dc. P. Giss. 19 (59)
Ἀλινὴ Ἀπολλωνίωι τῶι ἀδελφῶι πολλὰ χαίρειν.

A. D. 2dc. P. Giss. 22 (65)
Εὐδαιμονὶς Ἀπολλωνίωι τῶι —μοτάτωι υἱῶι πολλὰ χαίρειν.

A. D. 2dc. P. Giss. 23 (66)
Εὐδαιμονὶς Ἀλινῆι τῆι θυγατρὶ πολλὰ χαίρειν.
also: B. G. U. II 601 (245); 615 (268) ;III 775 (76).

A. D. 2d-3dc. P. Tebt. II 413 (287)
Ἀφροδίτη Ἀρσινοῆτι τῇ κυρίᾳ πολλὰ χαίρειν.

A. D. 2d-3dc. P. Fay. 127 (284)
Ταορσενοῦφις Ἰσίων(=ῳ) τῇ μητρὶ πολλὰ χαίρειν.

A. D. 3dc. P. Ryl. 244 (392)
Διόσκορος Εὔτι τῇ ἀδελφῇ πολλὰ χαίρειν.

A. D. 3dc. P. Ryl. 242 (390)
Ἐπίμαχους(- -χος) τῷ πατρεὶ πολλὰ χαίρειν.

A. D. 3dc. P. Oxy. X. 1296 (250)
Αὐρήλιος Δῖος Αὐρηλίῳ Ὡρείωνι τῷ γλυκυτάτῳ μου πατρὶ πολλὰ χαίρειν.

A. D. 3dc. P. Oxy. XIV. 1769 (184)
Ἀμμωνᾶς τῇ ἀδελφῇ μου πολλὰ χαίρειν.

A. D. 3dc. P. Oxy. XIV 1665 (120)
Αὐρήλιος Σαραπίων Αὐρηλίῳ Κλαυδίωι τῷ πατρὶ πολλὰ χαίρειν.

A. D. 3d-4thc. P. S. I. III 236 (93)
Ζώιλος ξυστάρχης Παυλείνῳ ἀδελφῷ ξυστάρχῃ πολλὰ χαίρειν.

---

A— to B— πλεῖστα χαίρειν.

B. C. 2 P. Oxy. IV 742 (241)
Ἀντᾶς Φαύστωι πλεῖστα χαίρειν.

B. C. 1 P. Oxy. IV. 744 (243)
Ἰλαρίωνα(=ίων) Ἄλατι τῆι ἀδελφῆι πλεῖστα χαίρειν. (καὶ Βεροῦτι τῇ κυρίᾳ μου καὶ Ἀπολλωνάριν).

A. D. 98-130 B. G. U III 811 (126)
Κορνήλιος Ἀπολλῶτι τῶι ἀδελφῷ πλεῖστα χαίρειν.

A. D. 2dc. P. Oxy. XII 1481 (239)
Θεωνᾶς Τεθεῦτι τῆι μητρὶ καὶ κυρίᾳ πλεῖστα χαίρειν.

A. D. 2dc. P. Oxy. III 528 (263)
Σερῆνος Εἰσιδώρᾳ τῇ ἀδελφῇ καὶ κυρίᾳ πλαῖστα χαίρειν.

A. D. 2dc. B. G. U. II 423 (84)
Ἀπίων Ἑπταμάχῳ τῶι πατρὶ καὶ κυρίῳ πλεῖστα χαίρειν.

A. D. 2dc. P. Tebt. II 414 (288)
Θενπετσῶκις Θεναπύνχι τῇ ἀδελφῇ πλῖστα χαίρειν.

A. D. 2dc. P. Giss. 21 (64); also: P. Giss. III 81 (74); 97 (90);
Εὐδαιμονὶς Ἀπολλωνίωι τῶι υἱῶι πλεῖστα χαίρειν

A. D. 2dc. P. Giss. 17 (56)
Ταῦς Ἀπολλωνίωι τῶι κυρίωι πλεῖστα χαίρειν.

A. D. 2dc. P. Oxy. XIV. 1757 (180)
Ὡρεῖς Ὡρίωνι τῶι ἀδελφῶι πλεῖστα χαίρειν.
also: B. G. U. II 602 (246); 632 (297); IV 1040 (47).

A. D. 2dc-3dc. P. S. I. III 177 (34)
Ἰσιδώρα Ἑρμίᾳ τῷ κυρίῳ ἀδελφῷ πλεῖστα χαίρειν.
also: B. G. U. I 93 (111); 261 (261); 332 (326); II. 384 (42); 385 (43); 449 (108); 635 (283); P. Strass. 38 (133).

A. D. 3dc. P. Meyer 20 (80)
Ἀθηνόδωρος Σελβείνᾳ τῇ ἀδελφῇ πλεῖστα χαίρειν.

A. D. 3dc. P. Fay. 130 (286)
Μύσθης Σεραπάμμωνι τῷ ἀδελφῷ πλεῖστα χαίρειν.

A. D. 3dc. P. Gen. 139 (112)
Ἡραὶς Ἀγριππίνωι τῶι υἱῷ πλεῖστα χαίρειν.

A. D. 3dc. P. Flor. III 365 (87)
Διοσκουρίδης Παθερμούθῳ τῷ πατρὶ πλῖστα χαίρειν.

A. D. 3dc. P. Tebt. II 420 (296)
Αὐρήλιος Σαραπίων Πωλίωνι τῷ ἀδλφῷ καὶ Διογένι τῷ πατρὶ πλεῖστοι χαίρειν.

A. D. 3dc. P. Oxy. XIV. 1676 (134)
Φλαούιος Ἡρκουλανὸς Ἀπλωναρίῳ τῇ γλυκυτάτῃ καὶ τειμιωτάτῃ πλεῖστα χαίρειν.

A. D. 3dc. P. Oxy. XIV. 1681 (141)
Ἀμμώνιος Ἰουλίῳ καὶ Ἱλάρῳ τοῖς ἀδελφοῖς πλεῖστα χαίρειν.

see also: P. Oxy. I 121 (188); VI. 937 (305); VII 1066 (220); IX 1218 (261); XIV 1668 (124).

A. D. 3d-4thc. P. Gen. 9 (113).
Σαραπάμμων Νεφωτιανῷ τῷ πατρὶ πλεῖστα χαίρειν.

---

A— to B— τῶι φιλτάτωι χαίρειν.

A. D. 38 P. Ryl. 229 (378)
Ἀμμώνιος Ἀφροδισίωι φιλτάτωι χαίρειν.

A. D. 40 P. Ryl. 230 (379); also 231 (380); 231a.
Ἀμμώνιος Ἀφροδισίωι τῶι φιλτάτωι χαίρειν.

A. D. 55-6 B. G. U. III 824 (139)
Παπηρεὶς Καλήτει τῷ φιλτάτωι χαίρειν.

A. D. 57 P. Oxy. II 269 (250)b
Τρύφων Ἀμμωνᾶτι τῷ Μάκρῳ τῷ φιλτάτῳ χαίρειν.

A. D. 83 B. G. U. III 844 (168)
Ἡρώιδης Ἀπολλωνίωι τῶι φιλτάτωι χαίρειν.

A. D. 95 P. S. I. IV 317 (50)
Κάστωρ Πτόλλιδι τῶι φιλτάτωι χαίρειν.

A. D. 98 P. Lips. 106 (309)
Ἡρακλείδης Ἀπολλωνίωι τῷ φιλτάτῳ χαίρειν.

A. D. 1stc. P. B. M. 356 (252)
Προκλήιος Πεκύσει τῶι φιλτάτωι χαίρειν.

A. D. 1stc. P. Oxy. II 298 (298)
————ωι τῶι φιλτάτωι χαίρειν.

A. D. 2dc. P. Giss. 25 (69)
Συρίων Αἰλουρᾶι τῶι φιλτάτωι χαίρειν.

A. D. 2dc. P. Giss. 26 (70); also 27 (73)
Ἀπολλώνιος Ἡρακλείωι τῶι φιλτάτωι χαίρειν.

A. D. 2dc. P. Oxy. XIV 1759 (181)
Δημήτριος Θέωνι τῷ φιλτάτῳ χαίρειν.

A. D. 2dc. P. Oxy. VII 1062 (216)
Μάρκος Ματρέαι τῶι φιλτάτωι χαίρειν.

A. D. 2dc. P. Fay. 125 (281)
Πτολεμαῖος Ἥρωνι τῶι φιλτάτῳ χαίρειν.

A. D. 2dc. B. G. U. I 249 (248)
Χαιρήμων Ἀπολλωνίωι τῶι φιλτάτωι χαίρειν.

also: B. G. U. I 248 (246); IV. 1031 (32); P. Ryl. 232 (382); P. Tebt. II 315 (114)

A. D. 2d-3dc B. G. U. III 884 (200)
Θεόκτιστος Ἀπολλωνίῳ τῶι φιλτάτωι χαίρειν.

A. D. 2d-3dc. B. G. U. I 48 (62)
Κύλινδρος Ἀπολλωνίωι τῶι φιλτάτωι χαίρειν.
A. D. 3dc. P. B. M. II 479 (255)
Τιθοεὶς Εἰρηνίωνι τῷ φιλτάτῳ χαίρειν.
A. D. 256 P. Ryl. 236 (385)
Σύρος Ἡρωνείνῳ τῷ φιλτάτῳ χαίρειν.
A. D. 3dc. P. Rein. 54 (161)
Πάλας Ἡρωνείνῳ τῷ φιλτάτῳ χαίρειν.
A. D. 3dc. (250-260). P. Flor. II 180 (238)
Ἀπίανος Ἡρωνείνῳ τῶ φιλτάτῳ χαίρειν.
also: ibidem, 183, 185, 189, 190, 194, 195, 209, 212, 213, etc.
A. D. 3dc. P. S. I. IV 308 (40)
Σαραπιὰς Εὐδαιμονίδι —— τῇ φιλτάτῃ χαίρειν.
also: P. B. M. III 973b (213).
A. D. 3d-4thc. P. S. I. IV. 286 (14)
——ων Διογένει τῶι φιλτάτωι χαίρειν.

---

A— to B—τῶι φιλτάτωι πλεῖστα χαίρειν.

A. D. 3 P. Tebt. II 408 (282)
Ἱππόλιτος Ἀκουσιλάῳ τῷ φιλτάτῳ πλεῖστα χαίρειν.
A. D. 16 P. Tebt. II 410 (285)
Ἑρμίας Ἀκουσιλάωι τῶι φιλτάτωι πλεῖστα χαίρειν.
A. D. 104 P. Oxy. VIII 1155 (257)
Θωνᾶς Ἀπίονι τῷ φιλτάτῳ πλῖστα χαίρειν.
A. D. 2dc. P. Ryl. 243 (392)
Δημάριν καὶ Εἰρήνη Σύρῳ τῶι φιλτάτῳ πλεῖστα χαίρειν.
A. D. 2d-3dc. P. Oxy. 533 (270)
Ἀπίων Ἀπίωνι τῶι υἱῷ καὶ Ὡρίωνι τῶι φιλτάτῳ πλεῖστα χαίρειν.
A. D. 3d-4thc. P. Oxy. XII 1493 (250)
Θῶνις Ἡρακλήῳ τῷ φιλτάτῳ πλεῖστα χαίρειν.

---

A— to B—τῶι τιμιωτάτωι χαίρειν.

A. D. 84 B. G. U. III 596 (240)
Δίδυμος Ἀπολλωνίωι τῶι τιμιωτάτωι χαίρειν.
A. D. 1stc. P. Oxy. II 299 (300)
Ὧρος Ἀπίωνι τῷ τειμειωτάτωι χαίρειν.
A. D. 2dc. P. Oxy. XIV 1673 (130)
Ἑρμῆς Σαραπιακῶι τῶι τιμιωτάτωι χαίρειν.
A. D 2dc. P. Oxy. XII 1583 (282)
Διογένης Διοσκορᾶτι τῷ τιμιωτάτῳ χαίρειν.
A. D. 2dc. P. Oxy. VI 931 (296)
Θεόπομπος Σαραπίωνι τῶι τιμιωτάτωι χαίρειν.

A. D. 2dc. P. Jand. I 8 (39); also: 9 (42).
Ἰσχυρίων Ἀντωνίνωι τῶι τιμιωτάτωι χαίρειν.
A. D. 2dc. P. Giss. 15 (54); also: 16 (55).
Ἑρμαῖος Ἀπολλωνίωι τῶι τιμιωτάτωι χαίρειν.
A. D. 2dc. P. Giss. III 73 (62); also: 75 (63).
Ἀντώνιος Δῖος Ἀπολλωνίωι τῶι τιμιωτάτωι χαίρειν.
also: P. Giss II 47 (63); A. D. 118-19 P. Giss. III 69 (56).
A. D. 2d-3dc. P. Oxy. XIV 1663 (117)
Τούρβων Κλέωνι τῶι τιμιωτάτωι χαίρειν.
A. D. 3dc. (about 250) P. Flor. II 181 (140); also: 184 (143).
Ἀπολλώνιος Ἡρωνείνῳ τῷ τιμιωτάτῳ χαίρειν.
A. D. 3dc. P. Tebt. II 419 (295)
Ἥρων Ἥρωνι τῷ τιμιωτάτῳ χαίρειν.
A. D. 3dc. P. Oxy. XIV 1766 (183)
A——υλις Ὡρείωνι τῶι τιμιωτάτωι χαίρειν.
A. D. 3d-4thc. P. Oxy. XIV 1771 (185)
Αὐρήλιος Σερῆνος Αὐρηλίῳ Ὡρίωνι τῶι τιμειωτάτωι χαίρειν.

---

A— to B— τῶι τιμιωτάτωι πλεῖστα χαίρειν.

A. D. 25 P. Oxy. II 292 (292)
Θέων Τυράννωι τῶι τιμιωτάτωι πλεῖστα χαίρειν.
A. D. 2dc. P. Oxy. XIV 1758 (181)
Διογενὶς Διδυμᾷ τῶι τιμιωτάτωι πλεῖστα χαίρειν.
A. D. 2dc. P. Tebt. II 314 (113)
Χαιρέας Μα—τῷ τιμιωτάτῳ πλεῖστα χαίρειν.
A. D. 2d-3dc. B. G. U. I 276 (272)
A—— Πτολεμαίῳ τῷ τιμιωτάτῳ πλεῖστα χαίρειν.
A. D. 3dc. P. Tebt. II 418 (294)
Σωτήριχος Ὡριγένει τῷ τιμιωτάτῳ πλεῖστα χαίρειν.

---

A— to B— τῶι ἰδίωι (πλεῖστα) χαίρειν.

A. D. 50 B. G. U. I 37 (52)
Μυσταρίων Στοτόητι τῶι ἰδίωι πλεῖστα χαίρειν.
A. D. 94 P. Fay. 110 (261)
Λούκιος Βελλῆνος Γέμελλος Ἐπαγάθωι τῶι ἰδίωι χαίρειν.
also: A. D. 95-6 P. Fay 111 (265); A. D. 99, 112 (166); A. D. 100, 120 (276); A. D. 104, 116 (271).
A. D. 100 (about) P. Fay. 121 (277)
Βελλῆνος Σαβῖνος Γεμείνωι τῶι ἰδίωι χαίρειν.
A. D. 100 (about) P. Fay. 122 (273)
Βελλῆνος Σαβῖνος Ἐπαγάθωι τῶι ἰδίωι χαίρειν.
A. D. 2dc. (late) P. Oxy. 932 (298)
Θαὶς Τιγρίῳ τῷ ἰδίῳ χαίρειν.

A. D. 2dc. P. Oxy. XII 1584 (283)
Θέων Διογενίδι ἰδίαις ἀδελφαῖς χαίρειν.

---

A— to B— τῶι κυρίωι χαίρειν.

A. D. 1stc (late) P. Oxy. II 300 (301)
Ἰνδικὴ Θαεισοῦτι τῇ κυρίᾳ χαίρειν.

A. D. 2dc. P. Oxy. I 113 (178)
Κορβόλων Ἡρακλείδῃ τῶι κυρίωι χαίρειν.

A. D. 2dc. P. Oxy. XII 1482 (240)
Μῶρος Ἐπιμάχῳ τῶι κυρίωι μου χαίρειν.

A. D. 2dc. P. Giss. 13 (51); also: 14 (53)
Ἐπαφρόδειτος Ἀπολλωνίωι τῶι κυρίωι χαίρειν.

A. D. 2dc. P. Giss. III 77 (67)
Τεεὺς Ἀλινῆ τῇ κυρίᾳ χαίρειν.

A. D. 3dc. P. Oxy. VII 1068 (223)
Σατορνῖλος κυρίῳ μου Ἀπολλωνίου(=ῳ) χαίρειν.

---

A— to B— χαίρειν καὶ ἐρρῶσθαι.

B. C. 2dc. (164-158) P. Par. 49
Διονύσιος Πτολεμαίωι χαίρειν καὶ ἐρρῶσθαι.

B. C. 131-0 P. Reville Mel. p. 295 (Archiv II 517)
Ἐσθλάδας τῶι πατρὶ καὶ τῆι μητρὶ χαίρειν καὶ ἐρρῶσθαι.

B. C. 118 P. Tebt. I 12 (75)
Μεγχῆς Ἡρώδει τῶι ἀδελφῶι χαίρειν καὶ ἐρρῶσθαι.

B. C. 114 P. Tebt. I 57 (167)
Πετενεφιῆς ———— χαίρειν καὶ ἐρρῶσθαι.

B. C. 113 P. Tebt. 20 (90)
Πολέμων Μεγχεῖ χαίρειν καὶ ἐρρῶσθαι.

B. C. 2dc. (late) P. Tebt. 55 (165)
Μουσαῖος Μεγχεῖ τῶι ἀδελφῷ χαίρειν καὶ ἐρρῶσθαι.

B. C. 2dc. B. G. U. IV. 1009
———— τῶι ἀδελφῶι χαίρειν καὶ ἐρρῶσθαι.

---

A— to B— χαίρειν καὶ ὑγιαίνειν.

A— to B— (πλεῖστα) χαίρειν καὶ (διὰ παντὸς) ὑγιαίνειν.

B. C. 28 B. G. U. IV 1204 (343)
Ἰσιδώρα Ἀσκληπιάδηι τῶι ἀδελφῶι χαίρειν καὶ ὑγιαίνειν διὰ παντός.

B. C. 28 B. G. U. IV 1206 (347); also: 1205 (346).
Ἰσιδώρα Ἀσκλᾶτι τῶι ἀδελφῶι χαίρειν καὶ διὰ παντὸς ὑγιαίνειν καθάπερ εὔχομαι.

B. C. 27-6 B. G. U. IV 1208 (349)
(Τρύφων) τῶι ἀδελφῶι χαίρειν καὶ διὰ παντὸς ὑγιαίνειν.

B. C. 23 B. G. U. IV 1209 (351)
Τρύφων Ἀσκληπιάδηι τῶι ἀδελφῶι χαίρειν καὶ ὑγιαίνειν.

B. C. 22 P. Oxy. VII 1061 (214)
Διογένης Διονυσίωι τῶι ἀδελφῶι πλεῖστα χαίρειν καὶ ὑγιαίνειν.

A. D. 5 P. Tebt. II 409 (284)
Δωρίων Ἀκουσιλάωι τῶι διοικητῆι πλεῖστα χαίρειν καὶ διὰ παντὸς ὑγιαίνειν.

A. D. 16 P. Oxy. IV 746 (246)
Θέων Ἡρακλείδηι τῶι ἀδελφῶι πλεῖστα χαίρειν καὶ ὑγιαίνειν.

A. D. 22 P. Oxy. II 294 (294)
Σαραπίων Δωρίωνι τῷ ἀδελφῷ χαίρειν καὶ διὰ παντὸς ὑγιαίνιν.

A. D. 27 P. Oxy. II 293 (293)
Διονύσιος Διδύμῃ τῆι ἀδελφῇ πλεῖστα χαίρειν καὶ διὰ παντὸς ὑγιαίνειν.

A. D. 32 P. Oxy. XII 1480 (238).
Ἑρμογένης Ἀρυώτῃ τῷ προφήτῃ καὶ φιλτάτῳ πλῖστα χαίρειν καὶ διὰ παντὸς ὑγιένειν.

A. D. 37–41 P. Oxy. XIV 1672 (129)
Δημήτριος καὶ Παυσανίας Παυσανίαι τῶι πατρὶ πλεῖστα χαίρειν καὶ ὑγιαίνειν.

Also: A. D. 39 B. G. U. 1078 (122).

A. D. 75 B. G. U. 597 (241)
Χαιρήμων Ἀπολλωνίωι τῶι ἀδελφῶι πλεῖστα χαίρειν καὶ ὑγιαίνειν.

A. D. 2dc. B. G. U. III 846 (170)
Ἀντῶνις Λόνγος Νειλοῦτι τῇ μητρὶ πλῖστα χαίρειν καὶ διὰ πάντων εὔχομαί σαι ὑγιαίνειν.

A. D. 2dc. B. G. U. I 27 (41)
πολλὰ χαίρειν καὶ διὰ παντὸς εὔχομαί σε ὑγιένεν καὶ (ἐγὼ) αὐτὸς ὑγιένω.

---

To B— A— χαίρειν.

A. D. 2dc. P. Ryl. 234 (383)
Ἀπολλωνίωι ——— ὑπηρέτης τῷ κυρίῳ χαίρειν.

A. D. 3dc. P. Oxy. XIV 1671 (128)
Κυρίῳ μου Ζωίλῳ Διονύσιος χαίρειν.

A. D. 3dc. P. Oxy. VIII 1157 (259)
Κυρίᾳ μου ἀδελφῇ Διονυσίᾳ Πατερμοῦθις χαίρειν.

A. D. 3dc. P. Oxy. XIV 1678 (137)
Κυρίᾳ μου μητρεὶ Θέων χαίρειν.

A. D. 3dc. P. Oxy. VIII 1158 (260)
Κυρίῳ μου ἀδελφῷ Διοδώρῳ Λούκις καὶ Σαραπίωνι πολλὰ χαίρειν.

A. D. 3d-4thc P. Oxy. X 1160 (263)
Κυρίῳ μου πατρὶ Ὠριγένης Τρόφιμος πολλὰ χαίρειν.
A. D. 3d-4thc. P. Oxy. I 123 (190)
Κυρίῳ μου υἱῷ Διονυσοθέωνι ὁ πατὴρ χαίρειν.
A. D. 4thc. P. Oxy. 1495 (252)
Κυρίῳ ἀδελφῷ Ἀπολλωνίῳ Νεῖλος χαίρειν.
A. D. 4thc. P. Oxy. XIV 1682 (143)
Κυρίᾳ μου ἀδελφῇ Ἀντιοχείῃ Ἡρακλείδης χαίρειν.

---

## MISCELLANEOUS.

B. C. 81 P. Grenf. II 38 (62)
Πασίων Νίκωνι τῶι πατρὶ πολλὰ χαίρειν καὶ [διὰ παντὸς ἐρρ]ωμένων διευτυχεῖν.
A. D. 2dc. P. Oxy. I 115 (186)
Εἰρήνη Ταοννώφρει καὶ Φίλωνι εὐψυχεῖν.
A. D. 2dc. B. G. U. III 845 (169)
[. . ]ρεῖνος τῇ μητρὶ πλεῖστα πολλὰ χαίρειν.
A. D. 3dc. P. S. I. IV 299 (36)
Τῇ κυρίᾳ ἀδελφῇ Τιτιανὸς εὖ πράττειν.
A. .D 3d-4thc. P. S. I. III 207 (68)
Κυρίῳ μου πατρὶ Στεφάνῳ Ἱέραξ εὖ πράττειν.
A. D. 108 P. Fay. 117 (272)
Λούκιος Βελλῆνος Γέμελλος Σαβίνωι τῶι υειῶι χαίρειν καὶ διὰ παντὸς εὖ ἔχειν (εὐτυχεῖν ? Ziemann P. 313 Note)
A. D. 3dc. P. Oxy. XII 1490 (247)
Ἡρακλείδης Σαραπίωνι τῷ ἀξιολογωτάτῳ χαίρειν.
A. D. 41 B. G. U. IV 4079 (123)
Σαραπίων Ἡρακλείδῃ τῷ ἡμετέρῳ χαίρειν.

---

## (From A—) (to B—) (χαίρειν).

B. C. 13 B. G. U. IV 1141 (257)
Ἐρωσῆτι πλεῖστα χαίρειν.
A. D. 3dc. P. Tebt. II 423 (300)
Αὐρηλίῳ Νεμεσίωνι φροντιστῇ χαίρειν.
A. D. 3dc. P. Oxy. 1770 (185)
Κυρίᾳ μου μητρὶ ἅμα τοῖς κυρίοις μου ἀδελφοῖς πλεῖστα χαίρειν.
A. D. 3dc. P. Oxy. VII 1065 (219)
Στεφάνῳ παρὰ Ἡφαιστίωνος.
A. D. 3dc. P. Oxy. XII 1570 (279)
Παρὰ Διογενίδος Σαραπάμμωνι χαίρειν.
A. D. 3dc. P. Oxy. XII 1573 (279)
Παρὰ Σεουήρου γυμνα. Σαραπίωνι τῷ φιλτάτῳ χαίρειν.
A. D. 295 P. S. I. III 205 (65)
Παρὰ Θεοδοτίου Ἀντιόχῳ χαίρειν.

A. D. 299 P. Oxy. XII 1572 (279)
Παρὰ Σαραπίωνος Δημητριανῷ δεσπότῃ χαίρειν.

---

## Χαίροις.

A. D. 1st c. P. B. M. II 144 (253)
Χαίροις κύριέ μου Ἀθηνόδωρε Ἀλέξανδρος ἐπασπάζομαι.

A. D. 2d c. P. Oxy. III 526 (262)
Χαίροις Καλόκαιρε Κύριλλός σε προσαγορεύω.

A. D. 2d c. (late) P. Oxy. VI 933 (299)
Χαίροις κύριέ μου Ἀπολινάριε παρὰ Διογένους φίλου.

A. D. 2d-3d c. P. Oxy. VII 1063 (217)
Χαίροις τέκνον Ἀμόι.

A. D. 3d c. P. Strass. 37 (131)
Χαίροις Ἀμμωνιανὲ παρὰ τοῦ πατρὸς Ἀπολλωναρίου.

A. D. 3d c. P. Tebt. II 417 (293)
Χαίροις πολλά.

A. D. 3d-4th c. P. Oxy. I 112 (177)
Χαίροις κυρία μου Σερηνία παρὰ Πετοσείριος.

A. D. 264 P. Flor. II 140 (93)
Χαίροις κύριέ μου Ἀλύπι Ἀνουβίων σε προσαγορεύω.

A. D. 3d c. (end) P. S. I. 206 (66)
Χαίροις ἀδελφὲ Δημήτριε Πα—ρας σαι προσαγορεύω.

A. D. 3d-4th c. P. Iand. 12 (49)
Χαίροις Ἀφυμοῦ παρὰ Σωρίδος.

---

## Χαῖρε.

A. D. 2d c. B. G. U. III 821 (146)
Χαῖρε κύριέ μου πάτερ Ἡραίσκος σε ἀσπάζομαι.

A. D. 2d c. P. Rein. 48 (149)
Χαῖρε κύριέ μου Σαραπόδωρε.

A. D. 2d c. P. B. M. III 899 (208)
Χαῖρε τέκνον Ἄρειε ἀπὸ Ἑρμαίου πατρός.

A. D. 2d-3d c. B. G. U. II 435 (95)
Χαῖρε Οὐαλεριανὲ παρὰ τοῦ ἀδελφοῦ.

A. D. 3d c. P. Fay. 129 (285)
Χαῖρε κύριε τιμιώτατε.

A. D. 3d c. P. Oxy. VIII 1156 (258)
Χαῖρε κύριέ μου Ἀντᾶ παρὰ Ἀνουβίωνος.

A. D. 3d c. P. Flor. III 345 (76)
Χαῖρε κύριέ μου Ἑρμᾶ.

A. D. 3d c. P. Oxy. XIV. 1667 (123)
Χαῖρε Ἀπίων τιμιώτατε Δωρίων σε προσαγορεύω.

A. D. 3d c. P. Oxy. XIV 1677 (136)
Χαῖρε Ἀφροδείτη Ἀγαθός σε ἀσπάζομαι.

A. D. 3dc. P. Oxy. XIV. 1675 (133)
Χαῖρε Ἰσχυρίων.

A. D. 3d-4thc. P. Oxy. XII 1492 (249)
Χαῖρε ἱερὲ υἱὲ Δημητριανὲ Σῶτάς σε προσαγορεύω.

A. D. 4thc. P. S. I. III 208 (69)
Χαῖρε ἐν κυρίῳ ἀγαπητὲ ἀδελφὲ Πέτρε Σῶτάς σε προσαγορεύω.

Note also:

A. D. 3dc. P. Oxy. XIV. 1664 (118)
Χαῖρε κύριέ μου Ἀπίων Φιλοσάραπίς σε προσαγορεύω εὐχόμενός σε σώζεσθαι πανοικησίᾳ καὶ εὖ διάγειν.

A. D. 3dc (late) P. Oxy. XII 1587 (284)
[Χαῖροις or Χαῖρε κύριέ μου] Σαραπίων Ἀμμώνιός σε [προσαγορεύω.]

A. D. 3d-4thc. P. Oxy. I 122 (189)
——ς Γαιανὸς χρηστέ μου ἀδελφὲ Ἀγήνωρ χαῖρε.

---

## 2. BUSINESS LETTERS

(Receipts, leases, loans, contracts, sales, etc.)

A— to B— χαίρειν.

B. C. 258-3 P. P. II 13 (37)
Ἀρχέστρατος Κλέωνι χαίρειν.

B. C. 250 P. P. II 32 (111); see also: P. P. III32 (71); II 40 (136) B. C. 240.
Ἁρμάις Βακχίωι χαίρειν.

B. C. 242 P. S. I. 390 (120)
Θευκλῆς Ζήνωνι Ἡρακλείτωι χαίρειν.

B. C. 225 P. Eleph. 28 (78)
Μνήσαρχος Ἀντιπάτρωνι χαίρειν.

see also: P. Eleph. 39, 9, 11, 12, 18, 10, B. C. 225-223

B. C. 176-65 P. Amh. II 55 (64)
Δημήτριος Σινωπεὺς τῆς β ἱππαρχίας (ἑβδομηκοντάρουρος) Μαρρῇ καὶ τοῖς μετόχοις χαίρειν.

B. C. 160 P. Leid. C (21)
Πτολεμαῖος Πτολεμαίου Μακεδ—— Δημητρίῳ Σώσου Κρητὶ τῶν προτέρων Εὐμήλου τακτομίσθῳ χαίρειν.

B. C. 146 P. Amh. II 56 (65); see also: II 57 (65).
Διόδωρος ὃς καὶ Πετροσοῦχος Μαρρείους προφήτης Σοκνοπαίου θεοῦ μεγάλου Ἀμμωνίωι χαίρειν.

B. C. 136 P. Grenf. II 17 (34)
Πατοῦς Πατοῦτος Τακῶιτι Πατοῦτος χαίρειν.

B. C. 132 P. Amh. II 58 (66)
Ἀκουσίλαος Τεσενούφιος Μαρρῆς(=ρεῖ) γρ. είερῖ Σουκενεπαίου θεοῦ μεγάλου χαίρειν.

B. C. 114 P. Amh. II 32 (38)
Φανίας Πρωτάρχου Πασικράτηι Ἀπολλωνίου χαίρειν.

B. C. 112 P. Tebt. I 107 (467)
Πτολεμαῖος Μενίσκου Μεγχεῖ χαίρειν.

B. C. 111 P. Rein. 11 (73)
Ἐμσιγῆσις ἡ καὶ Βερενίκη Λεωνίδου Περσίνη Διονυσίωι Κεφάλατος χαίρειν.

B. C. 73 or 44 P. Oxy. XIV 1639 (56)
Ὀρσενοῦφις καὶ Πεκῦσις ἀμφότεροι Πετοσίριος Πέρσαι τῆς ἐπιγονῆς Θέωνι καὶ Θοώνει τῶν κατοίκων ἱππέων χαίρειν.

B. C. 33-30 P. Ryl. 73 (21)
Ἀρνῆσις Σενθέως καὶ τούτου υἱοὶ Σενθεὺς καὶ Ὀννῶφρις οἱ γ τῶν ἀπὸ Σετρεμπάειτος καὶ Εὔβιος Πνεφερῶτος Ἁρμιύσει Ψεμπνούτιος προβατοκνηνοτρόφων Εὐημερείας χαίρειν.

A. D. 15 P. Hawara (Archiv V 41 p-480)
Κόιντος Ζηνᾶς Κοίντου υἱὸς Γαίωι Ἰουλίωι Ζωσίμου χαίρειν.

A. D. 16 P. Ryl. 183 (225); also 183a (226); P. B. M. III 1168 (135) A. D. 18.
Ἀνχορίνφις Ἡρακλείδου προστάτης ἰδίων ὄνων Ἀπολλωνίου τοῦ Ἀλεξάνδρου ἐπισπουδαστοῦ Ἀφροδισίῳ καὶ Πετερμουθίωνι τοῖς δυσὶ Ἀσκληπιάδου χαίρειν.

A. D. 36 P. Oxy. II 267 (243); also: A. D. 54 P. Oxy II 264 (234)
Τρύφων Διονυσίου Πέρσης τῆς ἐπιγονῆς Σαραεῦτι Ἀπίωνος μετὰ κυρίου Ὀννώφριος τοῦ Ἀντιπάτρου χαίρειν.

A. D. 57 P. Oxy. II 269 (250)
Διόσκορος Ζηνοδώρου Πέρσαι τῆς ἐπιγονῆς Τρύφωνι Διονυσίου χαίρειν.

also: A. D. 69 P. Hamb. 2 (6); A. D. 70 P. Gen. 3 (35).

A. D. 73 P. Tebt. II 387 (241)
Πανῆσις Πακήβκις Διοσκόρῳ Μάρωνος χαίρειν.

A. D. 90 P. Amh. II 103 (131)
Εὐτυχίδης Ἀχιλλίωνος Σαραπίωνι Εὐτυχίδους γεωργῷ χαίρειν.

also: P. B. M. I 260 (261); II 285 (201); A. D. 91 P. Flor. I 85 (168)

A. D. 93 C. P. R. 12 (41)
Λούκιος Σεναγουβᾶς Διονυσίωι Διδύμου χαίρειν.

A. D. 99 P. Fay. 100 (241)
Ἀφροδοῦς Σατύρου μετὰ κυρίου τοῦ συγγενοῦς Ἀμμωνίου τοῦ Ἡρακλείδου Σαμβᾷ τῷ καὶ Διδύμῳ τραπεζίτῃ χαίρειν.

see also: B. G. U. IV 1066 (104) A. D. 98.

A. D. 103 P. Oxy. III 511 (242)
Ἁρμιῦσις ὁ καὶ Ἡρακλᾶς Διδύμῳ Σαραπίωνος δημοσίῳ ἀφροδισιαστῇ χαίρειν.

see also: A. D. 102 B. G. U. I 44 (58); P. B. M. II 172 (205) A. D. 105.

A. D. 110 C. P. R. 13 (42)
———μων Ὡρίωνος Πέρσης τῆς ἐπιγονῆς Ἀμμωνίωι Περικλέου χαίρειν.
see also: A. D. 113-4 B. G. U. I 68 (81); A. D. 115 B. G. U. I 60(63)

A. D. 120 P. Ryl. 168 (201)
Πετεχῶν Ἀρεῶτος Ἑρμίᾳ Σαβουρίωνος χαίρειν.
see also: B. G. U. I 69 (83)

A. D. 124 P. Ryl. 180 (222);
Νωρβανὸς Ὀρέστης Ἑρμίᾳ Σαβουρίωνος χαίρειν.

A. D. 125 P. Hib. 104 (132)
Δημητρία ἡ καὶ Τασεῦς Ἀπολλονίδου μετὰ κυρίου τοῦ ἐμαυτῆς υἱοῦ Ἀρείου Νεάρχου τοῦ καὶ Μεγχῆος Ἀνουβίωνι Σεραπίωνος γεοργῶι χαίρειν.
also: P. Amh. II 87 (108); P. B. M. III 1173 (207); P. Gen. 56 (37); A. D. 124 P. Gen 300 (36); A. D. 127 P. Amh. II 105 (132); also: A. D. 123 P. B. M. III 839 (140); A. D. 128 P. Tebt. II 379 (223); A. D. 130 P. Oxy. III 500 (209); A. D. 137 P. Gen. 21 (40);

A. D. 139 P. Ryl. 163 (190)
Ἑρμαῖος Διογένους——— Ἑρμοπολείτης ἀναγραφόμενος ἐπ' ἀμφόδου Πόλεως Λιβὸς———μετὰ κυρίου τοῦ αὐτῆς πατρὸς Δίου Ἀντιμάχου χαίρειν.

A. D. 141-2 P. Oxy. I 98 (160)
Χαιρήμων Θέωνος τοῦ Θέωνος μητρὸς Τοτοεῦτος ἀπ' Ὀξυρύγχων πόλεως Ἀρχίᾳ ἀπελευθέρῳ Ἀμοίταιος Ζωίλου ἀπὸ τῆς αὐτῆς πόλεως χαίρειν.
also: A. D. 141 P. Tebt. II 372 (209); A. D. 142 P. Gen. 104 (41); P. B. M. III 1132b (141); P. Oxy. IV 728 (212); A. D. 145 P. Flor. I 23 (47).

A. D. 149 P. Tebt. II 394 (253)
Δίδυμος ὁ καὶ Λοῦρις Λυσιμάχου Λυσιμάχῳ Πασίωνος χαίρειν.
also: A. D. 150 P. Oxy. IV 732 (224); A. D. 153 B. G. U. I 155 (168)

A. D. 155 P. Oxy. IV 724 (204)
Πανεχώτης ὁ καὶ Πανάρης τῶν κεκοσμητευκότων τῆς Ὀξυρυγχειτῶν πόλεως διὰ Γεμέλλου φίλου Ἀπολλωνίῳ σημιογράφῳ χαίρειν.
also: A. D. 158-9 P. Oxy. VIII 1123 (215); B. G. U. III 800 (97).

A. D. 159 P Fay. 99 (240).
Διδύμη ἡ καὶ Ματρώνα Ἀσκληπιάδου μετὰ κυρίου τοῦ κατὰ μητέρα μου ἀνεψίου Ἥρωνος τοῦ Ἀπολλωνίου Ἥρωνι Σαταβοῦτος γεωργῷ χαίρειν.
also: P. Giss. 29 (77); A. D. 162 P. Oxy. VIII 1132 (229); A. D. 168 P. B. M. II 470 (212); A. D. 171 P. Ryl. 164 (192); A. D. 173 P. Oxy. III 512 (244); A. D. 179 P. Hamb.

39 (158); P. B. M. II 339 (200); A. D. 183 P. B. M. II 341 (213); A. D. 184 P. Oxy. III 513 (245).

A. D. 187 P. Oxy. I 91 (153)

Χωσίων Σαραπίωνος τοῦ Ἁρποκρατίωνος μητρὸς Σαραπιάδος ἀπ' Ὀξυρύγχων πόλεως Τανεντήρει Θώνιος τοῦ Θώνιος μητρὸς Ζωιλοῦτος ἀπὸ τῆς αὐτῆς πόλεως μετὰ κυρίου Δημητρίου Ὡρίωνος μητρὸς Ἀρσινόης ἀπὸ τῆς αὐτῆς πόλεως χαίρειν.

A. D. 188 P. Tebt. II 396 (256)

Διόδωρος ὁ καὶ Ἀμάτιος υἱὸς Ἥρωνος τοῦ καὶ Σαραπίωνος ἐξηγητεύσαντος Ταορσεῦτι Εὐτύχου χαίρειν.

Also: P. B. M. II 343 (213); A. D. 189 B. G. U. I 71 (85); A. D. 2dc. P. Oxy. III 505 (230);

A. D. 3dc. B. G. U. I 24 (37)

Αὐρήλιος Ἡρακλείδης Ὥρου Αὐρηλίᾳ Διοδώρᾳ χέρειν.

also: A. D. 201 B. G. U. I 156 (169); A. D. 203-4 P. Ryl. 181 (223);

A. D. 214 P. Ryl. 184 (226)

Σερηνίλλα διὰ Ἡρακλείδου Μαρίωνι γεωργῷ χαίρειν.

also: A. D. 216-219 P. B. M. IV. 851 (48); A. D. 225 P. Oxy. VI 909 (257); VII 1040 (184); A. D. 246 P. Ryl. 177 (217);

A. D. 247 P. Grenf. II 68 (104)

Αὐρήλιος Πετοσῖρις Πετοσίριος νεκροτάφος ἀπὸ Ἰβειτῶν πόλεως Αὐρηλίῳ Πετεχῶντι υἱῷ Τμάρσιος ἀπὸ κώμης Κύσεως χαίρειν.

A. D. 249 P. Oxy. XIV 1636 (42)

Αὐρήλιος Σερῆνος ὁ καὶ Σαραπίων Ἀγαθείνου μητρὸς Ταποσειριάδος ἀπ' Ὀξυρύγχων πόλεως Αὐρηλίῳ Πανεσπεῖ Πτόλλιδος μητρὸς Ἀν—— ἀπὸ κώμης Σεφύρεως χαίρειν.

A. D. 255 P. Oxy. X 1277 (217)

Αὐρηλία Σαραπιὰς Ἀρείου ἀστὴ χωρὶς κυρίου χρηματίζουσα τέκνων δικαίῳ κατὰ τὰ Ῥωμαίων ἔθη Αὐρηλίῳ Θέωνι Ἀμμωνίου τοῦ καὶ Ἀπύγχιος ἀπ' Ὀξυρύγχων πόλεως χαίρειν.

A. D. 263 P. Oxy. VII 1054 (209)

Πέκυλλος Πολυδεύκι χαίρειν.

also: P. Oxy. VI 964 (318); A. D. 267 P. Oxy. VII 1055 (210);

A. D. 268-9 P. Oxy. XIV 1646 (77)a

Κληρονόμοι Οὐιβίου Πουπλίου οὐετρανοῦ τῶν ἐντειμῶς ἀπολελυμένων ἀπὸ ὀφφικιαλίων ἐπάρχου Αἰγύπτου γενομένου βουλευτοῦ τῆς λαμπροτάτης πόλεως τῶν Ἀλεξανδρέων δι' ἐμοῦ Πλουτογένους γραμματεύτου Αὐρηλίῳ Σερήνῳ τῷ καὶ Σαραπίωνει χαίρειν.

also: P. Oxy. XIV 1646 b(77); A. D. 271 C. P. R. 9 (28);

A. D. 279 P. Oxy. XIV 1713 (162)
Αὐρήλιος Σερῆνος ὁ καὶ Σαραπίων ἀπὸ τῆς λαμπρᾶς καὶ λαμπροτάτης Ὀξυρυγχειτῶν πόλεως Αὐρηλίῳ Ἁρποκρατίωνι καὶ ὡς χρηματίζει χαίρειν.

A. D. 289 P. Oxy. XIV 1642 (65)
Αὐρήλιος Δημητριανὸς καὶ ὡς χρηματίζω Ἀ——ω Διδύμῳ τῷ ἀδελφῷ χαίρειν.
also: B. G. U. I 13 (19); A. D. 298 P. Oxy. XIV 1643 (70).

A. D. 290-304 P. Grenf. II 72 (114)
Αὐρήλιος Σοῦρις Πετεχῶντος μητρὸς Τβήκιος ἀπὸ κώμης Κύσεως τῆς Ἰβιτῶν πόλεως ὡς (ἐτῶν) μη οὐλὴ ἐπὶ τοῦ ἀριστεροῦ ποδὸς Αὐρηλίῳ Ψεντφθοῦτι Πετενσφώτου μητρὸς Σευρίσριος ἐξωπυλίτῃ Διοσπόλεως καταμένοντι ἐν νεκροπόλει Ἀπτύτεως χαίρειν

---

To B—— from A——.

(Offers to rent, buy, etc.)

B. C. 13 B. G. U. IV 1052 (69) contract.
Πρωτάρχωι παρὰ Θερμίου τῆς Ἀπίωνος μετὰ κυρίου τοῦ Ἀπολλωνίου τοῦ Χαιρέου καὶ παρὰ Ἀπολλωνίου τοῦ Πτολεμαίου.
see also B. G. U. IV 1054 (76); 1055 (78); 1057 (84);

A. D. 13 P. Oxy. IX 1188 (203). βούλομαι ὠνήσασθαι.
Κοίντωι Ἀττίωι Φρόντωνι παρὰ Διδύμου τοῦ Ἡρακλείδου.

A. D. 26 P. Ryl. 166 (197) βούλομαι μισθώσασθαι.
Γαίωι Ἰουλίωι Ἀμαράντωι παρὰ Ὀρσενούφιος πρεσβυτέρου τοῦ Ἀφροδισίου τῶν ἀπὸ Εὐημερίας τῆς Θεμίστου μερίδος.

A. D. 39 P. Ryl. 167 (199) β.μ.
Κάστορι Ἀσκληπιάδου παρὰ Σερᾶτος τοῦ Σεραπίωνος.

A. D. 56-7 P. Ryl. 171 (205) β.μ.
Εὐσχήμονι οἰκονόμωι τῆς ἐν τῶι Ἀρσινοείτηι Τιβερίου Κλαυδίου Δορυφόρου πρότερον Ναρκισσιανῆς οὐσίας παρὰ Πάπου τοῦ Τρύφωνος τῶν ἀπὸ Ἡρακλείας τῆς Θεμίστου μερίδος καταγεινομένου ἐν ἐποικίωι Ἀντωνίας Δρούσου διὰ Ψενεριεῦτος Πέρσου τῆς ἐπιγονῆς.
also: A. D. 78 P. Amh. II 85 (105); β. μ.

A. D. 89 P. Hamb. 5 (17) β.μ.
Λουκίωι Οὐαλερίωι Γάλλωι ἀπολυσίμωι ἱππῖ παρὰ Νεοπτολέμου τοῦ κτλ.
also: A. D. 88 P. B. M. I 163 (182) β.μ ; A. D. 94 P. B. M. 216 (186) β.μ.; A. D. 98 P. Iand. 26 (80);

A. D. 2dc. P. Oxy. III 498 (214) contract.
Ἀντωνίᾳ Ἀσκληπιάδι τῇ καὶ Κυρίᾳ διὰ Ἀπολλωνίου ἐπιτρόπου παρὰ Ἀσκλᾶτος Ἀλεξάνδρου καὶ

'Απολλωνίου 'Αμόιτος μητρὸς Ταύριος ἀμφοτέρων ἀπ' 'Οξυρύγχων πόλεως.

A. D. 128 P. Amh. II 38 (109) β.μ.

Εὐτυχίδῃ Σαραπίωνος παρὰ Κάστορος Πανεχώτου τῶν ἀπὸ κώμης 'Ακώρεως καταγεινομένωι ἐν κώμηι Μνάχει.

also: A. D. 116-7 P. Tebt. II 309 (103); A. D. 131 P. Tebt. II 374 (214) β.μ.

A. D. 140 P. Tebt. II 375 (215) β. μ.

'Ηρακλείδῃ τῷ καὶ Νίννῳ Μύσθου καὶ τῇ τούτου μητρεὶ 'Ισιδώρᾳ 'Ηρακλείδου παρὰ 'Ισίωνος τοῦ Ἥρωνος ἀπὸ τῆς μητροπόλεως ἀπὸ ἀμφόδου Μακεδόνων.

also: A. D. 149 P. B. M. II 314 (189) β.μ.; A. D. 151 B. G. U. I 227 (227); A. D. 154 C. P. R. 31 (157) β.μ.; A. D. 159 P. Amh. II 81 (113); β.μ.

A. D. 161 P. Fay. 93 (230) β. μ.

Κάστορι 'Αντιφίλου Σωσικοσμίῳ τῷ καὶ 'Αλθαιεῖ παρὰ Σαραπίωνος 'Αρτεμιδώρου τοῦ Πτολεμαίου ἀπὸ ἀμφόδου Χηνοβοσκίων 'Ετέρων.

also: A. D. 162 P. Tebt. II 376 (217) β.μ.; A. D. 157 B. G. U. I 166 (176); A. D. 162-3 P. Amh. II 92 (115); A. D. 168 P. Grenf. II 57 (92) β.μ.; A. D. 180-192 P. Amh. II 97 (123); A. D. 181 P. Amh. II 93 (167); A. D. 186 B. G. U. I 39 (54) β.μ.;

note also A. D. 162 P. B. M. II 168 (190) B— from A—.

A. D. 196-7 P. Ryl. 169 (203) β. μ.

Νεωτερίδι τῇ καὶ Μαξιμιναίνῃ 'Ερμοπολιτίδι διὰ 'Ισιδώρου προνοητοῦ παρὰ Προοῦτος 'Ερμίνου καὶ Χιχόιτος ἀδελφοῦ τῶν αὐτῶν γονέων γεωργῶν 'Ερμοπολιτῶν.

also C. P. H. 119 VI 3dc. A. D.

A. D. 208 P. Ryl. 172 (206) β.μ.

Φλαυίᾳ Πετρωνίλλῃ τῇ καὶ Τιτανιάδει μετὰ κυρίου τοῦ ἀνδρὸς Γαίου Οὐαλλερίου Πάνσα γυμνασιαρχήσαντος παρὰ Καν—ερέως καὶ 'Εριήους ἀδελφοῦ.

also A. D. 210 P. Tebt. II 377 (219) β.μ. A. D. 217 P. Strass. 2 (12) β.μ.

A. D. 238 P. Ryl. 100 (71) β.μ.

Τοῖς πρεσβυτέροις Μαγδώλων Μιρῆ τοῦ ἐνεστῶτος β (ἔτους) παρὰ Αὐρηλίου Μέλανος Φίβιος ἀπὸ κώμης Μαγδώλων Μιρῆ.

A. D. 265 P. Tebt. II 378 (221) β.μ.

Αὐρηλίοις Σαραπάμμωνι παρήλικι καὶ 'Ηρακλείᾳ χωρὶς κυρίου χρηματίζουσα ἀμφοτέροις Ἥρωνος ἀπὸ —— εως τοῦ δὲ Σαραπάμμωνος μετὰ κηδεστρίας τῆς ἀδελφῆς 'Ηρακλείας τῆς προκειμένης παρὰ Αὐρηλίου Δημητρίου καὶ ὡς χρηματίζει.

Compare also: A. D. 280 P. Oxy. XIV 1631 (15).

B. C. 99-98 P. Good. I 9 (12)
Παρὰ Πατῆτος τοῦ Πανεβχώνιος.

A. D. 3dc. P. Oxy. VI 974 (320)
Παρὰ Σαρᾶ Διονυσίῳ γεωργῷ χαίρειν.

A. D. 3dc. P. Oxy. VIII 1141 (240)
Παρὰ Ἰουλίου Διογένους Θωνίῳ οἰνοπαραλημπτῇ χαίρειν.

A. D. 293 P. Oxy. VIII 1140 (239)
Παρὰ Σεύθου Σαραπίωνι γεωργῷ χαίρειν.

---

## 3. PETITIONS, COMPLAINTS, APPLICATIONS.

To B— χαίρειν A—.

B. C. 272-1 ? P. S. I. VI 551 (1)
Ζήνωνι χαίρειν Ὧρος.

B. .C 258-7 P. S. I. 435 (161)
Ἀπολλωνίωι χαίρειν Ζώιλος.

B. C. 254 P. S. I. 352 (86)
Ζήνωνι χαίρειν Ἀρτεμίδωρος.

B. C. 255-4 P. P. II 4 (6)
Κλέωνι ἀρχιτέκτονι χαίρειν οἱ δεκατάρχοι τῶν λατόμων ἀπὸ τῆς ἐγβατηρίας.
also P. P. II 4 (12);

B. C. 255-4 P. P. II 4 (11)
Κλέωνι χαίρειν Δημήτριος.

B. C. 3dc. P. Lille I 7 (60)
Βασιλεῖ Πτολεμαίωι χαίρειν Διονυσόδωρος.

B. C. 3dc. P. S. I. 414 (140)
Ζήνωνι χαίρειν Μένων ἀμπελουργός. ὀφείλεταί μοι.

B. C. 3dc. P. S. I. 440 (166)
Ζήνωνι χαίρειν οἱ ἱερόδουλοι τῆς Βουβαστίου ὄντες αἰλουροβοσκοί. καλῶς ποιῶν ὁ βασιλεὺς κτλ.

B. C. 3dc. P. S. I. 441 (162)
Ζήνωνι χαίρειν Παῆσις. ἵνα μὴ συμβαίνηι κτλ.

B. C. 3dc. P. S. I. 541 (125)
Βασιλεῖ μεγάλωι Πτολεμαίωι χαίρειν Αἴγυπτος.

B. C. 3dc. P. S. I. 418 (144)
Ζήνωνι χαίρειν Πύρων. καλῶς ποιήσεις κτλ.

B. C. 3dc. P. S. I. 420 (145)
Ζήνωνι χαίρειν Σεμθεύς. συνέταξάς μοι κτλ.

B. C. 250-49 P. S. I. 372 (101); B. C. 250 P. Hib. I 35 (176)
Ζήνωνι χαίρειν Ὧρος Πεταρμώτιος.

B. C. 248-7 P. S. I. 383 (160)
Βασιλεῖ Πτολεμαίωι χαίρειν Θήρων

B. C. 248-7 P. S. I. 384 (112)
Ζήνωνι χαίρειν Εὐφαμίδας τῶγ Κλεισίου
also: B. C. 3dc. P. S. I. 419 (144); B. C. 256-5 P. S. I. 341 (77);

B. C. 3dc. P. S. I. VI 589 (34)
Ζήνωνι χαίρειν Ἑρμίας. καλῶς ἂν ποιήσαις κτλ.
see also P. S. I. 341, 399, 402, 422, 488, 571, B. C. 258-252; 3dc.

B. C. 222 P. Lille I 1 (58)
Βασιλεῖ Πτολεμαίωι χαίρειν Πτολεμαῖος Μακεδὼν τῶν Πυθαγγέλου καὶ Πτολεμαίου τοῦ υἱοῦ αὐτοῦ ἐπιλάρχης κληροῦχος.

B. C. 222 P. Lille 2 (65)
Βασιλεῖ Πτολεμαίωι χαίρειν Ἀσία.

B. C. 221 P. Lille II 9 (90)
Βασιλεῖ Πτολεμαίωι χαίρειν Ἐποῆρις τῆς Πανῆτος ἰσιονόμος κατοικοῦσα Ἀθηνᾶς κώμην τῆς Θεμίστου μερίδος.
see also P. Lille II 3, 4, 5, 6, 7, 11, 13, 14, 23, 25, etc. B. C. 222-218. cp. also P. Hibeh I 34 B. C. 243-2.

B. C. 163-2 P. Par. 26
Βασιλεῖ Πτολεμαίωι καὶ Βασιλίσσηι Κλεοπάτραι τῆι ἀδελφῆι θεοῖς φιλομήτορσι χαίρειν Θαυὴς καὶ Ταοὺς δίδυμαι αἱ λειτουργοῦσαι ἐν τῶι πρὸς Μέμφει μεγάλωι Σαραπείωι.
also: P. B. M. I 45 (35) and 23 (37) B. C. 160-158. P. Leid. B. (9) B. C. 164;

B. C. 157 P. Amh. II 33 (38)
Βασιλεῖ Πτολεμαίωι καὶ Βασιλίσσηι Κλεοπάτραι τῆι ἀδελφῆι θεοῖς φιλομήτορσι χαίρειν Μαρεπάθις Σισούχου καὶ Πατκῶς Ὀννώφριος κτλ. βασιλικοὶ γεωργοὶ τῶν ἀπὸ τῆς Σοκνοπαίου Νήσου τῆς Ἡρακλείδου μερίδος τοῦ Ἀρσινοίτου νομοῦ.

B. C. 141 P. Rein. 7 (54)
Βασιλεῖ Πτολεμαίωι καὶ Βασιλίσσηι Κλεοπάτραι τῆι ἀδελφῆι καὶ Βασιλίσσηι Κλεοπάτραι τῆι γυναικὶ [θεοῖς] Εὐεργέταις χαίρειν Κέφαλος Διονυσίου τῶν ἐν τῶι Ἑρμοπολίτηι μισθοφόρων καταγινομένων δ' ἐν τῆι Ἀκώρεως.

B. C. 118 P. Tebt. I 43 (146)
Βασιλεῖ Πτολεμαίωι καὶ Βασιλίσσηι Κλεοπάτραι τῆι ἀδελφῆι καὶ Κλεοπάτραι τῆι γυναικὶ θεοῖς Εὐεργέταις χαίρειν Μεγχῆς κωμογραμματεὺς Κερκεοσίρεως τῆς Πολέμωνος μερίδος τοῦ Ἀρσινοίτου καὶ ὁ τούτου ἀδελφὸς Πολέμων.
also: B. C. 115 P. Fay. 11 (100); B. C. 103 P. Fay 12 (103);

B. C. 99 P. Leid. G (41) b. also: P. Leid H (47) b.
Βασιλεῖ Πτολεμαίωι τῶι καὶ Ἀλεξάνδρωι θεῶι φιλομήτορι καὶ βασιλίσσηι Βερενικῆι τῆι ἀδελφῆι θεᾶι φιλαδέλφωι χαίρειν Πετῆσις Χενούφιος ἀρχενταφιαστὴς Ὀσοράπιος καὶ Ὀσορμεύιος θεῶν ἀειζωίων.
Compare also:

A. D. 200-2 P. Oxy. IV 705 (162)

Τοῖς εὐμενεστάτοις Αὐτοκράτορσι Σεουήρῳ καὶ Ἀντωνίνῳ τοῖς πάντων ἀνθρώπων σωτῆρσι καὶ εὐεργέταις Αὐρήλιος Ὡρείων γενόμενος στρατηγὸς καὶ ἀρχιδικαστὴς τῆς λαμπροτάτης πόλεως τῶν Ἀλεξανδρέων χαίρειν.

---

To B— from A—

(On account of the identity of form in the opening formula we include in this section with the Petitions all communications from and to officials, such as apographai, epicrisis, applications for state monopolies, official reports, notices of death, birth, etc.)

B. C. 3dc. P. Lille I 8 (62)

ὑπόμνημα Νικάνορι παρὰ Φίβιος τοῦ Πάσιτος γεωργοῦ ἐξ Ὀξυρύγχων τοῦ Ἀρσινοίτου.

B. C. 3dc. P. Lille I 9 (64)

ὑπόμνημα Ἀσκληπιάδηι οἰκονόμωι παρ' Ἀπόλλωνος τοῦ ἐξειληφότος τὴν διάθεσιν τοῦ ἐλαίου.

B. C. 3dc. P. S. I. 400 (129)

ὑπόμνημα Ζήνωνι παρὰ Ἀγάθωνος.

B. C. 3dc. P. S. I. 407 (135); see also ibidem 408, 409, 413, 442.

ὑπόμνημα Ζήνωνι παρὰ Θευφίλου ζωγράφου.

B. C. 260-59 P. P. II 2 (2). also: P. P. II 1.

Διοφάνει στρατηγῶι παρ' Ὀνήτορος καὶ Ἀσκληπιάδου καὶ Μουσαίου.

B. C. 252 P. P. II 20 (64); also: P. P. II 20 (61); 38 (121); B. C. 250 P. P. II 6 (17); 32 (108)

Ἡρακλείδηι οἰκονόμωι παρὰ Θεοφίλου τοῦ παρ' Ἀντικλέους.

B. C. 250 P. P. III 34 (72)

προσάγγελμα Σεμθεῖ κωμογραμματεῖ Λυσιμάχιδος παρὰ Δωσιθέου Θραϊκός.

B. C o P. S. I. 378 (106)

ὑπόμνημα Ζήνωνι παρὰ Περδιάκου.

B. C. 246 P. P. II 18 (58)

Διονυσοδώρωι οἰκονόμωι τῆς Ἡρακλείδου μερίδος παρὰ Ἀπολλωνίου τοῦ Θέωνος ἐκ Πτολεμαίδος τῆς νέας.

also: P. P. II 8 (20); B. C. 241 P. P. II 12 (31); B. C. 240 P. P. III 32 (66); 28 (59)e.

B. C. 241-40 P. Hib. 72 (222)

Δωρίωνι ἐπιστάτηι παρὰ Πετοσίριος ἀρχιερέως.

also: P. P. II 9 (24); 10 (25); 10 (26); P.P. III 29 (62); 30 (62); P. P. III 29 (62)e;

B. C. 223 P. Eleph. 19 (62); also: P. Eleph. 20 (63); 21 (67);

Ἀπολλοδώρωι παρὰ Πλατοῦτος τοῦ μάχου.

B. C. 225-4 P. Eleph. 27 (45); B. C. 200 P. Eleph. 24 (71); 25 (72);

Μίλωνι τῶι παρὰ Εὐφρονίου πράκτορι ἱερῶν παρὰ Πινύριος τοῦ Ἐστφήνιος καὶ Ψινταήτιος μικροῦ Ἐστφήνιος.

B. C. 163 P. Leid. D (24); also: P. Leid. E (29). B. C. 160.

Σαραπίωνι τῶν διαδόχων καὶ ὑποδιοικητῆι παρὰ Πτολεμαίου τῶν ἐν κατοχῆι ὄντων ἐν τῶι μεγάλωι Σαραπιείωι ἔτος τοῦτο ἑνδέκατον,

also P. B. M. I 20, 21, 33, 35, 42, 44, B. C. 163-161. B. C. 164-3 P. B. M. I 22 (7); P. Amh. II 34 (41) B. C. 157 about P. Amh. II 36 (45) B. C. 135; 35 (42) B. C. 132.

B. C. 119 P. Tebt. I 41 (142)

Κρονίωνι ἀρχιφυλακίτηι Κερκεοσίρεως παρὰ Ἁρμιύσιος κωμάρχου καὶ τῶν ἐκ τῆς αὐτῆς βασιλικῶν γεωργῶν.

also: B. C. 117 P. Tebt. I 40 (140); B. C. 116-111 P. B. M. II 401 (12); B. C. 115 to 110: P. Tebt. I 30, 39, 31, 42, 44, 45, 46, 48, 49, 51, 52, 50, 53; P. Rein. 17 (93); 18 (95) B. C. 109, 108.; B. C. 2dc. P. Grenf. I 42 (73); B. G. U. III 1012 (352);

B. C. Ptolemaic. P. Gizeh (Archiv. II p. 80) 10371

Ἀμφικλεῖ συγγενεῖ καὶ ὑπομνηματογράφωι παρὰ τῶν ἐν Κροκοδείλων πόλει τῆς Θηβαίδος ἱερείων τοῦ Σούχου καὶ τῶν ἄλλων.

also: ibidem 10277, 10323;

B. C. 1stc. P. B. M. I 50 (48)

Μητροδώρωι ἐπιμελήτηι παρὰ Ἀπύγχιος Ἰναρώιτος.

B. C. Ptolemaic. P. P. III 72 (200)

Εἰμούθηι βασειλεικῶι γραμματεῖ παρὰ Πάσειτος τοῦ Σοκμήνιος βασιλικοῦ γεωργοῦ ἐκ Ταμαύεως τῆς Ἡρακλείδου μερίδος τοῦ Ἀρσινοίτου νομοῦ.

also: P. P. III 72 (201); 67 (194); 73 (203); 68 (194);

B. C. 1stc. B. G. U. IV 1187 (324)

Ἀνδρομάχωι συγγενεῖ καὶ στρατηγῶι καὶ ἐπὶ τῶν προσόδων παρὰ Κάστορος τοῦ Πολυδεύκου τῶν ἐκ κώμης Τοκώεως.

B. C. 93-60 P. Tebt. II 283 (41)

Ἀπολλωνίωι τῶι διεξάγοντι τὰ κατὰ τὴν ἐπιστρατηγίαν Τεβτύνεως παρὰ Ταρμιύσιος τῆς Πετεσούχου τῆς ἐκ Τεβτύνεως.

also: B. C. 89 P. Ryl. 68 (9); B. C. 86 P. Tebt. I 54 (163);

B. C. 71-70 P. Grenf. I 38 (69); also: B. C. 34 P. Ryl. 69 (10);

Νούμηνι ἀρχισωματοφύλακι καὶ στρατηγῶι παρὰ Πωκᾶτος τοῦ Ὀνῶτος φυλακείτου ἀμίσθου.

B. C. 19 P. Grenf. I 45 (77)

Ἀπολλωνίῳ κωμογραμματεῖ Θεαδελφίας παρὰ Πνεφερῶτος τοῦ Φανεμιέως δημοσίου γεωργοῦ.

also: B. C. 114 to 110 B. G. U. IV 1060, 1061, 1197; B. G. U. II 352;

B. C. 4-3 P. Oxy. XII 1457 (116)

Ἀρίστωνι καὶ Πτολεμαίῳ τοῖς ἐξειληφόσι τὴν ἑξαδραχμήαν τῶν ὄνων παρὰ Θοώνιος τοῦ Θώνιος.

also: B. C. 1 or A. D. 1 B. G. U. IV 1189; A. D. 2 B. G. U. IV 1201 (343);

A. D. 12 B. G. U. III 757 (65)

Οὐαλερίωι Οὐάρωι στρατηγῶι παρὰ Ἡρακλείους τοῦ Κοζίνθου τῶν ἀπὸ Αὐτοδίκης δημοσίων γεωργῶν.

also: A. D. 14-15 P. B. M. II 357 (165); 445 (166);

A. D. 19-20 P. Oxy. II 252 (205)

Θέωνι καὶ Εὐτυχείδῃ τοπογραμματεῦσι καὶ κωμογραμματεῦσι παρὰ Θοώνιος τοῦ Ἀμμωνίου.

also: A. D. 20 P. Oxy. II 254 (207); 281 (271);

A. D. 23 P. Oxy. II 244 (193)

Χαιρέαι στρατηγῶι παρὰ Κηρίνθου Ἀντωνίας Δρούσου δούλου.

also: A. D. 26 P. Oxy. II 245 (195);

A. D. 29 P. Ryl. 125 (120)

Σεραπίωνι ἐπιστατῇ φυλακειτῶν παρὰ Ὀρσενούφιος τοῦ Ἁρπαήσιος ἡγουμένου κώμης Εὐημερίας τῆς Θεμίστου μερίδος.

also: A. D. 28-50. P. Ryl. from 126 to 152.

A. D. 37 P. Fay. 29 (138)

Ἡρακλείδῃ κωμογραμματεῖ Εὐημερίας παρὰ Μύσθου τοῦ Πενεουήρεως τῶν ἀπὸ Εὐημερίας τῆς Θεμίστου μερίδος.

also: A. D. 30-45 P. Oxy. II 282 (273); A. D. 40-41 P. B. M. II 177 (167); A. D. 44 P. Oxy. II 279 (269);. A. D. 44-50 P. Oxy. II 251, 255, 283; P. Oxy. I 38 (81);

A. D. 50 P. Oxy. II 284 (275)

Τιβερίωι Κλαυδίωι Πασίωνι στρατηγῷ παρὰ Ἀλεξάνδρου τοῦ Ἀπολλωνίου τῶν ἀπ' Ὀξυρύγχων πόλεως γερδίων λαύρας δρόμου Θοήριδος.

also: P. Tebt. II 299 (83); P. Oxy. II 285 (276); A. D. 54 B. G. U. I 112 (129); P. Ryl. 119 (106); A. D. 58 P. Oxy. II 268 (247); A. D. 60 B. G. U. II 650 (316); A. D. 61 P. Oxy. II 262 (232); A. D. 66 P. Oxy. II 246 (195); P. B. M. II 281 (65); A. D. 67 B. G. U. I 379 (39); A. D. 71 P. Tebt. II 302 (88);

A. D. 72 P. S. I. V 459 (35)

Ἀπολλωνίωι Ἀπολλωνίου ἐκλήμπτορι ζυγοστασίου μητροπόλεως καὶ νομῶν καὶ ἄλλων ὠνῶν παρὰ Θέωνος τοῦ Θέωνος τοῦ Ὥρου ἀπὸ κώμης Καρανίδος.

also: A. D. 77 P. Oxy. II 263 (232)

A. D. 80 P. Oxy. II 249 (200)

Ἐπιμάχωι καὶ Θέωνι βιβλιοφύλαξι παρὰ Διογᾶτος τοῦ Τεῶτος τοῦ Κενταύρου μητρὸς Ἀπίας τῆς Πρωτᾶτος τῶν ἀπ' Ὀξυρύγχων πόλεως.

also: P. Oxy. II 248 (198); A. D. 83 P. Oxy. XII 1462 (185); A. D. 84 P. Ryl. 107 (84); A. D. 86 P. Oxy. VII 1028 (161); A. D. 90 P. Oxy. I 72 (135); P. Oxy. II 247 (197); IV 713 (180); A. D. 99 B. G. U. I 226 (226); A. D. 100 B. G. U. IV 1068 (107);

A. D. 2dc. P. Ryl. 121 (114)

Ἥρωνι ἱερεῖ ἐξηγητῇ παρὰ Σαραπιοδώρου τοῦ Ἀπολλωνίου παλαιστροφύλακος τοῦ μεγάλου γυμνασίου.

A. D. 2dc. P. Grenf. II 62 (98)

Ἱέρακι στρατηγῷ Ἀρσινοίτου Ἡρακλείδου μερίδος παρὰ Ἀπύγχιος καὶ μετόχων πραιτόρων ἀργυρικῶν Σοκνοπαίου Νήσου.

also: P. Strass. I 57 (141); 2dc A. D. P. Tebt. II 330 (143); 327 (137); A. D. 108 B. G. U. IV 1036 (38); A. D. 109 P. Ryl. 108 (85); P. Oxy. III 482 (170); A. D. 111-2 P. Fay. 36 (149); A. D. 114 B. G. U. I 22 (36);

A. D. 115 P. Amh. II 70 (84)

Φήλικι Κλαυδίωι Οὐίνδικι τῶι κρατίστωι ἐπιστρατήγωι παρὰ ἀρχόντων Ἑρμοῦ πόλεως.

also: A. D. 116 P. Oxy. I 74 (137); A. D. 117 P. Ryl. 96 (64); A. D. 118 P. Giss. II 43 (54); A. D. 119 P. Giss. III 61 (39); P. Oxy. XII 1547 (270); A. D. 123 P. Oxy. VI 898 (221); A. D. 127 P. Tebt. II 323 (131); A. D. 129 P. Hamb. 6 (22); P. Fay. 31 (140);

A. D. 129 P. Oxy. I 75 (138)

Διογένει καὶ Θέωνι τῷ καὶ Πτολεμαίῳ βιβλιοφύλαξι παρὰ Θέωνος Θέωνος τοῦ Θέωνος μητρὸς Θερμοῦθος Ἀπίωνος ἀπ' Ὀξυρύγχων πόλεως.

also: P. Oxy. III 477, 478, 486, 484, A. D. 132-138; XII 1472 A. D. 136; P. Ryl. 193 (79) A. D. 134; 113 (96) A. D. 133; 105 (82) A. D. 136; P. Tebt. II 331 (143) A. D. 131; 329 (140) A. D. 139; P. Amh. II 73 (88) A. D. 129-30; 77 (84) A. D. 139; P. Gen. 19 (38) A. D. 130-31; 18 (39) A. D. 136; P. Hamb. 7 (24), A. D. 131-2; B. G. U. I 53 (67) A. D. 133; P. Fay. 32 (142) A. D. 131; P. Hawara (Archiv. V. p. 308) A. D. 131; P. Strass. 70 (206) A. D. 138; P. Grenf. II 45 (71) A. D. 136; 45 (72) b A. D. 137; P. B. M. II 208 a A. D. 138; P. Ryl. 83 (45) A. D. 138-161.

A. D. 140-1 P. Tebt. II (160)

Ἀρτεμιδώρωι βασιλικῶι γραμματεῖ Ἀρσινοείτου Θεμίστου μερίδος παρὰ Καπίτωνος κωμογραμματέως Θεογονίδος.

also: P. Grenf. II 49 (77); P. Fay. 106 (25); A. D. 142 B. G. U. I 17 (27); A. D. 144 B. G. U. III 729 (33); A. D. 146 P. Tebt. II 294 (63); P. Gen. 30 (5); 54 (42); A. D. 147 P. Amh. II 74 (89); P. Tebt. II 321 (128); A. D. 148 P. Grenf. I 47 (79); B. G. U. 340 (332); P. Gen. 32 (27); A. D. 149 P. S. I. III 160 (11); A. D. 150 P. Fay. 26 (133); 28 (137);

P. Oxy. IX 1198 (220); A. D. 151 P. Fay. 27 (135); P. Tebt. II 300 (85); A. D. 154 P. Amh. II 69 (83); P. Ryl. 98a (68); A. D. 156 P. Gen. 21 (44); P. Oxy. XII 1550 (272); III 487 (183); P. Ryl. 115 (100); A. D. 157 B. G. U. I 195 (204);

A. D. 158 P. Ryl. 106 (83)

*Ἀπολλωνίδῃ καὶ Διδύμῳ γραμματεῦσι μητροπόλεως παρὰ Καπίτωνος συντρόφου ἀπελευθέρου Πτολεμᾶς μητρὸς Τασουχαρίου ἀναγραφομένου ἐπ' ἀμφόδου Ἀπολλωνίου Ἱερακείου.*

also: A. D. 161 P. Meyer 4 (18); P. Grenf. II 56 (89); P. Ryl. 111a (91); A. D. 162 P. Grenf. II 56 (91); P. Oxy. VII 1032 (169); A. D. 163 P. Fay. 33 (144); A. D. 167 P. Ryl. 120 (111); P. Tebt. II 304 (94); A. D. 169 B. G. U. I 168 (177); A. D. 171 P. Fay. 108 (259);

A. D. 172 P. Ryl. 98 (67)

*Ἰσίωνει καὶ τοῖς λοιποῖς ἐπιτηρηταῖς θ μισθοῦ βαφικῆς παρὰ Ἥρωνος Ἡρώδου τοῦ Θεογίτονος ἀπὸ ἀμφόδου Σεκνεπτονείου.*

also: A. D. 170 P. Oxy. I 76 (139); A. D. 173 P. Oxy. I 51 (108); P. Fay. 20 (139); A. D. 174 P. Tebt. II 317 (120); A. D. 175. Gen. 20 (2); A. D. 176 P. Tebt. II 332 (145); 303 (93); A. D. 178 P. Amh. II 71 (86); P. Oxy. III 485 (176); A. D. 180 P. Strass. 34 (122); P. Gen. 4 (26); A. D. 181 P. Tebt. II 320 (127); P. Oxy. I 79 (142); B. G. U. I 60 (75); A. D. 182 P. Oxy. III 475 (159); A. D. 183 B. G. U. I 28 (42);

A. D. 184 P. Amh. II 78 (97)

*Αὐρηλίῳ Ἀντωνείνῳ ἑκατοντάρχῳ παρὰ Στοτοήτιος Ἀγχώφεως ἀπὸ κώμης Σοκνοπαίου Νήσου.*

also: A. D. 186 P. Fay. 41 (158); P. Gen. 103 (49); A. D. 189 P. Tebt. II 292 (58); 322 (129); A. D. 190 P. Tebt. II 336 (150); 301 (86); A. D. 191 B. G. U. I 72 (86); P. Tebt. II 328 (139); A. D. 193 B. G. U. I 46 (60); II 454 (113); 515 (162); P. B. M. II 342 (173) A. D. 195;

A. D. 194 P. Ryl. 116 (102)

*Ἡρακλείδῃ στρατηγῷ Ἑρμοπολίτου παρὰ Σαπρίωνος τοῦ καὶ Ἑρμαίου υἱοῦ Σαραπίωνος κοσμητεύσαντος καὶ γυμνασιαρχήσαντος Ἑρμοῦ πόλεως τῆς μεγάλης.*

also: P. Tebt. II 338 (154); B. G. U. III 1022 (12); P. Grenf. II 61 (95); A. D. 3dc. P. Oxy. XIV 1405 (1); P. Gen. 21 (3); P. Oxy I 70 (130); P. Grenf. II 79 (125) A. D. 200 B. G. U. I 25 (38); P. Tebt. II 334 (147); A. D. 201 P. Oxy. I 54 (111); A. D. 203 B. G. U. I 45 (59); P. Oxy. VIII 1113 (189); A. D. 206 P. Tebt. II 340 (158)a, b; A. D. 207 P. Gen. 10 (22); A. D. 208 P. Tebt. II 324 (132); A. D. 209 B. G. U. I 2 (2).

A. D. 210 P. Flor. I 6 (22)

Καλουεντίῳ Ἀδιουτόρι τῷ κρατίστῳ διοικητῇ παρὰ Διδύμου Μαικηνᾶ κοσμητεύσαντος καὶ γυμνασιαρχήσαντος βουλευτοῦ Ἑρμοῦ πόλεως τῆς μεγάλης ἀρχαίας καὶ λαμπρᾶς.

also: A. D. 211 P. Oxy. I 56 (114); B. G. U. I 98 (118); A. D. 215 P. Oxy. XII 1463 (187); A. D. 216 P. Tebt. II 333 (146); B. G. U. I 321 and 322; A. D. 217 P. Oxy. IX 1202 (230); A. D. 219 P. Oxy. XII 1460 (181).

A. D. 220-1 P. Grenf. I 49 (81)

Αὐρηλίωι Σαβεινιανῷ τῷ κρατίστῳ ἐπιστρατήγῳ παρὰ Αὐρηλίου Πτολεμαίου τοῦ καὶ Σεμπρονίου Ἀπολιναρίου Ἀντινοέως

also: P. B. M. II 353 (112); A. D. 222 B. G. U. I 35 (51); A. D. 224 P. Tebt. II 339 (156); A. D. 226 P. Oxy. XII 1459 (179);

A. D. 237 P. Grenf. II 67 (101)

Αὐρηλίῳ Θέωνι πρωνοητῇ γυμνασίου παρὰ Αὐρηλίου Ἀσκληπιάδου Φιλαδέλφου ἡγουμένου συνόδου κώμης Βακχιάδος.

also: A. D. 240 P. Oxy. XII 1549 (271); A. D. 246 P. Amh. II 72 (87); A. D. 247 P. Amh. II 81 (101); A. D. 255 P. Flor. I 9 (26); A. D. 259 P. Ryl. 110 (88); A. D. 263 P. Oxy. XII 1467 (195); A. D. 265 P. Flor. I 2 (5);

A. D. 266 P. Tebt. II 326 (136)

Ἰουεννίωι Γενεαλίωι τῷ λαμπροτάτωι ἐπάρχωι Αἰγύπτου παρ' Αὐρηλίας Σαραπιάδος Ἀντινοίδος.

also: A. D. 269 P. Ryl. 117 (103) b; A. D. 280 P. Ryl. 114 (97); A. D. 283 P. Oxy. I 55 (112); A. D. 284 P. Oxy. VIII 1115 (196); A. D. 287 P. S. I. 164 (17); A. D. 2d-3dc B. G. U. I 4 (4), 36 (51); A. D. 3dc. C. P. H. 62 II.

A. D. 303 P. Oxy. I 71 (131)

Κλωδίωι Κουλκιανῶι τῷ διασημοτάτῳ ἐπάρχωι Αἰγύπτου παρὰ Αὐρηλίου Δημητρίου Νείλου ἀρχιερατεύσαντος τῆς Ἀρσινοιτῶν πόλεως.

---

From A——

B. C. 119 P. Tebt. I 9 (70)

Παρὰ Μεγχείους κωμογραμματέως Κερκεοσίρεως.

B. C. 115 P. Tebt. I 30 (118)e.

Παρὰ τῶν γραμματέων.

B. C. 113 P. Tebt. 38 (134)

Παρ' Ἀπολλοδώρου τοῦ ἐξειληφότος τὴν διάθεσιν καὶ τὸ τέλος τοῦ ἐλαίου τῆς αὐτῆς εἰς τὸ δ (ἔτος).

B. C. 2dc. P. Grenf. I 41 (73); also P. Good. I 5 (9);

Παρὰ Πετεύριος.

B. C. 18 P. Grenf. 46 (78)

Παρὰ Πνεφερῶτος τοῦ Πανεμειήους τῶν ἀπὸ Θεαδελφίας δημοσίων γεωργῶν.

A. D. 1st c.? P. Ryl. 124 (119);
Παρὰ Ἱππάλου τοῦ Ἀχῖτος δημοσίου γεοργοῦ τῶν ἀπὸ κώμης Εὐημερίας τῆς Θεμίστου μερίδος.
also: P. Ryl. 82 (43) A. D. 113; A. D. 167 P. Ryl. 104 (81); B. G. U. I 198 (208) A. D. 162-3; P. Tebt. II 293 (61) A. D. 187;

A. D. 188 B. G. U. III 926 (259)
Παρὰ Αὐρηλίου Πλουτογένους ἐπιτρόπου.

A. D. 202-3 P. Oxy. XII 1548 (271); also P. Oxy. VIII 1111 (184);
Παρὰ Πλουτίωνος Πλουτίωνος τοῦ Πλουτίωνος μητρὸς Ταψόιτος ἀπ' Ὀξυρύγχων πόλεως.

A. D. 157 P. Oxy. III 479 (167); also A. D. 160 P. Oxy. VIII 1109 (180)
Παρὰ Δημητροῦτος Ἀμόιτος τοῦ Φιλοξένου μετὰ τοῦ κυρίου τοῦ υἱοῦ Ἀμόιτος Ἀπερῶτος.

A. D. 3dc. P. S. I. IV 292 (21)
Παρὰ Αὐρηλίου Ἑρμίου Λεωνίδου μητρὸς Πτολεμᾶς ἀπό——.

A. D. 3dc. P. Ryl. 245 (393)
Παρὰ Ἀρείου.

A. D. 3d-4thc. P. Fay. 38 (154)
Παρὰ Δομιττίου Ἀννιανοῦ ἑκατοντάρχου.

A. D. 3dc. P. Oxy. I 78 (141)
Παρὰ Αὐρηλίου Σαραπᾶτος.

A. D. 254 P. Flor. 118 (67); also A. D. 260 P. Fay. 133 (288) A. D. 262 P. Ryl. 238 (387)
Παρὰ Ἀλυπίου.

A. D. 254 P. Flor. 182 (142)
Παρὰ Ἁρπάλου.

A. D. 256 P. Flor. 172 (127)
Παρὰ Ἀπιάνου.

---

## 4. LETTERS FROM AND TO OFFICIALS

A—— to B—— χαίρειν.

B. C. 270-233 P. Grenf. II 14 (26)a
Ἀπολλώνιος Ἀσκληπιάδει χαίρειν.

B. C. 265 P. Hibeh I 39 (181)
Ξάνθος Εὐφράνορι χαίρειν.

B. C. 264-227 P. Grenf. 14 (26)b
Ἀπεννεὺς Ἀσκληπιάδει χαίρειν.

B. C. 266-257 P. S. I. 322 (63)
Ἀπολλώνιος Ζήνωνι χαίρειν.

B. C. 262 P. Hib. I 42 (184); also ibidem 40, 41, 43;
Καλλικλῆς Ἀριθμούθηι χαίρειν.

B. C. 261 P. S. I. 324 (64); also ibidem 325.
Ἀπολλώνιος Ἀπολλοδότωι χαίρειν.

B. C. 260 P. P. II 2 (3); also P. Lille I 5 (47)
Μοσχίων Διοφάνει χαίρειν.

B. C. 258 P. S. I. 328 (66)
Οἱ ἱερεῖς τῆς 'Αφροδίτης 'Απολλωνίωι διοικητῆι χαίρειν.
also: B. C. 258-251 P. P. II 13, 4; P. Hib. I 44, 45, 46, 47, 48, 49, 50, (186 seqq.);

B. C. 251 P. S. I. 361 (92)
Μαίμαχος Ζήνωνι χαίρειν.

B. C. 250 P. P. II 8 (19)
Βασιλεὺς Πτολεμαῖος Λυκομείδηι χαίρειν.

B. C. 250 P. Hib. I 80 (235); also 56 (202);
'Επιχάρης Χαιρήμονι χαίρειν.
also: P. Lille I 12 (77); P. Hamb. 27 (115); P. Hib. I 55 (202); P. P. II 6 (17); III 42 (111);

B. C. 250 P. P. II 42 (138)
Κλέανδρος οἰκονόμοις νομάρχαις βασιλικοῖς γραμματεῦσι φυλακίταις μυριαρούροις κωμάρχοις κωμογραμματεῦσι χαίρειν.
also: B. C. 248 P. Hib. I 76 (231); 86 (248)b;

B. C. 248 P. Hib. I 102 (276)
Κυρηναῖος τῶν Ζωίλου ἰδιώτης Εὐκάρπωι ἰατρῶι χαίρειν.
also: B. C. 248-241: P. Hib. I 51, 52, 53, 57, 58, 59, 60, 61, 62, 71, 72, 73, 78. P. P. II 12 (32); 38 (122); P. Lille I 13, 14, 15, 18.

B. C. 241-39 P. P. II 9 (22)
Θεόδωρος Διοτίμωι χαίρειν.
also: B. C. 241-232: P. P. II 9 (22), 9 (24), 38 (123); P. Hamb 25 (108); P. Hib. I 82a, 82b, 82c, 71c, 81d,

B. C. 232-1 P. Hib. I 75 (230)
Θεόδωρος τοῖς ἐν Ταλάηι φυλακίταις χαίρειν.
also: B. C. 231-218: P. Hib. I 66, 67, 68, 69, 70, 103;

B. C. 218 P. Lille 4 (36)
Μαρσύας Στρατοκλεῖ τακτομίσθωι χαίρειν.

B. C. 3dc. P. Grenf. II 14 (26)
'Ασκληπιάδης Πολυκράτει χαίρειν.

B. C. Ptolemaic P. P. III. 77 (209); also ibidem 86, 115, 89,
'Απολλώνιος 'Αμμωνίωι χαίρειν.

B. C. 2dc. P. Amh. II 41 (49); also 38 (41); P. Grenf. II 37 (62);
Διόδωρος τοῖς ἱερεῦσι τοῦ Σοκνοπαίου καὶ ῎Ισιος Νεφορσείους χαίρειν.

B. C. 170 P. Fay. 13 (105)
.ελθοῦς ἐξειληφὼς τὴν ζυτηρὰν Θεαδελφίας εἰς τὸ ιβ (ἔτος) Ψάιτι καὶ τοῖς μετόχοις ταριχευταῖς χαίρειν.

B. C. 157 P. Amh. II 33 (38)
Βασιλεὺς Πτολεμαῖος 'Απολλωνίωι χαίρειν.

B. C. 158-7 P. B. M. I 23 (37); also P. Grenf. I 11 (27)b; 13 (32) B. C. 152 (141).

Δημήτριος Διοσκούδει χαίρειν.

B. C. 149 (or 137) P. Graec. Ber. 6 ab P. 11306

'Ασκληπιάδης Φιλίνωι τῶι εἰσάγοντι τοῖς ἀπὸ τοῦ Πανοπολίτου καὶ τοῖς μεμερισμένοιςτόποις δικασταῖς χαίρειν.

B. C. 145 P. Tebt. I 32 (124)d

Σῶσις καὶ Αἴγυπτος Παγκράτει χαίρειν.

B. C. 124 P. Fay. 14 (106)

Σίμων καὶ Πτολεμαῖος οἱ προκεχιρισμένοι πράκτορες τοῦ ἀναπεφωνημένου Νουμηνίῳ στεφάνου Φιλέᾳ Τρύφωνος χαίρειν.

also: B. C. 119-114 P. Tebt. I 10, 14, 16, 17, 18, 21, 28, 30 a, b, c 100; P. Grenf. I 22 (48);

B. C. 114 P. Tebt. I 13 (77)

Μεγχῆς κωμογραμματεὺς Κερκεοσίρεωςτῆς Πολέμωνος μερίδος Πτολεμαίωι χαίρειν.

B. C. 114 P. Tebt. 26 (103)

Ὧρος τοῖς τοπογραμματεῦσι καὶ κωμογραμματεῦσι χαίρειν.

also: B. C. 113 P. Tebt. I 38 (134); 27 (105) a,b,e,f; B. C. 112 P. Tebt. I 22 (92); 31 (122) a.b.c.; 33 (1271); 35 (130) P. Fay. 15 (107); P. Amh. II 31 (34); B. C. 108 P. Grenf. II 23 (40) a, b, c,

B. C. 1stc. P. Fay. 18 (112)b; also 18 (114)a; 16 (108); P. Grenf. II 39 (65);

'Οννῶφρεις γραμματεὺς κτηνοτρόφων Βακχιάδος 'Ακουσιλάωι σιτολόγωι τῆς αὐτῆς χαίρειν.

B. C. 99 P. Leid. H (47); also P. Leid. G (41) a (royal rescript)

Τιμόνικος τῶι τοῦ 'Ανουβείου ἐπιστάτει χαίρειν.

B. C. 73 P. Tebt. I 37 (33); B. C. 77 P. Tebt. I 102 (445);

'Απόλλων Πετεσούχωι χαίρειν.

B. C. 30-1 A. D. P. Tebt. II 382 (228)

Σπασίνης καὶ 'Απολλωφάνης Διονυσίωι καὶ 'Ασκληπιάδηι χαίρειν.

B. C. 28 P. Fay. 43 (165); also B. C. 27 B. G. U. II 543 (188);

'Αρπαησίων Νῖλος 'Ακουσιλάῳ 'Ακουσιλάου χαίρειν.

B. C. 16 P. Fay. 44 (167); also B. G. U. IV 1202 (344);

'Απολλώνιος ὁ παρὰ 'Αρχίου 'Οννώφρι λάξῳ τῆς Θεμίστου μερίδος χαίρειν.

A. D. 1stc. (late) P. Oxy. I 47 (104); also 44 (100);

'Αχιλλεὺς ὁ προκεχειρισμένος ὑπὸ Πύρρου τοῦ ἀσχολημένου τοὺς καταλοχισμοὺς τῆς Αἰγύπτου τοῖς ἀγορανόμοις χαίρειν.

see also: A. D. 13 P. Oxy. IX 1188 (203); A. D. 14-37 P. Ryl. 94 (62); A. D. 15 P. B. M. II 256 (95);

A. D. 23 P. Tebt. II 289 (52);
Ἀπολλώνιος στρατηγὸς Ἀκοῦτι τοπάρχῃ Τεβτύνεως χαίρειν.
also: P. B. M. III 1213-15 (121) A. D. 65-66.

A. D. 74 P. Oxy. XIV 1661 (115)
Ἀρθοῶνος Ἡρακλείδηι τῷ διοικητῆι χαίρειν.

A. D. 77 P. Oxy. II 242 (186)
Ἀλέξανδρος καὶ οἱ μέτοχοι τοῖς ἀγορανόμοις χαίρειν.
also A. D. 79 P. Oxy. II 243 (190) a, b; A. D. 86 P. Grenf. II 42 (68); P. Oxy. I 48 (105);

A. D. 95 P. Oxy. I 45 (101)
Φανίας καὶ Ἡρακλᾶς καὶ Διογένης ὁ καὶ Ἑρμαῖος διασχολούμενοι τοὺς καταλοχισμοὺς τοῖς ἀγορανόμοις χαίρειν.
also: A. D. 98 P. Oxy. II 241 (185); A. D. 100 P. Oxy. I 46, 49, 50; A. D. 101 P. Grenf. II 44 (70); A. D. 104 P. Ryl. 81 (42);

A. D. 107 P. Amh. II 64 (70)
Σουλπίκιος Σίμιλις Ἡρακλείδηι στρατηγῶι Ἑρμοπολίτου χαίρειν.

A. D. 125 P. Meyer 6 (41).
Ἀνδρόνεικος ὁ ἱερεὺς καὶ ἀρχιδικαστὴς τῷ τῆς Ἡρακλειδου μερίδος τοῦ Ἀρσινοίτου στρατηγῷ χαίρειν.
also: A. D. 123 P. Tebt. II 296 (70); P. Oxy. I 107 (174); A. D. 129 P. Oxy. VII 1024 (153); A. D. 134 P. Oxy. III 515 (250); A. D. 136 P. B. M. II 255 (117);

A. D. 139 P. Grenf. II 46 (74)
Λούσιος Σπάρσος Κερεάλι στρατηγῷ Ἀρσινοείτου Ἡρακλείδου μερίδος χαίρειν.

A. D. 146 P. Ryl. 84 (46)
Μοινατίδης Μερούλᾳ στρατηγῷ Ἑρμοπολίτου χαίρειν.
also: P. Meyer 3 (12) A. D. 148; A. D. 150 P. Fay. 26 (133); A. D. 156 P. Ryl. 115 (100); A. D. 158 P. Gen. 15; A. D. 160 P. Oxy. III 516 (251);

A. D. 179 P. Oxy. I 88 (151)
Λάμπων Ἀμμωνίου προνοητὴς οἴκου γυμνασιάρχου Ὀξυρύγχων πόλεως σειτολόγοις μέσης τοπαρχίας Πέτνη τόπων χαίρειν.
also: A. D. 180 P. Oxy. I 96 (158); A. D. 191 P. Grenf. I 48 (80); A. D. 193 B. G. U. II 646 (311); A. D. 195 P. Ryl. 86 (49); A. D. 197 P. Tebt. II 357 (193); A. D. 2d-3dc P. Oxy. XII 1510 (258);

A. D. 3dc. C. P. H. 119
Αὐτοκράτωρ Καῖσαρ Πούβλιος Λικίννιος Γαλλιηνὸς Εὐσεβὴς Εὐτυχὴς Σεβαστὸς Αὐρηλίῳ Πλουτίωνι χαίρειν.
also: C. P. H. 121 (66);

A. D. 3dc. P. Iand. 36 (97)

Αὐρήλιος Ἰσίδωρος φροντιστὴς Τησχίας Ἀκοῦτος τοῦ Μύστου Αὐρηλίῳ Νεφωντιανῷ φροντιστῇ Φιλαδελφίας χαίρειν.

A. D. 3dc. P. Grenf. II 63 (98)

Ἀνουβίων βουλευτὴς σιτολόγων Γερμανῷ ἀπελευθέρῳ χαίρειν.

also: 3dc. A. D. P. Fay. 88 (222); P. Oxy. I 62 (120);

A. D. 206 P. Oxy .VIII 1100 (164)

Σουβατιονὸς Ἀκύλας στρατηγοῖς ζ νομῶν καὶ Ἀρσινοίτου χαίρειν.

also: A. D. 207-9 P. Gen. 20 (50); P. Tebt. II 313 (110) A. D. 210-11.

A. D. 248 B. G. U. I 8 (9)

Μάγνιος Ῥουφεινιανὸς στρατηγοῖς ἐπιστρατηγίας Ἑπτὰ νομῶν καὶ Ἀρσινοίτου χαίρειν.

also: A. D. 265 P. Flor. I 2 (5); A. D. 280 P. Oxy. IX 1190 (210);

A. D. 284-304 P. Oxy. XII 1544 (269)

Αὐρήλιος Φιλίμουσος πραγματευτὴς τοῦ κρατίστου Αὐρηλίου Ἀμμωνίωνος Αὐρηλίῳ Μαξίμῳ πραγματευτῇ χαίρειν.

A. .D 288 P. Oxy. I 58 (116);

Σερβαῖος Ἀφρικανὸς στρατηγοῖς ἐπιστρατηγίας Ἑπτὰ νομῶν καὶ Ἀρσινοίτου χαίρειν.

A. D. 300 P. Oxy. XII 1429 (84)

Αὐρήλιος Μακρόβιος μισθωτὴς ἀσχολήματος στυπτηρίας δι' ἐμοῦ Καισαρίου γραμματέως Αὐρηλίῳ Ἰσακ χιριστῇ χαίρειν.

Note also: A. D. 25 P. Oxy. II 244 (193)b;

Χαιρέας Ἑρμίᾳ στρατηγῷ Κυνοπολίτου πλεῖστα χαίρειν.

---

A—— to B—— τῷ φιλτάτῳ (πλεῖστα) χαίρειν.

A. D. 25-6 P. Oxy. II 291 (290)

Χαιρέας Τυράννωι τῶι φιλτάτωι πλεῖστα χαίρειν.

A. D. 2d-3dc. P. Oxy. I 63 (121)

Πανήσιος Ἀρχελάωι τῶι φιλτάτωι χαίρειν.

A. D. 117 P. Oxy. IX 1189 (207)

Ἀκύλιος Πυλίων στρατηγὸς Ἡρακλεοπολίτου Ἀπολλωνίῳ στρατηγῶι Ὀξυρυγχείτου τῶι φιλτάτωι χαίρειν.

A. D. 128 P. Oxy. XII 1422 (74);

——Δημήτριος στρατηγὸς ——κοπολείτου Ἀγαθῷ Δαίμονι στρατηγῶι Ὀξυρυγχείτου τῶι ——φιλτάτωι χαίρειν.

A. D. 157 P. Ryl. 78 (37)

———— Ἡρακλείδηι στρατηγῶι Βουσιρίτου τῶι φιλτάτωι ———— χαίρειν.

A. D. 158 P. Gen. 255
——ος Ἐπαφροδίτωι τῶι φιλτάτωι χαίρειν.

A. D. 3dc. P. Oxy. I 57 (115)
Αὐρήλιος Ἀπολινάριος στρατηγὸς Ὀξυρυγχείτου Ἀπίωνι στρατηγήσαντι Ἀνταιοπολίτου τῶι φιλτάτωι χαίρειν.

A. D. 3dc. P. Oxy. VI 890 (207)
Λούκιος Σεπτίμιος Αὐρήλιος Σαραπίων ὁ καὶ Ἀπολινάριος καὶ ὡς χρηματίζω ἔναρχος πρύτανις τῆς Ὀξυρυγχειτῶν πόλεως Αὐρηλίῳ Λεονίδῃ στρατηγῷ τῶι φιλτάτωι χαίρειν.

also: A. D. 214-15 B. G. U. II 362 (7);

A. D. 221 P. Oxy. I 61 (120)
Αὐρήλιος Σαραπίων ὁ καὶ Μουμιανὸς γενόμενος —νυνὶ στρατηγὸς—— διὰ Αὐρηλίου Ὡρίωνος γραμματέως Αὐρηλίῳ Διογένει καὶ τοῖς σὺν αὐτῷ δημοσίοις τραπεζίταις Ὀξυρυγχίτου τοῖς φιλτάτοις χαίρειν.

A. D. 246 P. Oxy. XIV 1662 (116)
Αὐρήλιος Βίων ὁ καὶ Ἀμμώνιος γυμνασίαρχος βουλευτὴς ἔναρχος πρύτανις τῆς Ὀξυρυγχιτῶν πόλεως Αὐρηλίῳ Δίῳ τῷ καὶ Περτίνακι στρατηγῷ τοῦ αὐτοῦ νομοῦ τῷ φιλτάτῳ χαίρειν.

A. D. 274 B. G. U. IV 1073 (114)
Ὀξυρυγχιτῶν τῆς λαμπρᾶς καὶ λαμπροτάτης πόλεως ἡ κρατίστη βουλὴ διὰ Αὐρηλίου Εὐπόρου τοῦ καὶ Ἀγαθοῦ Δαίμονος γενομένου κοσμητοῦ ἐξηγητοῦ ὑπομνηματογράφου τῆς λαμπροτάτης πόλεως τῶν Ἀλεξανδρέων πραγ(----) καὶ ὡς χρηματίζει βουλευτοῦ ἐνάρχου πρυτάνεως βιβλιοφύλαξι ἐνκτησέων τοῖς φιλτάτοις χαίρειν.

also: A. D. 292 P. Oxy. I 59 (117); A. D. 294 P. Oxy. VI 891 (208); A. D. 3dc. C. P. H. 119 IV (57);

A. D. 3dc. C. P. H. 192 (51)
Ἑρμοῦ πόλεως τῆς μεγάλης ἀρχαίας καὶ σεμνοτάτης καὶ λαμπροτάτης ἡ κρατίστη βουλὴ Αὐρηλίῳ Δημητρίῳ τῷ καὶ Φιλέρωτι ἀγορανόμῳ βουλευτῇ τῷ φιλτάτῳ χαίρειν.

---

A—— to B—— τῷ τιμιωτάτῳ χαίρειν.

A. D. 2dc. P. Giss. 65a (48)
Κορνήλιος Ἀπολλωνίωι τῶι τιμιωτάτωι χαίρειν.

A. D. 118 P. Giss. 11 (45)
Παπείρεις Ἀπολλωνίῳ στρατηγῷ Ἀπολλωνοπολείτου Ἑπτακωμίας τῷ τιμιωτάτῳ χαίρειν.

A. D. 127 P. Oxy. I 34 (68); also A. D. 135 B. G. U. I 73 (87);
Ἀπολλώνιος Ὡρίωνι τῷ τιμιωτάτῳ χαίρειν.

A. D. 3dc. P. Ryl. 206 (279)b; also P. Rein. I 20 (99) A. D. 250.
Αὐρήλιος Σαραπίων κοσμητεύσας βουλευτὴς Αὐρηλίοις Θῶνι καὶ Ἀπίωνι τοῖς τειμιωτάτοις χαίρειν.

---

A—— to B——.

B. C. 256 P. S. I. IV 344 (80)
Φινέας Μαιμάχωι.

B. C. 119 P. Tebt. I 11 (73)
Μεγχῆς Πετεσούχου κωμογραμματεὺς Κερκεοσίρεως τῆς Πολέμωνος μερίδος τοῦ Ἀρσινοίτου Δωρίωνι Εἰρηναίου τῶν πρώτων φίλων.

B. C. 116 P. Tebt. I 111 (471)
Ἀρβῆχις Ἐργέως Ἀπολλωνίωι καὶ Ἡρακλείδει τοῖς σιτολογοῦσιν.

B. C. 30-1 A. D. P. Tebt. II 382 (228)a
Ἡρακλῆς Ἀκουσιλάου Μακεδὼν τῶν κατοίκων ἱππέων Ἀκουσιλάωι τῶι νεωτέρωι μου ἀδελφῷ.

A. D. 23 P. Oxy. II 269 (227)
Θέων Ἀμμωνίου Πέρσης τῆς ἐπιγονῆς Δημητρίῳ τῷ τεταγμένῳ πρὸς τῇ τοῦ Διὸς φυλακῇ.

A. D. 59 P. Oxy. II 260 (229)
Ἀντιφάνης Ἀμμωνίου τῶν ἀπ' Ὀξυρύγχων πόλεως τοῖς παρὰ Τιβερίου Κλαυδίου Ἀμμωνίου στρατηγοῦ καὶ ἐπὶ τῶν προσόδων Ὀξυρυγχείτου.
also A. D. 81-96 P. Oxy. VIII 1105 (175);

A. D. 182 P. Oxy. III 457 (159); A. D. 161 P. Gen. 45 (46);
Ἱέραξ στρατηγὸς Ὀξυρυγχείτου Κλαυδίῳ Σερήνῳ ὑπηρέτῃ.

A. D. 269 P. Ryl. 117 (103)
Αὐρήλιος Τύραννος καὶ Ἀμμώνιος στρατηγὸς Ἑρμοπολίτου Ἑρμῇ ὑπηρέτῃ ——τ. ου

A. D. 2d-3dc P. Tebt. II 370 (207)
Σαραπιὰς Σαραπίωνος διὰ Δηκίωνος Σαραπίωνος ἀδελφοῦ κυβερνήτου πλοίου πρότερον Λεογησ—— ὁρμοφύλαξι ὅρμου Ἄλσους μητροπόλεως καὶ σιτολόγοις μητροπόλεως.

A. D. 3d P. Tebt. II 424 (302)
Σαραπάμμων Πιπερᾶτι.
Compare P. Oxy. XII 1489 (246)

---

To B—— A——.

A. D. 66 P. Oxy. II 239 (183)
Τῷ γράφοντι τὸν Ὀξυρυγχίτην Ἐπίμαχος Παυσίριος τοῦ Πτολεμαίου μητρὸς Ἡρακλείας τῆς Ἐπιμάχου τῶν ἀπὸ κώμης Ψώβθεως τῆς κάτω τοπαρχίας.
also A. D. 87 P. Hamb. 4 (16); A. D. 130 B. G. U. II 647 (312);

A. D. 133 P. Oxy. I 100 (163)

Τοῖς ἀγορανόμοις Μάρκος Ἀντώνιος Δεῖος καὶ ὡς χρηματίζω στρατηγήσας Ἀλεξανδρείας νεώκορος τοῦ μεγάλου Σαράπιδος.

A. D. 105-6 P. Iand. 30 (89)

Σαραπίωνι βασιλικῶι γραμματεῖ Ἀρσινοΐτου Θεμίστου μερίδος Ἀβοῦς Μύσθου καὶ Τιθοείους καὶ—ἀπὸ κώμης Θεαδελφίας τῆς αὐτῆς μερίδος.

A. D. 135 P. Oxy. I 106 (173)

Ἀγορανόμοις Ὀξυρύγχων πόλεως Ἀπολλώνιος Πτολεμαίου ὑπηρέτης.

A. D. 158 P. Fay. 24 (131)

Διοδώρῳ στρατηγῷ Ἀρσινοΐτου Θεμίστου καὶ Πολέμωνος μερίδων Πουσεῖμις Ὀρσενούφεως τοῦ Πετεραίπιος ἀρχεφόδου ἐποικίου Δάμα.

A. D. 185 P. Ryl. 85 (48)

Δαμαρίωνι στρατηγῶι Ἑρμοπολίτου Ἀντώνιος Ἰουστεῖνος δουπλικάριος διαπεμφθεὶς ὑπὸ Οὐαλερίου Φροντείνου ἐπάρχου τῆς ἐν Κόκτῳ εἴλης Ἡρακλειανῆς.

also: P. Amh. II 107 (134); 108 (135); A. D. 196 P. Fay. 42 (163);

A. D. 211 P. Hawara (Archiv V p. 390)

Αὐρηλίῳ Κύρῳ ἑκατοντάρχῃ Τούρβων Ἀπολλωνίου μητρὸς Ἡροῦτος ἀπὸ ἀμφόδου Ἱερᾶς Πύλης.

A. D. 211 P. Grenf. II 62 (97)

Κρηνολήϊῳ Κουιντιλλιανῷ ἑκατοντάρχῳ Δημήτριος Σατύρου Ἄνθου Σύρου μητρὸς Διοδώρας ἀπὸ ἀμφόδου Βιθυνῶν ἄλλων τόπων.

A. D. 216 P. Oxy. XII 1458 (177); also A. D. 223 P. Oxy. I 77 (140).

Αὐρηλίωι —— βασιλικῶι γραμματεῖ Αὐρήλιος Αἰλουρίων ἔναρχος κοσμητὴς βουλευτὴς τῆς Ἀθριβιτῶν πόλεως πρὶν δὲ τυχῖν τῆς Ῥωμαίων πολιτικῆς Αἰλουρίων Ζωΐλου Νεοκόσμιος ὁ καὶ Ἀλθαιεύς.

also: A. D. 238-44 P. Oxy. I 80 (143);

A. D. 244-5 P. Oxy. I 81 (144)

Αὐρηλίῳ Δίῳ τῷ καὶ Περτίνακι στρατηγῷ Ὀξυρυγχίτου Αὐρήλιος Ἀπίων Διονυσίου μητρὸς Ταρμαλόιος ἀπ' Ὀξυρύγχων πόλεως.

A. D. 260-1 P. Oxy. XII 1555 (273)

Αὐρηλίῳ Πτολεμαίῳ τῷ καὶ Νεμεσιανῷ στρατηγῷ Ὀξυρυγχείτου Αὐρήλιος Φιλαντίνοος ὁ καὶ Μῶρος Βησαρίωνος καὶ ὡς χρηματίζω.

A. D. 275 P. Oxy. XII 1455 (172); also 1456;

Αὐρηλίῳ —— στρατηγῷ Ὀξυρυγχίτου Αὐρήλιος Θεόδωρος Ὡρίωνος τοῦ Θῶνος μητρὸς —— ἀπὸ τῆς λαμπρᾶς καὶ λαμπροτάτης Ὀξυρυγχιτῶν πόλεως πράτης ἐλαίου χρηστοῦ.

A. D. 286 P. S. I. III 162 (15)

Αὐρηλίῳ Φιλιάρχῳ τῷ καὶ Ὡρίωνι στρατηγῷ Ὀξυρυγχίτου Αὐρήλιος Ψευαμοῦνος Ἱέρακος μητρὸς Πενβῆτος ἀπὸ Κώμης Φοβώου οἰκοδόμος.

---

To B—— A—— χαίρειν.

B. C. 261 P. S. I. 326 (65)

Ζήνωνι Ἀρτεμίδωρος χαίρειν.

A. D. 135 B. G. U. I 19 (30)

Πετρωνίῳ Μαμερτείνῳ τῷ κρατίστῳ ἡγεμόνι Μένανδρος γενόμενος βασιλικὸς γραμματεὺς Ἀρσινοείτου χαίρειν.

A. D. 139 B. G. U. III 747 (53)

Αὐιδίωι Ἡλιοδώρωι τῷ κρατίστωι ἡγεμόνι Πτολεμαῖος στρατηγὸς Κοπτείτου χαίρειν.

A. D. 160 P. Hamb. 35 (150)

Ἱέρακι στρατηγῷ Ἀρσινοίτου Ἡρακλείδου μερίδος Οὐαλέριος καὶ Σαραπίων καὶ Γεβινᾶς καὶ οἱ λοιποὶ οἷς ἐκέλευσας προσταθῆναι κώμης Φιλαδελφείας τῶι κυρίωι χαίρειν.

A. D. 190 P. Iand. 34 (96);

Σερήνῳ βασιλικῷ γραμματεῖ Ἀρσινοίτου Πολέμωνος μερίδος Σαραπίων Παθώτου προφήτης ἱεροῦ Ἑρμοῦ καὶ Ἀφροδίτης κώμης Τεμ——κτλ. καὶ οἱ λοιποὶ ἱερεῖς τοῦ αὐτοῦ ἱεροῦ χαίρειν.

A. D. 3dc. P. S. I. IV 303 (35) petition.

Αὐρηλίῳ Διογένει γενομένῳ ὑπομνηματογράφῳ διοικοῦντι τὸν Μενδήσιον Αὐρήλιος Σαραπίων ὁ καὶ Ἀπολλώνιος ἐξηγητὴς βουλευτὴς τῆς λαμπροτάτης Ἀλεξανδρείας τῷ φιλτάτῳ χαίρειν.

---

To B. ——

B. C. 223 P. Eleph. 15 (54)

Πανίσκωι.

B. C. Ptolemaic P. P. III 57 (164)

Πύθωνι.

B. C. Ptolemaic P. P. III 104 (249), also ibidem 105; 106; 53; 46;

Ἀχοάπει.

B. C. 3dc. P. Grenfell II 14 (26)d.

Ἀριστοδώρωι.

B. C. 238 P. Hibeh I 81 (237)b.

Νικάνορι.

B. C. 201 P. Tebt. I 8 (67).

Ἀφροδισίωι.

B. C. 158-5 P. B. M. I 23 (37)
Δημητρίωι.
B. C. 117 P. Tebt. I 40 (140)b
Μεγχεῖ κωμογραμματεῖ.
B. C. 113 P. Tebt. I 27 (105); also ibidem 27 g, h; 33(127) b;
Ἀσκληπιάδει.
B. C. 113 P. Tebt. I 27 (105)d
Ἑρμίαι Ἀρνελτώτου τοῦ ἐν τῶι Ὥρου βασιλικοῦ γραμματέως.
B. C. Ptolemaic P. Tebt. III Introd. p. 36.
Θέωνι ἐπιμελήτηι τῶν κάτω τόπων τοῦ Σαύτου.
A. D. 1stc. P. Ryl. 80 (41)
Πρεσβυτέροις τῶν ὑπογεγραμμένων κωμῶν.
A. D. 1stc. P. Gen. 35 (7); also A. D. 13 P. Oxy. IX 1188 (203);
Νεμεσίωνι βασιλικῶι γραμματεῖ Ἀρσινοείτου Ἡρακλείδου μερίδος.
also: A. D. 135 P. Oxy. IX 1195 (216);
A. D. 145 P. Tebt. II 325 (135); also A. D. 156 P. Ryl. 88 (52);
Τῷ κωμογραμματεῖ Τεπτύνεως.
A. D. 158 P. Good. I 19 (24)
Σιτολόγοις Καρανίδος.
A. D. 3dc P. Fay. 37 (153); also P. Grenf. II 66 (100);
Ἀρχεφόδῳ κώμης Ψενύρεως.
A. D. 210 P. Oxy. IX 1196 (217); also ibidem 1197;
Ἀνουβίωνι στρατηγῷ Ὀξυρυγχείτου.
A. D. 229 P. Oxy. XII 1500 (254)
Ἀχιλλᾶ τραπεζίτῃ.
Note also: B. C. 258-3 P. P. II 13 (33) Κλέωνι χαίρειν. B. C. 250 P. P. II 23 (69) Ἀσκληπιάδει βασιλείωι γραμματεῖ χαίρειν. B. C. 240 P. P. III 42 (105) Θεοδώρωι Δρίμακος χαίρειν. B. C. 114 P. Tebt. I 15 (82) a, b; 26 (103) b: Ὥρωι χαίρειν. A. D. 23 P. Tebt. II 348 (181) Ἀκουσιλάωι χειριστῇ χαίρειν. A. D. 156 B. G. U. 171 (179) Σιτολόγοις κώμης Καρανίδος χαίρειν.

---

From A— to B—.

B. C. 223 P. Eleph. 17 (38)
ὑπόμνημα παρὰ Ξένωνος Μίλωνι τῶι παρ' Εὐφρονίου πράκτορι ἱερῶν.
A. D. 3dc. P. S. I. 213 (72)
Παρὰ τοῦ στρατηγοῦ πεδιοφύλαξι Νεσμίμεως.
A. D. 3dc. P. Oxy. XII 1421 (72)
Παρὰ τοῦ στρατηγοῦ κωμάρχαις καὶ δημοσίοις κωμῶν Ταампέμου καὶ Σερύφεως.
A. D. 3d-4thc P. Oxy. I 65 (123)
Παρὰ τοῦ στατίζοντος βενεφικιαρίου κωμάρχοις κώμης Τερύθεως.
also: P. Oxy. I 64 (122); XII 1505, 1506, 1507;

From A— to B— χαίρειν.

A. D. 259 P. Flor. II 204 (171); also A. D. 263 P. Flor. II 233 (203);
Παρὰ Ἰσχυρίωνος Ἡρωνείνῳ φροντιστῇ χαίρειν.

A. D. 265 P. Oxy. XII 1419 (68)
Παρὰ τοῦ πρυτάνεως Θωνίῳ πράκτορι πολιτικῶν χαίρειν.

A. D. 274-80 P. Oxy. XII 1514 (259)
Παρὰ Νεμεσᾶ Ἕρμωνος Μαξίμῳ πραγματευτῇ χαίρειν.

A. D. 309 P. Oxy. XII 1499 (254)
Παρὰ τοῦ πρυτάνεως Ἀπολλωνίῳ τραπεζίτῃ χαίρειν.

Varia

B. C. Ptolemaic P. P. III 36 (74) Petition
Νικάνορι ἐπιμελήτηι.

B. C. 241 P. P. III 43 (129) Petition.
Ἑρμογενῆι.

B. C. 255-4 P. P. II 4 (10) Complaint. Also: B. C. 250 P. P. II 19 (60)
Δημήτριος Κλέωνι χαίρειν.

B. C. 2dc. P. Tebt. I 36 (132) Official.
Ἀπολλώνιος Κρίτωνι ——— πολλὰ χαίρειν καὶ ἐρρῶσθαι.

B. C. 100 P. Tebt. I 34 (129) Political patronage.
Φιλόξενος Ἀπολλῶτι τῶι ἀδελφῶι χαίρειν καὶ ἐρρῶσθαι.

B. C. 99 P. Leid. H (47) b
Βασιλεὺς Πτολεμαῖος ὁ ἐπικαλούμενος Ἀλέξανδρος καὶ Βασίλισσα Βερενίκη ἡ ἀδελφὴ Ἀπολλοδώρωι χαίρειν καὶ ἐρρῶσθαι.

---

## *B. COMMENTARY*

The foregoing chronological tables of epistolary formulas show that the basic phrases of the opening-forms were in use as far back as the papyrological evidence reaches, and that they remained in use throughout the Ptolemaic and Roman periods, at least until the approach of the Byzantine period, the "terminus ad quem" of our investigation. These basic formulas are: A— to B— χαίρειν; To B— from A—. The former is used in all sorts of letters: private letters, business letters, communications between officials, as well as in letters from or to officials. The latter is used in applications of various kinds: for rental or purchase, for notices of birth or death, for census and other official registrations, for complaints about injuries received, with a request for redress, etc. Ziemann rather arbitrarily states that these latter communications can not be classified as letters. Technically these communications are known as ὑπομνήματα, and since they are nowhere called ἐπιστολαί or γράμματα, "igitur seiungenda sunt ab epistulis."[1] According to the definitions given above[2] ὑπομνήματα are rightly classed with letters, though they differ somewhat in form and content. Even though such documents were at times presented in person, their nature did not require the personal presentation by the writer; and several features of them—such as the great detail in description of person, place, injuries received—seem to indicate that the writer did not present the document in person, since in such a case they would be rather superfluous.

The following table shows, according to the evidence of the papyri now extant, what epistolary opening formulas were current during the Ptolemaic and the Roman periods.

| | inclusive | | inclusive |
|---|---|---|---|
| A—— to B—— χαίρειν | B. C. 3dc | —— | A. D. 3dc |
| A—— to B—— ———— | B. C. 3dc | —— | A. D. 3dc |
| To B—— from A ——— | B. C. 3dc | —— | A. D. 3dc |
| To B———— (χαίρειν) | B. C. 3dc | —— | A. D. 3dc |
| To B—— χαίρειν A——— | B. C. 3dc | —— | B. C. 1stc |
| From A ————— | B. C. 2dc | —— | A. D. 3dc |
| To B—— A————— | A. D. 1stc | —— | A. D. 3dc |
| To B—— A——χαίρειν | A. D. 2dc | —— | A. D. 3dc |
| From A— to B———— | A. D. 3dc | —— | A. D. 3dc |
| From A— to B— χαίρειν | A. D. 3dc | —— | A. D. 3dc |
| Χαίροις ————— | A. D. 1stc | —— | A. D. 3dc |
| Χαῖρε ————— | A. D. 2dc | —— | A. D. 3dc |

At present we are not concerned with the grammatical explanation of the various epistolary formulas. This task has been undertaken by G. A. Gerhard.[3] It is our aim to show what epistolary formulas were in use during the six hundred years which elapsed between the founding of Alexandria and the elevation of Byzantium to the position of capital of the Roman empire. We

[1]Zieman F. p. 264

[2]Supra page 4.

[3]Philologus 64 (1905) Untersuchingen zur Geschichte des Griechischen Briefes.

refrain on purpose from entering upon the field which Gerhard has tried to cover, since to our mind no satisfactory results can be obtained until we know more about the origin of the epistolary phrases. The Alexandrian scholars, in a sense, were as far remote from the origin of these epistolary phrases as we are; and though the various suggestions made by them and their successors are plausible enough, as long as historical proof is lacking they remain mere hypotheses.

A— to B— *χαίρειν.*

Throughout the Ptolemaic and Roman periods the formula: A—— to B—— *χαίρειν* is by far the most common. It is used by superiors writing to their inferiors, and by inferiors writing to their superiors. One need but read the opening phrases given above to realize that no distinction was made as to rank or superiority. Children use this formula in writing to their parents, and servants in writing to their masters. In the Christian era another formula came into use in which the order of the names was reversed, but it did not supplant the older form during the Roman period; judging from the evidence at hand one may say that the older form was used at least as frequently as the reversed formula.

In familiar letters there was a tendency of giving expression to the friendship existing between the writer and his correspondent by the addition of appropriate words to the salutation. The same tendency may be noticed in the letters of officials who were apparently on familiar terms. Thus the simple formula: A—— to B—— *χαίρειν* was not infrequently expanded in the following manner:

A—— to B——

| | | |
|---|---|---|
| *τῶι πατρὶ (μητρὶ κτλ.) χαίρειν.* | B. C. 3dc- | A. D. 3dc |
| *πολλὰ χαίρειν.* | B. C. 2dc- | A. D. 3dc |
| *πλεῖστα χαίρειν.* | B. C. 1stc- | A. D. 3dc |
| *τῶι φιλτάτωι χαίρειν.* | A. D. 1stc- | A. D. 3dc |
| *τῶι φιλτάτωι πλεῖστα χαίρειν.* | A. D. 1stc- | A. D. 3dc |
| *τῶι τιμιωτάτωι χαίρειν.* | A. D. 1stc- | A. D. 3dc |
| *τῶι τιμιωτάτωι πλεῖστα χαίρειν.* | A. D. 1stc- | A. D. 3dc |
| *τῶι ἰδίωι χαίρειν.* | A. D. 1stc- | A. D. 2dc |
| *τῶι κυρίωι χαίρειν.* | A. D. 1stc- | A. D. 3dc |

Not all these forms occur with the same frequency. Though not exhaustive, the tables given above are fairly complete as far as the papyri are concerned which are extant in the main collections. In the period covered in our investigation we have noticed twenty-one times the phrase: πολλὰ χαίρειν. The phrase: τῶι κυρίωι χαίρειν occurs the same number of times; τῶι φιλτάτωι χαίρειν sixty-three times; τῶι τιμιωτάτωι χαίρειν thirty times; τῶι ἰδίωι χαίρειν ten times. Ziemann had noticed πλεῖστα χαίρειν about sixty times, with the fourth century included.[4] We have found the same number, not including the fourth century A. D. or later. We hesitate to attach any value to these numbers. As has been pointed out before, the papyri now extant have come into our possession, not according to any selective plan which preserved what was best, but by the good fortune of the explorers who chanced upon their hiding places. Another fortunate discovery may bring to light many documents of one class rather than of another, and thus change their relative importance. Or documents may be found which antedate those we now have, and thus compel us to change our chronology. The earliest extant letter containing the phrase: πλεῖστα χαίρειν was dated B. C. 2, until the publication of P. Oxy. VII 1061 (214)[5] which is dated B. C. 22. In 1911 Ziemann had to state concerning the occurrence of the phrase: πολλὰ χαίρειν: "Perdurat usque ad saeculum III post C."[6] But the P. Ryl., P. Oxy. X and XIV, and the P. S. I., not only brought to light other letters containing this phrase, but also showed it to have been in use till the fourth century A. D.

The phrases: τῶι φιλτάτωι, τῶι τιμιωτάτωι, τῶι κυρίωι τῶι ἰδίωι, came into use when the Roman republic changed into an empire. From this time on, and especially in the third century, these opening formulas become explicit, and even pompous, enumerating the various titles of offices held formerly or at the time.

Under "Business Letters" have been included documents of various kinds, dealing with commercial affairs. Many of these documents are letters only in the broader meaning of the word. Such are agreements of sale( for instance P. Ryl. 163, 164; P. B. M. II 339; P. Tebt. II 379; etc.); loans( B. G. U. I 69; P. Oxy. VII 1040; P. Ryl. 177; P. Grenf. II 72; P. Tebt. II 387; etc.); receipts (P. Fay. 99; P. B. M. II 343; P. Tebt. II 396; P. Rein. 11; P. Ryl. 183; P. Amh. II 103, etc.); contracts (P. Oxy I 91; IV 724; P. Grenf II 17; P. Ryl. 181, etc.); but since we are treat-

[4]Ziemann p. 299. [5]Supra p. 22. [6]Ziemann l. c.

ing of the letter-*form*, we could not well exclude them. In their opening formulas they agree with the letters proper.

The documents just now mentioned differ from other commercial documents which are not drawn up in epistolary form, mainly in the following particulars. They are drawn up in the first person, not in the third as is usual in contracts and commercial agreements. If the date is expressed, it is placed at the end, as in letters, and not at the beginning. From the real letter these commercial agreements in epistolary form do not differ except, perhaps, in one respect: in accordance with their nature the opening formula is somewhat more explicit, giving the various names by which the writer is known, as well as the names of parents or guardians.

In official letters the use of this formula by inferiors writing to superiors becomes less frequent during the first three centuries of the Christian era. Compare P. Tebt. II 370; P. Oxy. XII 1510; P. Ryl. 81; 115; P. Grenf. I 48; etc. It remains the common formula for superiors and equals.

A—— to B—— χαίρειν καὶ ἐρρῶσθαι.

This formula seems to be a development of the opening phrase combined with the initial salutation or health wish. We have noticed its occurrence between ten and twenty times; all practically during the late Ptolemaic period. It was used in both familiar and official letters.

A—— to B—— χαίρειν καὶ (διὰ παντὸς) ὑγιαίνειν.

We meet more frequently with the above formula, which appears to have resulted from a combination of the opening formula with the health-wish. In point of time it comes after the preceding form. Its first occurrence in extant papyri is in the latter half of the first century B. C. It continues into the third century A. D., but is quite rare.

A—— to B——.

This formula is very rare, occurring about a dozen times throughout the entire period, and only once among familiar letters, as far as we have noticed. (P. B. M. I 42 B. C. 172). Its first occurrence in extant papyri seems to be P. S. I. IV 344, B. C. 256. It is found also in the third century A. D. (P. Tebt. II 424).

To B—— from A——.

This formula is used in commercial letters, in applications and similar documents, and in official communications. The business letters beginning with this formula are mostly offers to rent a piece of land, a house, or anything else, under certain conditions: they are leases in letter form. The usual phrase with which these letters begin is: βούλομαι μισθώσασθαι, or an equivalent phrase. Since these letters partake of the nature of contracts, the opening formulas are rather specific, tending to identify the writer and his correspondents with a certain degree of exactness.

Applications and related documents, as well as official letters, beginning with this formula, are found throughout both the Ptolemaic and the Roman periods. Often the initial word in the dative case is preceded by the word ὑπόμνημα. It may be doubted whether this word really belongs to the form. The great majority of these documents have no such word preceding the formula. Though it occurs in some of the earliest papyri, other documents, quite as early, are without it. Here again we are without any historical proof as to the origin of the formula; and we are compelled to leave the question in abeyance.

It may not be amiss to remark that, if the word ὑπόμνημα is a part of the formula, whether expressed or understood, its primary meaning was mostly lost sight of. It can not be inferred that it is a "follow-up" document, for it rarely contains a reference to preceding correspondence. The great detail with which the request is expressed would be quite unnecessary, if the matter had been previously explained to the persons concerned.

To B— χαίρειν A—.

Petitions addressed to rulers of the land or to high officials almost invariably begin with this formula. There can no longer be any doubt that these petitions were addressed to magistrates as well as to the king; nor is there any need of confining petitions with this formula addressed to magistrates "ad priorem saeculi III partem" as Ziemann does,[7] thus modifying the opinion of Laqueur.[8] The P. S. I., published since Ziemann wrote, contain nearly two dozen petitions addressed to magistrates during the third century B. C. Doubtless in the course of time we shall find similar documents; and they may push their date forward to the

[7]Ziemann p. 260. [8]Quaestiones Epig. et Papyr. selectae. 1904.

second century B. C. All documents with this formula now extant belong to the early Ptolemaic period.

Ziemann, following Wilcken, has pointed out the correct place of the period in this formula, namely after the nominative (To B— χαίρειν A—.) and not after χαίρειν (To B— χαίρειν.) In the table above in some instances we have printed the first words following the address-formula. It would be impossible to construe the sentence, if the nominative were connected with them.

P. Oxy. IV 705 is a petition addressed to the Roman emperors. Its formula is different from that of the Ptolemaic petition, namely: To B— A— χαίρειν.

To B————(χαίρειν).
From A————————.

These formulas are evidently abbreviations of the standard formulas in use at the time. They are found passim throughout the entire period. Various explanations have been attempted. Wilcken in a note on "Eine Epikrisis-Eingabe aus Oxyrhynchus" says: "Da das Präskript unvollständig ist, so liegt eine Kopie vor."[9] In the P. Ryl. page 81 the editor remarks that this explanation would not apply to P. Ryl. 104, since this document has the autograph of the writer: "Ηρων ἐπιδέδωκα. He thinks that writers of applications, made out in duplicate, were apt to omit the heading in one copy, and refers to P. Oxy. 1111, 1; 1113, 2. In P. P. III 46 (137) it is suggested that on the official copy, kept in the archives, the address was abreviated. It may be observed in this connection that, when official letters went through "regular channels", the result was often a "chain" letter, each respective official attaching a copy of the orders received by him to his forwarding note. At times six or seven letters, attached the one to the other, would reach the last official in line. In such "chain" letters the address was sometimes written in full; sometimes only the formula: To B——, was used.[10] The same holds of endorsements on applications or petitions, when such documents were sent by a higher official with his approval to a subordinate for execution. In regard to P. Grenf. I 45, P. Good. 5(9), Wilcken has suggested that these two letters are attempts at bribery, and that for this reason the name of the addressee has been omitted.

[9]Grundzüge und Chrestomathie der Papyruskunde I 2 p. 252. note 217.
[10]Cp.P.P.II 23; 12; III 42; 53; P. Grenf. II 14d.

Thus the recipient would not be compromised in case the letter should fall into the wrong hands. But the writer would be less fortunate! The same suggestion is made regarding P. Tebt. I 9. If these suggestions are correct, it is clear that these letters are exceptions to the rule and they are of no assistance in explaining similar forms of address in documents where there is no question of bribery.

A curious form is P. Hib. I 81: Ἀρτεμίδωρος. This is apparently the entire address. This papyrus, as well as the grain receipts of Karanis[11] and similar short forms may be due to the influence of the ostraca. Potsherds are not suitable for long communications. The writer naturally condenses his message as much as possible. Nominative forms as address-formulas (A———.) are commonplace in Wilcken, Ostraka II; the dative form is not so common.[12] For hurried and less important messages such brief forms may have been quite satisfactory.

To B—— A—— (χαίρειν).

The collections of papyri published during the last ten years almost doubled the number of extant texts exhibiting this formula. The earliest occurrence of this formula in papyri now extant seems to be P. S. I. 361, dated B. C. 261. But its next occurrence is apparently in the first century of the Christian era. It was thought that this formula was used to show greater deference to the addressee. However, it is used in familiar letters also, by brothers to sisters, and by father to son. It occurs about forty times among the papyri so far published.

From A—— to B—— (χαίρειν).

A still later formula arises from the mixture of the two main types. It is used in familiar letters, business letters, and official communications, generally with the greeting attached. Only about twenty texts with this formula have come to our notice; they all belong to the third century A. D.

Χαίροις. Χαῖρε.

Quite a different formula from those in common use is the optative or the imperative of the verb χαίρειν. Letters beginning with this formula occur during the first three centuries of the

[11]Stud. Class. Phil. III
[12]Ostraca II page 303, 305 etc.

Christian era. As far as we have noticed the two formulas are found less than thirty times among the extant papyri. We have classed them all among the familiar letters. Ziemann claims: "Quae epistulae magna ex parte scriptae sunt ab hominibus ineruditis,"[13] and then quotes two of the letters which apparently had been written by slaves. We can not share his view, nor do we see any ground upon which it could be based. Slaves are not necessarily "homines ineruditi." With the exception of the opening formula these letters do not differ from other familiar letters. The spelling is no worse than that of other documents of the same period. No explanation is vouched for this form. Only we must bear in mind that, while certain formulas are customary in private correspondence, none are obligatory, and a writer was at liberty to choose a less formal mode of address. Future discoveries may show that this independence of form was far more common than we at present are inclined to believe.

[13]Ziemann p. 296.

## II. THE CLOSING FORMULA

In the epistolary papyri of the Ptolemaic and the Roman periods we find that certain letters regularly have for their closing formula the expression: ἔρρωσο (ἔρρωσθε), or its modifications; others end with the verb: εὐτύχει, later changed into διευτύχει; while a third group of letters has no special formula at all, but simply omits the final salutation. With due allowance for exceptions we may perhaps say that familiar letters belong to the first group; that petitions and formal complaints belong to the second group; and that business communications of various kinds generally belong to the third group. Official letters ordinarily end with the phrase: ἔρρωσο, or its modifications; yet a large number of official letters are found without any final salutation.[1] If we could attach much value to definite numbers, we might observe that the closing salutation is missing in about one third of the official letters beginning with the formula: A—— to B—— χαίρειν. But letters of an official nature, beginning with other opening formulas, are quite frequently without any salutation at the end.

It is not our purpose to investigate the origin of the closing formulas. The papyri do not furnish any evidence on which to base such a discussion. Both phrases, ἔρρωσο as well as εὐτύχει, are found in the earliest epistolary papyri extant. Both were still in use at the end of Roman period. In the first century A. D. διευτύχει began to displace the form εὐτύχει, and succeeded in doing this during the second and third centuries. Its earliest occurrence seems to be B. C. 13-12 B. G. U. IV 1197 (338); also B. C. 10 P. B. M. II 354 (163). There are but a few instances of this form during the first century A. D., i.a. P. B. M. II 177 (167) A. D. 40; P. Tebt. II 302 (88) A. D. 71; P. Amh. II 68 (75) late 1stc. A. D. During the next two centuries it occurs more frequently. Even during the first century A. D. its use must have been much more common than the papyri now show. It is not probable that a form should occur but half a dozen times during hundred and and twenty years, and then replace the older form which had been

[1]The Roman emperors used εὐτύχει. Cf. Lafoscade o. c.

in use for more than four hundred years. Here also future discoveries of papyri may show the real proportion.

How unsafe it is, at the present stage of papyrological study, to rely upon definite numbers, may be shown in the case of the form ἔρρωσο. During the last century of the Roman period this form was being supplanted by a modification of it: ἐρρῶσθαί σε εὔχομαι. Ziemann[2] found that of about 66 private letters among the papyri of the second century A. D., 29 had the old form, and 36 the new form. But several important collections of papyri have been published since. They brought the number of private letters in the second century A. D. to 93, of which 46 have ἔρρωσο, and 47 ἐρρῶσθαί σε εὔχομαι. Any addition to the papyri so far extant may change the relative position.

Only a few forms have come to our notice differing from the rest. They occur only once: B. C. 164-158 P. Paris 49 (Witk. p. 69) ὑγίαινε; B. C. 99 P. Good. 9 (12) ὑγιαίνει; A. D. 2dc. P. Oxy. I 115 (181) εὖ πράττετε. These "hapax legomena" need not detain us.

A— to B— χαίρειν.

As has been shown in the preceding chapter, the opening formula A—— to B—— χαίρειν, with its modifications, is used in familiar letters, business letters, and official communications. Of a group of 655[3] letters beginning with this formula 284 have the closing formula ἔρρωσο, 142 close with the phrase ἐρρῶσθαί σε εὔχομαι, six have the same formula without the personal pronoun: ἐρρῶσθαι εὔχομαι, and two have a formula thus far not found in other papyri—to our knowledge,: ἐρρῶσθαι ὑμᾶς βούλομαι A. D. 193 B. G. U. II 646 (311) and A. D. 206 P. Oxy. VIII 1100 (164). Five letters beginning with the same opening formula have the closing phrase εὐτύχει. The remaining 216 letters of this group have no closing salutation at all. Of these 655 letters, therefore, beginning with the formula A—— to B—— χαίρειν, 434 end with the salutation ἔρρωσο or one of its modifications. Of the 284 letters ending with ἔρρωσο 150 are familiar letters, 17 may be classed as business letters, and 117 are official communications. Also, of the 142 letters ending with ἐρρῶσθαί σε εὔχομαι

[2]Ziemann p. 337.

[3]A much larger number of letters with this formula are found among the papyri extant. When we had taken notes on about 1500 letters, we confined ourselves to reading the remainder, noting only differences from the usual type.

116 must be classed as familiar letters, and 23 as official communications. Hence, adding the five familiar letters ending in ἐρρῶσθαι εὔχομαι, we have 271 familiar letters ending with the word ἔρρωσο or one of its modifications. If we consider in this connection that of the 216 letters ending without any salutation only 49 are familiar letters, and that many of these 49 are in so fragmentary condition that it can not be determined what, if any, closing phrase they had, we feel safe in concluding that in the ordinary familiar letter of the Ptolemaic and the Roman periods the closing phrase was ἔρρωσο or one of its modifications. It is not likely that future additions to our papyri collections will materially change this conclusion.

Under business letters we have brought together a number of papyri of varied nature: receipts, contracts, agreements, and some real letters pertaining to business. All have opening formulas of the epistolary type; but only the last mentioned persists in that type. The rest are mostly receipts, contracts, commercial agreements. Receipts usually end without any salutatory formula, having only the signature of the writer. Contracts and agreements commonly end with a clause asserting the legal validity of the instruments. Of 91 business communications beginning with the formula A— to B— χαίρειν only 20 end with ἔρρωσο or ἐρρῶσθαί σε εὔχομαι. The rest have no special closing formula. If in this number had been included the numerous receipts extant, the difference would be still greater.

As has been stated above, of the official letters beginning with the formula A— to B— χαίρειν about one-third have no special closing salutation. In a goodly part of this one-third the absence of the salutation is due to the fragmentary state of the papyrus. Various reasons have been suggested for the absence of the closing formula in the other official letters: lack of erudition on the part of the writer; the practice of omitting the salutation in duplicates; carelessness; etc. Friendly communications between magistrates, though referring to official business, are rather in the nature of familiar letters. Communications confined strictly to official business are more likely to be without a final salutation, which in such cases would be merely conventional.

To B— χαίρειν A—.

During the Ptolemaic period petitions addressed to the king or to higher magistrates began with the formula: To B— χαίρειν A——. Of the 55 letters of this kind 50 have the closnig formula εὐτύχει, while one, P. S. I. 372 (106) B. C. 250-49, has the form ἔρρωσο. In four the closing phrase is missing. With so great a disparity in the numbers one feels safe in concluding as to what was the usual phrase.

To B—— A—— (χαίρειν).

During the later Roman period the order of names in the principal opening formula was, at times, reversed, resulting in the formula To B—— A—— χαίρειν. Not infrequently the word χαίρειν was omitted. The closing phrase is missing as a rule when the opening phrase lacks the salutation: To B—— A——. When the opening phrase has the greeting attached, the closing formula quite regularly is ἐρρῶσθαί σε εὔχομαι. Cp. 2dc. A. D. P. Ryl. 234 (383); A. D. 160 P. Hamb. 35 (160); A. D. 3dc. P. Oxy. VIII 1157, 1160, 1158; XIV 1671, 1678; A. D. 135 B. G. U. I 19 (30); A. D. 3d-4thc. P. Oxy. I 123 (190). For the formula To B—— A—— cp. A. D. 87 P. Hamb. 4 (16); A. D. 130 B. G. U. II 647 (312); A. D. 133 P. Oxy. I 100 (163) A. D. 135 ib. 106 (173); A. D. 223-245 ib. 77, 80, 81; A. D. 158 P. Fay. 24 (131); A. D. 196 ib. 42 (163); A. D. 185 P. Ryl. 85 (48); P. Amh. II 107, 108; etc. etc.

To B—— from A——.

Next to the formula A— to B— χαίρειν the opening phrase To B— from A— occurs most commonly. It was used in commercial communications, applications and similar documents, and in official letters. Its closing phrase varies accordingly. With proper allowance for exceptions it may be safely asserted that commercial letters—which usually are applications for leases, or similar documents,—are regularly without the final greeting. Official letters also commonly lack the closing salutation, when they are in the nature of reports, or notices of birth, death, etc., census or property returns, or sworn declarations. When they are in the nature of complaints addressed to minor officials, or petitions for redress on account of injuries received, etc., their final salutation is quite regularly εὐτύχει; or, from B. C. 13 on, occasionally, and from the second century A. D. on regularly, διευτύχει. It is of course not implied that the form διευτύχει was not employed before B. C. 13. It is quite likely that it was much older, since it occurred in inscriptions as early as B. C. 68.[4] Thus far, however, the papyri have not given us any evidence for its earlier occurrence.

With this opening phrase the closing formula ἔρρωσο occurs about a dozen times, more frequently in official letters than in others. Cp. B. C. 250 P. P. II 6 (17); B. C. 225 P. Eleph. 27 (75); B. C. 3dc P. Eleph. 25 (72); A. D. 66 P. Oxy. II 246 (195): A. D. 260 P. Flor. II 273 (239); etc.

## THE REMAINING FORMULAS

The apostrophic opening formula Χαίροις, Χαῖρε, belonging to the Christian era, is frequently followed by the closing salutation ἐρρῶσθαί σε εὔχομαι. Cp. P. Oxy. VI 933 (249); VII 1063 (217); XII 1492 (249); I 112 (177); B. G. U. III 821 (136); P. S. I. III 206 (66); P. Fay. 129 (285) etc. Often no final salutation is found, at times on account of the mutilated condition of the papyrus. The form εὐτύχει so far occurs once, P. Oxy. III 526 (262); the form διευτύχει also once in B. G. U. 248 (246) A. D. 2dc.

The opening formula To B—— nearly always lacks the final greeting. It has ἔρρωσο in P. P. II 9 (23) B. C. 241; ἐρρῶσθαί σε εὔχομαι in P. Oxy. VIII 1142 (240) late 3dc. A. D.; ἔρρωσο in P. Tebt. I 15 (32) B. C. 114; P. Tebt. I 26 (103).

The form From A— also is frequently without any final greeting. At times it has εὐτύχει: B. C. 113 P. Tebt. I 38 (134); B. C. 2dc. P. Grenf. I 41 (73); P. Good. 5 (9). It is found occasionally with ἔρρωσο: A. D. 3dc. P. Ryl. 245 (393); and with ἐρρῶσθαί σε εὔχομαι: A. D. 262 P. Ryl. 238 (387); A. D. 268 P. Fay. 133 (288); A. D. 254 P. Flor. II 118 (67); A. D. 3d-4thc P. Rein. 52 (157). Once it is found with ὑγιαίνει P. Good. 9 (12) B. C. 99.

We have noticed only a few instances in which the opening formula A— to B— is followed by the final greeting ἔρρωσο: B. C. 256 P. S. I. IV 344 (80); B. C. 172 P. B. M. I 42 (29); A. D. 81-95 P. Oxy. VIII 1105 (175). In all the other instances of this formula which we have noticed, about twenty-five, the final greeting was lacking.

The formula From A— to B— χαίρειν occurs but rarely. In P. Oxy. VIII 1140 (239) A .D. 293 and P. Oxy. XII 1570 (279) A. D. 3dc. it is followed by ἔρρωσο. In P. Flor. II 204 (171) A.

[4]Fay. inscr. No. 5 (p. 48) lin. 25 apud. Ziemann p. 325.

D. 260 the formula ἐρρῶσθαί σε εὔχομαι occurs. The formula From A— to B—, also infrequent, is found regularly without any closing formula.

By way of summary the following table is subjoined. Where the ending occurs only a few times, as an exception to the rule, it is not given in this table. The closing formulas are given in order of the frequency of their occurrence. ἔρρωσο is abbreviated as ἔρ., ἐρρῶσθαί σε εὔχομαι as ἐσε, εὐτύχει as εὐτ., διευτύχει as δι.

| | | |
|---|---|---|
| A— to B— χαίρειν | familiar | ἔρ., ἐσε, |
| | business | none, ἔρ., ἐσε, |
| | official | ἔρ., ἐσε, none. |
| A——— to B——— | | none. |
| To B— from A——— | petitions | εὐτ., δι., |
| | business | none. |
| | official | none. |
| To B— χαίρειν A—— | petitions | εὐτ. |
| To B— A————— | | none. |
| To B—— A—— χαίρειν | | ἐσε. |
| To B————— | | none. |
| From A————— | | none, ἐσε ,εὐτ. |
| From A— to B——— | | none. |
| From A— to B— χαίρειν | | ἔρ., ἐσε, none. |
| Χαίροις, Χαῖρε——— | | none, ἐσε. |

Since the formulas εὐτύχει and διευτύχει were employed mainly in rather formal communications, namely petitions addressed to the king or his magistrates, it does not at all seem strange that these formulas remained unchanged throughout the Ptolemaic and the Roman periods. The forms ἔρρωσο and ἐρρῶσθαί σε (ὑμᾶς) εὔχομαι were commonly used in familiar letters, and also in official letters between magistrates. As in the opening formulas, so also in the closing formulas the writer occasionally gave expression to the familiarity existing between him and his correspondent. To illustrate the amplifications of the regular salutatory closing phrases which thus came into use, the following quotations are appended. This list is not exhaustive; it gives, however, a fairly complete view of the main variations employed:

### ἔρρωσο

ἔρρωσο τέκνον 2dc. A. D. P. Oxy. III 531 (268); P. Giss. 21 (64);
ἔρρωσο κύριε P. Flor. III 332 (67); P. Giss. 13 (51); P. Giss III 77 (67);

P. Ryl. 233 (382); all 2dc. A. D.
ἔρρωσο Σελήνη ἀδελφή P. Amh. II 131 (160) early 2dc. A. D.
ἔρρωσο 'Απολλώνιε μετὰ τῆς ἀδελφῆς σου P. Giss. III 71 (60) 2dc. A. D.
ἔρρωσο κύριε ——— P. Giss. 17 (56) 2dc. A. D.
ἔρρωσθε πανοικίᾳ B. G. U. II 450 (109) 2d-3dc. A. D.
ἔρρωσό μοι ἀδελφέ P. Tebt. II 314 (113) 2dc. A. D.
ἔρρωσό μοι φίλτατε P. Giss. 16 (55) 2dc. A. D.
ἔρρωσό μοι τιμιώτατε P. Tebt. II 315 (114) 2dc. A. D.
ἔρρωσό μοι παράδοξε P. Oxy. XIV 1759 (181) 2dc. A. D.
ἔρρωσό μοι γλυκύτατε B. G. U. II 417 (78) 3dc. A. D.
ἔρρωσό μοι εὐτυχῶς. ἔρρωσόέμοί τε καί σοι εὐτυχῶς P. Oxy. I 118 (184) 3dc. A. D.
ἔρρωσό μοι πολλοῖς χρόνοις ὑγιαίνων μετὰ καὶ τῶν σῶν P. Hamb. 54 (194) 2d-3dc. A. D.
τά δ' ἄλλα ἔρρωσο P. Oxy. X 1292 (244) A. D. 30.
τὰ δ' ἄλλα ἔρρωσό μοι σὺν τοῖς σοῖς πᾶσι P. Giss. 24 (68) 2dc. A. D.

ἐρρῶσθαί σε (ὑμᾶς) εὔχομαι.

ἐρρῶσθαί σε εὔχομαι ἀδελφέ P. Oxy. XIV 1642 (65) A. D. 289; P. Flor. II 208 (174) A. D. 256; P. Oxy. XII 1491 (248) early 4thc A. D.
ἐρρῶσθαί σε εὔχομαι πάτερ P. Flor. II 180 (139 )A. D. 253; 184 (143) A. D. 250 about; P. Oxy. X 1296 (250) 3dc. A. D.
ἐρρῶσθαί σε εὔχομαι τιμιώτατε P. Giss. 27 (73) 2dc. A. D. ; B. G. U. I 73 (87) A. D. 135; P. Ryl. 238 (387) A. D. 262; C. P. H. 119 (57) 3dc. A. D.;
ἐρρῶσθαί σε εὔχομαι τιμιώτατου πάντων P. B. M. III 1173 (207) A. D. 125.
ἐρρῶσθαί σε εὔχομαι φίλτατε P. Oxy. XII 1422 (74) A. D. 128; P. Ryl. 78 (37) A. D. 157; B. G. U. IV 1031 (32) 2dc. A. D.; P. Fay 125 (281) 2dc A. D.; P. Oxy. I 63 (121) 2d-3dc. A. D. ; P. Oxy. XIV 1662 (116) A. D. 246; C. P. R. 20 (99) A. D. 250; P. Ryl. 236 (385) A. D. 256; P. Flor. II 194 (1601) A. D. 259; also ibid. 195,212, 213, 215, 227, 238, 242, 233; B. G. U. IV 1073 (114) A. D. 274; P. Oxy. I 159 (117) A. D. 292; P. Oxy. VI 891 (208) A. D. 294; P. Rein. 54 (166) A. D. 3d-4thc.
ἐρρῶσθαί σε εὔχομαι φίλτατε 'Ηράκλειε P. Giss. 26 (70) 2dc. A. D.
ἐρρῶσθαι ὑμᾶς εὔχομαι φίλτατοι ἀδελφοί C. P. H. 121 (66) 3dc. A. D.
ἐρρῶσθαί σε εὔχομαι γλυκυτάτηι P. Oxy. XIII 1767 (164) 2dc. A. D.
ἐρρῶσθαί σε εὔχομαι μετὰ τῶν τέκνων P. Amh. II 135 (164) 2dc. A. D.
ἐρρῶσθαί σε εὔχομαι κύριε P. Oxy. VI 933 (299) late 2dc. A. D.
ἐρρῶσθαί σε εὔχομαι κύριέ μου P. Giss. II 47 (63) 2dc. A. D.; III 64 (45) 2dc. A. D.; 69 (56) 118-119 A. D.; P. Ryl. 234 (383) 2dc. A. D.
ἐρρῶσθαί σε εὔχομαι ἐν Κυρίῳ Θεῷ P. Grenf. II 73 (115) late 3dc. A: D.
ἐρρῶσθαί σε ἐν Θεῷ εὔχομαι P. S. I. III 208 (69) 4thc. A. D.
ἐρρῶσθαι ὑμᾶς εὔχομαι πολλά P. Iand. 9 (42) 2dc. A. D.
ἐρρῶσθαί σε εὔχομαι πανοικεί 3dc. A. D. P. Oxy. XII 1586 (283); P. Iand. 129 (285); P. Oxy. XIV 1666 (121).

*ἐρρῶσθαί σε εὔχομαι ἡγεμὼν κύριε* B. G. U. I 19 (30) A. D. 135; P. Giss. II 41 (47) 2dc. A. D.
*ἐρρῶσθαί σε εὔχομαι πανοικεὶ κύριέ μου* P. Fay. 130 (286) 3dc. A. D.
*ἐρρῶσθαί σε εὔχομαι πολλοῖς χρόνοις* P. Oxy. I 112 (177); VI 936, 938; VII 1066, 1068; VIII 1157, 1158; XIV 1671, 1770; P. Ryl. 244 (392); all of the 3dc. A. D.
*ἐρρῶσθαί σε πολλοῖς χρόνοις εὔχομαι* P. Oxy. IX 1190 (210) A. D. 280.
*ἐρρῶσθαί σε εὔχομαι πολλοῖς χρόνοις κύριέ μου* P. Oxy. XII 1495 (252) 4thc. A. D.
*ἐρρῶσθαί σε εὔχομαι πολλοῖς χρόνοις κύριέ υἱέ* P. Oxy. I 123 (190) 3d-4thc. A. D.
*ἐρρῶσθαί σε εὔχομαι πολλοῖς χρόνοις κύριέ μου ἀδελφέ* P. Iand. 11 (46) 3dc. A. D.
*ἐρρῶσθαί σε εὔχομαι κυρία μου ἀδελφὴ πολλοῖς χρόνοις* P. Oxy. XIV 1682 (143) 4thc. A. D.
*ἐρρῶσθαί σε εὔχομαι πολλοῖς ἔτεσιν* P. Flor. III 365 (87) 3dc. A. D.
*ἐρρῶσθαί σε εὔχομαι πάτηρ πολλοῖς ἔτεσιν* P. Gen. 9 (113) 3d-4thc. A. D.
*ἐρρῶσθαί σε εὔχομαι εἰς τὸν ἀεὶ χρόνον* P. Fay. 117 (272) A. D. 108.
*ἐρρῶσθαί σε εὔχομαι πολλοῖς πραχθῆς εὖ ἐν χρόνοις* P. Flor. II 181 (140) 3dc. A. D.
*ἐρρῶσθαί σε κύριέ μου ἀδελφὲ πολλοῖς χρόνοις καὶ προκόπτειν εὔχομαι* P. Oxy. I 122 (189) 3d-4thc. A. D.
*ἐρρῶσθαι εὔχομαι εὖ πράττοντα* P. Oxy. III 527 (263) 2d-3dc. A. D.
*ἐρρῶσθαι ὑμᾶς εὔχομαι εὐτυχοῦντας.* P. Oxy. XIV 1768 (184) 3dc. A. D.; P. Flor. II 231 A. D. 257;
*ἐρρῶσθαί [σε] εὔχομαι τέκνον εὐτυχοῦντα δι' ὅλου* P. Oxy. IX 1219 (262) 3dc. A. D.
*ἐρρῶσθαί σοι εὔχομαι κύριέ μου εὐτυχοῦντα* P. Oxy. IX 1220 (263) 3dc. A. D.
*ἐρρῶσθαί σ' εὔχομαι κύριον εὐτυχοῦντα πανοικηκ(?)* P. Flor. II 273 (239) A. D. 260.
*ἐρρῶσθαί σε εὔχομαι φίλτατε εὐτυχοῦντα πανοικεί* P. Iand. 8 (39) 2dc. A. D.
*ἐρρῶσθαί σε εὔχομαι εὐκοποῦντα διὰ ὅλου βίου* P. S. I. IV 286 (14) 3d-4thc A. D.
*ἐρρῶσθαί σε καὶ εὐανθοῦντα εὔχομαι κύριέ μου υἱέ* B. G. U. IV 1080 (125) 3dc. A. D.
*ἐρρῶσθαί σε εὔχομαι κύριέ μου ὁλοκληροῦντα*—— P. Flor. III 373 (94) 3dc. A. D.
*ἐρρῶσθαί σε ὁλοκληροῦντα εὔχομαι* P. Oxy. XII 1490 (247) late 3dc. A. D.
*ἐρρῶσθαι ὑμᾶς εὔχομαι εὖ διάγοντας* P. Oxy. XIV 1668 (124) 3dc A. D.
*ἐρρῶσθαί σε εὔχομαι κατὰ νοῦν διάγοντα* P. Oxy. XIV 1665 (120) 3dc. A. D.

*ἐρρῶσθαί σε εὔχομαι κύριέ μου χρηστὲ καὶ εὐγενέστατε Ἀπίων διὰ βίου εὖ διάγοντα μεθ' ὧν ἡδέως διάγεις* P. Oxy. XIV 1664 (118) 3dc. A. D.
*ἐρρῶσθαί σε εὐτυχευδοξοῦντα πανοικησίᾳ εὔχομαι* P. Tebt. II 418 (294) 3dc. A. D.
*ἐρρῶσθαι [καὶ ὁλοκληρεῖν] σε εὐδοξοῦντα καὶ εὐτυχοῦντα καὶ εὐπραγοῦντα θεοῖς πᾶσι εὔχομαι* P. Oxy. XIV. 1766 (183) 3dc. A. D.
*ἐρρῶσθαί σ' εὔχομαι φίλτατε καὶ καλῶς ἔχειν πανοικεί* P.Flor. II 230 A. D. 256.
*ἐρρῶστέ σε εὔχομε ὁλοκληρεῖν* P. Oxy. XIV 1678 (137) 3dc. A. D.
*ἐρρώμένος μοι διατελοῖς μετὰ τῶν φιλτάτων κύριέ μου ἀσυγάριτε Ἀλύπι* P. Flor. II 140 (93) 264 A. D.
*ἐρρῶσθαι ὑμᾶς εὔχομαι τῷ Θεῷ διὰ παντὸς καὶ ἐν παντί* P. Oxy. XII 1492 (249) 3d-4thc. A. D.
*ἐρρῶσθαί σε κύριέ μου σὺν τῆι κρατίστηι ἀδελφῆι καὶ τῆι Κυρίλλῃ εὔχομαι. ἔρρωσο* P. Oxy. VI 931 (296) 2dc. A. D.
*Ἡρακλείδης ἔναρχος ἱεροποιὸς ἐρρῶσθαί σε εὔχομαι τιμιώτατε. ἔρρωσο* P. Giss. III 66 (49) 2dc. A. D.
*πρὸ πάντων ἐρρῶσθαί σε εὔχομαι τιμιώτατε πανοικεί. ἔρρωσο* P. Giss. III 75 (63) 2dc. A. D.

These quotations require no further comment. It will be noted that nearly all of them belong to the second and third centuries of the Christian era, and thus synchronize with the expanded opening formulas. At some future time, when more texts of these varied closing formulas are available, it will be possible to study their relative importance in their chronological development.

## III. THE DATING OF LETTERS

In this chapter we intend to show what formulas were used in the dating of letters during the Ptolemaic and the Roman periods. We shall try to give a fairly adequate and complete view of the formulas, as they are found in the epistolary papyri of the period. It is neither feasible nor desirable to give all the dates that occur. The frequency of the occurrence of a formula during a certain reign will be tentatively indicated by the quotation of the formula, with the addition of references to other papyri using the same formula. In these references we shall try to cover, as far as possible, the entire incumbency of the ruler. Throughout we shall present these formulas in chronological order.

We have given both the principal dates and the dates occurring within the document in the same section, preferring this arrangement to placing these dates under separate heads. The final or principal dates are quoted first; the dates occurring in the body of the letter are given last. It is to be noted that the years indicated at the head of each quotation pertain to the document from which the dating formulas are taken. These dating formulas belong occasionally to endorsements added to the document in question, and hence belong at times to later years.

Only a few examples will be given of the dating formulas in use before the reign of Augustus. They are quite the same throughout the entire period preceding the accession of Augustus. For the sake of convenience we have employed the following abbreviations in the formulas of the later Roman period.

| | | | |
|---|---|---|---|
| Αὐτοκράτορος | Α. | Αὐτοκρατόρων | Αων |
| Καίσαρος | Κ. | Καισάρων | Κων |
| τοῦ κυρίου | τ.κ. | | |
| Σεβαστοῦ | Σ. | Σεβαστῶν | Σῶν |
| Εὐσεβοῦς | Ε. | Εὐσεβῶν | Εῶν |
| Εὐσεβοῦς Εὐτυχοῦς | Ε.Ε. | Εὐσεβῶν Εὐτυχῶν | Εῶν Εῶν |
| Γερμανικοῦ | Γ. | Γερμανικῶν | Γῶν |
| Δακικοῦ | Δ. | Δακικῶν | Δῶν |
| Μεγίστου | Μ. | Μεγίστων | Μων |

*A. TEXTS*

MACEDONIAN NAMES.

B. C. 261 P. S. I. IV 324 (63): (ἔτους) κε Ἀρτεμισίου ιβ;
325 (65): (ἔτους) κε Δαισίου κα;
B. C. 258 P. S. I. IV 329 (67): (ἔτους) κη Δύστρου η;
435 (161): (ἔτους) κη Αὐδναίου θ.
B. C. 251 P. S. I. IV 364 (95): (ἔτους) λε Λώιου η;
B. C. 250 P. S. I. IV 375 (104): (ἔτους) λς Πανήμου κς.
B. C. 239 P. Hib. I 82 (239): (ἔτους) θ Ὑπερβερεταίου κζ etc.

EGYPTIAN NAMES.

B. C. 265 P. Hib. I 39 (181): (ἔτους) κα Θωὺθ ι.
B. C. 196 P. Amh. II 37 (46): (ἔτους) ι Φαῶφι α.
B. C. 114 P. Tebt. I 19 (89): (ἔτους) γ Παχὼν ιθ.
B. C. 1stc. P. Tebt. II 284 (43): (ἔτους) ιβ Χοίακ κ.
B. C. 81 P. Grenf. II 38 (62): (ἔτους) β τοῦ καὶ α (ἔτους) Φαρμοῦθι ιγ.
B. C. 28 B. G. U. IV 1206 (347): (ἔτους) γ Ἀθὺρ ς πρῶι.
B. C. 23 B. G. U. IV 1209 (351): (ἔτους ) ζ Μεχεὶρ κθ.
A. D. 1stc. P. Oxy. II 296 (296): (ἔτους) α μηνὸς Φαμενὼθ κη.
A. D. 1stc. P. Fay. 109 (260): (ἔτους) κ Παῦνι κε.
A. D. 199 P. Tebt. II 407 (279) a: (ἔτους) ζ Τῦβι κδ.
A. D. 256 P. Ryl. 236 (385): (ἔτους) γ Τῦβι ιε.
A. D. 262 P. Ryl. 238 (387): (ἔτους) θ Παχὼν κε.
Compare also: P. R l. 230 (379 )A. D. 40: (ἔτους) ε μηνὸς Νέου Σεβαστοῦ ς Σεβαστῆι.
P. R l. 231 (380) A. D. 40: (ἔτους) ε μηνὸς Σωτῆρος κα.
P. Ryl. 231a (381) A. D. 40 within: δ (ἔτους) μηνὸς Δρουσιέως κη.

MACEDONIAN—EGYPTIAN NAMES.

Ptolemaic P. P. III 53 (154): (ἔτους) ις Γορπιαίου δ Χοίαχ ια.
B. C. 260 P. P. III 2 (3): (ἔτους) κε Ἀπελλαίου ι Φαρμοῦθι ζ
B. C. 256 P. S. I. IV 341 (77): (ἔτους) λ Γορπιείου κη Θωὺθ κη.
also 342 (79): (ἔτους) λ Ὑπερβερεταίου ιζ Φαῶφι ιζ.
B. C. 249 P. Hib. I 77 (232): (ἔτους) λς Ἀρτεμισίου κγ Παχὼν κβ.
B. C. 222 P. Lille II 12 also ibidem 2, 3, 4, 11, (102): (ἔτους) δ Δίου γ Φαμενὼθ κς. (58): (ἔτους) κε Λώιου αζ Χοίακ κγ.
B. C. 221 P. Lille II 14 (112): (ἔτους) α Γορπιαίου λ Τῦβι ιγ.
also ibidem 18, 21, 22, 23, 25,
B. C. 218 P. Lille II 7 (82): (ἔτους) δ Δαισίου κζ Ἀθὺρ κθ.
also ibidem 13 (107);
P. Lille I 4 (36): (ἔτους) ε Ὑπερβερεταίου κη Φαμενὼθ κθ.
also ibidem: (ἔτους) ε Ἀπελλαίου ιγ Παχὼν ιγ.

B. C. 117 P. Tebt. I 25 (102): (ἔτους) νγ Ξανδικοῦ ιζ Μεχεὶρ ιζ
B. C. 113 P. Tebt. I 27 (105): (ἔτους) δ Περιτίου κγ Χοίαχ κγ.
also ibidem: (ἔτους) δ Δύστρου κα Τῦβι κα.
B. C. 99 P. Leid. G. (41): (ἔτους) ις Δίου κθ Θωοὺθ κθ.

---

B. C. 27 B. G. U. III 543 (188): ἔτους τρίτου Καίσαρος Τῦβι ιε
B. C. 13 B. G. U. IV 1053 (72): (ἔτους) ιζ Καίσαρος Φαρμοῦθι ζ
also: B. C. 19-18 P. Grenf. I 45, 46; B. C. 13 B. G. U. IV 1052, 1055, 1057; B. C. 4 P. Oxy. XII 1457 (176); B. C. 2 P. Oxy. IV 742, 743, 744; A. D. 3 P. Tebt. II 408 (282); A. D. 7 B. G. U. I 189 (198); A. D. 13 P. Oxy. IX 1188 (203); A. D. 15 P. B. M. II 256 (96).
B. C. 27 B. G. U. III 543 (188): τοῦ ἐνεστῶτος τρίτου ἔτους Καίσαρος.
B. C. 13 B. G. U. IV 1054 (76): ἀπὸ μηνὸς Φαρμοῦθι τοῦ ἐνεστῶτος ἑπτακαιδεκάτου ἔτους Καίσαρος.
B. C. 13 B. G. U. IV 1057 (84): ἀπὸ ιδ τοῦ ἐνεστῶτος μηνὸς Φαρμοῦθι τοῦ ιζ (ἔτους) Καίσαρος.
A. D. 7 B. G. U. I 189 (198): ἐν μηνὶ Μεχεὶρ τοῦ ἰσιόντος ἑβδόμου καὶ τριακωστοῦ ἔτους Καίσαρος.
A. D. 2 B. G. U. IV 1201 (343): τοῦ ἐνεστῶτος μηνὸς Παῦνει τοῦ λα (ἔτους) Καίσαρος.
A. D. 12 B. G. U. III 757 (65): τῆι ιγ τοῦ Παῦνι τοῦ μα (ἔτους) Καίσαρος.
cp. also: B. G. U. IV 1053 (72) B. C. 13; 1189 (327) B. C. 1; 1197 (338) B. C. 13;.
B. C. 6 B. G. U. IV 1198 (339): πέμπτου καὶ εἰκοστοῦ θεοῦ καὶ Σεβαστοῦ Καίσαρος ἔτους.

---

A. D. 15 P. Hawara (Archiv V p. 378): (ἔτους) α Τιβερίου Κ. Σ. Ἐπεὶφ ιδ.
also P. Ryl. 183 (225) A. D. 16; 94 (62) A. D. 15-37; P. B. M. II 256 (95) A. D. 15; P. Oxy. II 253 (206) A. D. 19; 259 (227) A. D. 23; P. Tebt. II 289 (52), 348 (181), A. D. 23; P. Oxy. IV 746 (246) A. D. 16; II 294 (294) A. D. 22; II 293 (293) A. D. 27; II 245 (195) A. D. 26; II 240 (184) A. D. 37; XII 1480 (238) A. D. 32; P. Fay 25 (133) A. D. 36;
A. D. 16 P. Tebt. II 410 (285): (ἔτους) γ Τιβερίου Κ. Σ. μηνὸς Νέου Σεβαστοῦ ιζ;
also: P. Ryl. 183 (226) A. D. 16; P. Oxy. X 1291 (243) A. D. 30;
A. D. 18 P. B. M. III 1168 (135): (ἔτους) δ Τιβερίου Κλαυδίου Κ. Σ. Γ. Α. Φαρμοῦθι κε.

---

A. D. 19 P. Oxy. II 252, 253 (205-6): τοῦ ἐνεστῶτος ε (ἔτους) Τιβερίου Κ. Σ.

A. D. 28 P. Ryl. 125 (120): τῷ Μεσορὴ μηνὶ τοῦ διεληλυθότος ιδ (ἔτους) Τιβερίου Κ. Σ.

A. D. 29 P. Ryl. 127 (123): νυκτὶ τῇ φερούσῃ εἰς τὴν ιζ τοῦ ἐνεστῶτος μηνὸς Σεβαστοῦ τοῦ ις (ἔτους) Τιβερίου Κ. Σ.

A. D. 32 P. Ryl. 132 (128): τῶι Παῦνι μηνὶ τοῦ ιη (ἔτους) Τιβερίου Κ. Σ.

Cp. also: P. Oxy. II 244 (193) A. D. 23; II 291 (290) A. D. 25; P. Tebt. II 348 (181) A. D. 23; P. Fay. 25 (133) A. D. 36; P. Ryl. 126 ,128, 129, 130, 131, 133, 134, 135, 136, 137, 138, 139, 140, A. D. 26-37;

A. D. 18 P. B. M. III 1168 (135): Τῦβι —— τοῦ ἐνεστῶτος δ (ἔτους) Τιβερίου Κλαυδίου Κ. Σ. Γ. Α.

A. D. 26 P. Ryl. 166 (197): ἀπὸ τοῦ ἐνεστῶτος τρισκαιδεκάτου ἔτους Τιβερίου Κ. Σ. ἕως τοῦ δωδεκάτου ἔτους Τιβερίου Κ. Σ.

---

A. D. 37 P. Fay. 29 (138): (ἔτους) α Γαίου Καίσαρος Σεβαστοῦ Γερμανικοῦ Μεσορὴ ιδ.

Cp. also: P. Ryl. 229 (378 )A. D. 38; B. G. U. IV 1078 (122) A. D. 39;

A. D. 36 P. Oxy. II 267 (243): (ἔτους) α Γαίου Κ. Γ. Νέου Σεβαστοῦ Α. Παχὼν κς Σεβαστῆι.

A. D. 39 P. Ryl. 167 (199): (ἔτους) δ Γαίου Κ. Σεβαστοῦ Γ. μηνὸς Σεβαστοῦ Σεβαστῇ γ.

cp. also P. Oxy. XIV 1672 (129) A. D. 37-41;

A. D. 38 P. Ryl. 145 (142): Τῦβι γ (ἔτους) γ Γαίου Κ. Σ. Γ.

A. D. 40 P. Ryl. 148 (145): (ἔτους) δ Γαίου Κ. Α. Σ. Παχὼν ιθ.

A. D. 40 P. Ryl. 150 (148): (ἔτους) ε Γαίου Κ. Α. Σ. μηνὸς Σωτῆρος κβ.

A. D. 40 P. Ryl. 151 (149): (ἔτους)ε Γαίου Κ. Α. Σ. Σωτῆρος κ Σεβαστῇ.

A. D. 37 P. Fay. 29 (138): ἐν τῷ Μεσορὴ μηνὶ τοῦ πρώτου (ἔτους) Γαίου Κ. Σ. Γ.

A. D. 36 P. Oxy. II 267 (243): τῇ τριακάδι τοῦ Φαῶφι τοῦ ἰσιόντος δευτέρου ἔτους Γαίου Κ. Γ. Νέου Σεβαστοῦ Α.

A. D. 37 P. Ryl. 141 (138): τῆι β τοῦ ἐνεστῶτος μηνὸς Παχὼν τοῦ α (ἔτους) Γαίου Κ. Α.

A. D. 37 P. Ryl. 142 (139): εἰς τὴν κβ τοῦ ἐνεστῶτος μηνὸς Μεσορὴ τοῦ α (ἔτους) Γαίου Κ. Σ. Γ.

cp. also: P. Ryl. 143, 144, 146, 147, 149; 167;

A. D. 40 P. Ryl. 148 (145): εἰς τὴν ιη τοῦ Παχὼν τοῦ ἐνεστῶτος δ (ἔτους) Γαίου Κ. Σ. Α.

cp. also P. B. M. II 177 (167) A. D. 40 - 41;

---

A. D. 41 B. G. U. IV 1079 (123): (ἔτους) α Τιβερίου Κλαυδίου Κ. Σ. Γ. Α. μηνὸς Καισαρείου ια.

cp. also: P. Ryl. 152 (150) A. D. 42; B. G. U. II 584 (230) A. D. 44; P. B. M. II 139 (200) A. D. 48; P. Oxy. II 264 (234) A. D. 54; P. Oxy. II 283 (273) A. D. 45; II 285 (276) A. D. 50; II 251 (203) A. D. 44; II 255 (215) A. D. 48; X 1258 (178) A. D. 45; P. Grenf. II 41 (67) A. D. 46; P. Tebt. II 299 (83) A. D. 50; B. G. U. I 37 (52) A. D. 50; P. Oxy. II 297 (297) A. D. 54;

Endorsement to P. Oxy. II 267 (243) A. D. 36: (ἔτους) γ Τεβρίου Γλαυτίου Κ. Σ. Γ. Αὐτοκρακάτορος Παοῖνι ιε!

A. D. 44 P. Oxy. II 251 (203): ἀπὸ τοῦ ἐνεστῶτος τετάρτου ἔτους Τιβερίου Κλαυδίου Κ. Σ. Γ. Α.

also: P. Oxy. II 279 (269) A. D. 44-5; II 255 (215) A. D. 48;

---

A. D. 57 B. G. U. IV 1095 (157): (ἔτους) γ Νέρωνος Κλαυδίου Κ. Σ. Γ. Α. Ἐπεὶφ ιβ.

A. D. 58 P. Oxy. II 268 (247): (ἔτους) δ Νέρωνος Κλαυδίου Κ. Σ. Γ. Α. μηνὸς Νερωνείου Σεβαστοῦ γ.

Cp. also: P. Oxy. II 269 (250) A. D. 57; 260 (229) A. D. 59; 262 (232), 250 (201) A. D. 61; B. G. U. I 112 (129) A. D. 59; B. G. U. II 612 (257) A. D. 57; P. Flor. I 79 (163) A. D. 60; B. G. U. III 748 (57) A. D. 62; P. Hamb. 2 (6) A. D. 69; P. B. M III 1213 (121) A. D. 65.

A. D. 55 B. G. U. III 824 (139): ἔτους δευτέρου Α. Νερ— Κ. Σ. Ε.

A. D. 66 P. Oxy. II 246 (195): (ἔτους) ιβ Νέρωνος Κ. τ. κ. Ἐπεὶφ λ.

A. D. 56 B. G. U. II 591 (236): εἰς τὸ τρίτον ἔτος Νέρωνος Κλαυδίου Κ. Σ. Γ. Α.

also: B. G. U. II 612 (257) A. D. 57; P. Oxy. II 262 (232) A. D. 61.

A. D. 56 P. Ryl. 171 (205): ἀπὸ τοῦ εἰσιόντος τρίτου ἔτους Νέρωνος Κλαυδίου Κ. Σ. Γ. Α.

also P. Amh. II 68 (75);

A. D. 57 P. Oxy. II 269 (250): τῇ τριακάδι τοῦ Καισαρείου μηνὸς τοῦ ἐνεστῶτος γ (ἔτους) Νέρωνος Κλαυδίου Κ. Σ. Γ. Α.

also: B. G. U. I 181 (186) A. D. 57; P. B. M. II 281 (65) A. D. 66; P. Hamb. 2 (6) A. D. 69;

---

A. D. 70 P. Gen. 3 (35): (ἔτους) β Α. Κ. Οὐεσπασιανοῦ Σ. Μεχεὶρ ια.

also: P. Tebt. II 387 (241) A. D. 73; P. Amh. II 85 (105) A. D. 78; B. G. U. II 597 (241) A. D. 75; III 981 (306) A. D. 79; P. Amh. II 130 (159) A. D. 70;

A. D. 74 P. Oxy. XIV 166 (115): (ἔτους) ζ Α. Κ. Οὐεσπασιανοῦ Σ. μηνὸς Νέου Σεβαστοῦ ις.

also: P. Oxy. II 242 (186) A. D. 77; 243 (190) A. D. 79;

A. D. 71 P. Tebt. II 302 (88): τῷ ἐνεστῶτι δ (ἔτει) Οὐεσπασιανοῦ
A. D. 72 B. G. U. I 184 (193): ἐπὶ δ (ἔτει) Α. Οὐεσπασιανοῦ Σ. Παῦνι ε.
A. D. 72 P. S. I. V 459 (35): ἀπὸ τοῦ ἐνεστῶτος πέμπτου ἔτους Α. Κ. Οὐεσπασιανοῦ Σ.
A. D. 78 P. Amh. II 85 (105) A.: ἀπὸ τοῦ ἐνεστῶτος δεκάτου (ἔτους) Οὐεσπασιανοῦ τ. κ.

---

A. D. 80 P. Oxy. II 249 (200): (ἔτους) γ Α. Τίτου Κ. Οὐεσπασιανοῦ Σ. Φαῶφι ιγ.
also: P. Oxy. II 248 (198) A. D. 80;

---

A. D. 81 P. Oxy. XII 1471 (208): (ἔτους) α Α. Κ. Δομιτιανοῦ Σ. Τῦβι ε.
also: B. G. U. II 536 (180); III 844 (168) A. D. 83; P. Ryl. 107 (84) A. D. 84.
A. D. 84 B. G. U. II 596 (240): (ἔτους) τρίτου Α. Κ. Δομιτιανοῦ Σ. Γ. Παχὼν ιε.
A. D. 86 P. Grenf. II 42 (68): (ἔτους) ς Α. Κ. Δομιτιανοῦ Σ. Γ. μηνὸς Νέου Σεβαστοῦ.
Cp. also: P. Oxy. I 48 (105) A. D. 86; 72 (135) A. D. 90; 45 (101) A. D. 95; P. Hamb. 4 (16) A. D. 87; P. Oxy. II 247 (197) A. D. 90; P. Fay 110 (261) A. D. 94; 111 A. D. 95-6; P. S. I. IV 317 (50) A. D. 95; P. Amh. II 103 (131), B. G. U. I 260 (261) A. D. 90; C. P. R. 12 (41) A. D. 93; P. Flor. I 85 (168) A. D. 91; P. Oxy. VII 1028 (161) A. D. 86; P. B. M. II 216 (186) A. D. 94;
A. D. 81 P. Oxy. XII 1471 (208): ἀπὸ Τῦβι τοῦ ἐνεστῶτος πρώτου ἔτους Α. Κ. Δομιτιανοῦ Σ.
A. D. 83-4 P. Oxy. XII 1467 (185): τῷ Παῦνι μηνὶ τοῦ διελθόντος δευτέρου ἔτους Α. Κ. Δομιτιανοῦ Σ. Γ.
cp. also: P. Oxy. II 258 (225) A. D. 86; 257 (217) A. D. 94; P. Hamb. 5 (17) A. D. 89; P. B. M. II 163 (182) A. D. 88; 285 (201) A. D. 90;
A. D. 86 P. Oxy. VII 1028 (161): τῷ α (ἔτει) ) Δομιτιανοῦ τ. κ.
A. D. 90 P. Amh. II 103 (131): τοῦ ἐνεστῶτος ἐνάτου ἔτους Δομιτιανοῦ Κ. τ. κ.
A. D. 93 C. P. R. 12 (41): τῆς τριακάδος τοῦ ἐνεσοῦτος (=στῶτος) μηνὸς Φαῶφι τοῦ ἐνεστῶτος τρισκαιδεκάτου ἔτους Δομιτιανοῦ Κ. τ. κ.

---

A. D. 97 P. Oxy. IV 713 (180): (ἔτους) α Α. Νερούα Κ. Σ. Φαμενὼθ ιθ.

---

A. D. 98 P. Iand. 26 (80): (ἔτους) δευτέρου Α. Κ. Νερούα Τραιανοῦ Σ. Γ. μηνὸς Σεβαστοῦ ιδ.
also: P. Fay 100 (241), B. G. U. I 226, III 811 (126), P. Fay 112 (166), P. Oxy. 481 (169) A. D. 99; B. G. U. IV 1068 (106),

P. Oxy. I 46 (103), 49 (107), P. Fay. 114 (269) A. D. 100; P. Leipz. 106 (309) A. D. 98; P. Grenf. II 44 (70) A. D. 101; P. Amh. II 64 (70) A. D. 102; P. Rein. 43 (139) A. D. 102; P. Oxy. III 511 (242) A. D. 103; B. G. U. IV 1063 (101) A. D. 100;

A. D. 98 B. G. U. IV 1066 (104): *ἔτους δευτέρου* A. K. *Νερούα Τραιανοῦ* Σ. *Θὼθ*——.

A. D. 100 B. G. U. III 829 (144): (*ἔτους*) *γ* A. K. *Νερούα Τραιανοῦ* Σ. Γ. *Δακικοῦ μηνὸς Τῦβι ιε.*

also: P. Oxy. VIII 1155 (257) A. D. 104; P. B. M. II 172 (205) A. D. 105; P. Oxy. III 483 (172) A. D. 108 ; VII 1029 (163) A. D. 107; B. G. U. IV 1036 (38) A. D. 108; P. Oxy. III 482 (170) A. D. 109; B. G. U. III 857 (179) ; P. Ryl. 82 (43), B. G. U. I 68 (81) A. D. 113;

A. D. 115 B. G. U. I 50 (63): *ἔτους ὀκτωκαιδεκάτου* A. K. *Νερούα Τραιανοῦ Ἀρίστου* Σ. Γ. Δ. *Τῦβι τριακάδι.*

A. D. 116 P. Oxy. I 74 (137): (*ἔτους*) *ιθ* A. K. *Νερούα Τραιανοῦ Ἀρίστου* Σ. Γ. Δ. *Μεχεὶρ β.*

A. D. 101 P. Fay. 115 (270): (*ἔτους*) *δ Τραιανοῦ τοῦ κυρίου μηνὸς Καισαρίου κη.*

also P. Fay. 116 (271) A. D. 104; 117 (272) A. D. 108; 118 (273) A. D. 110.

A. D. 98 P. Iand. 26 (80): *τοῦ ἐνεστῶτος δευτέρου ἔτους* A. K. *Νερούα Τραιανοῦ* Σ. Γ.

also: B. G. U. IV 1067 (105) A. D. 101;

A. D. 108 B. G. U. IV 1036 (38): *τῆι κζ τοῦ διεληλυθότος μηνὸς Τῦβι τοῦ ἐνεστῶτος ι* (*ἔτους*) A. K. *Νερούα Τραιανοῦ* Σ. Γ. Δ.

also: P. Fay. 36 (149) A. D. 111;

A. D. 98 P. Iand. 26 (80): *ἕως Χοίαχ μηνὸς τοῦ αὐτοῦ δευτέρου ἔτους Τραιανοῦ Καίσαρος τοῦ κυρίου.*

also: P. Grenf. II 44 (70) A. D. 101; P. Oxy. III 511 (242) A. D. 104; 483 (172 )A. D. 108; P. Ryl. 108 (85) A. D. 110; B. G. U. I 68 (81)A. D. 113; P. Tebt. II 309 (103) A. D. 116;

---

A. D. 118 P. Giss. I 4 (29): (*ἔτους*) *β* A. K. *Τραιανοῦ Ἀδριανοῦ* Σ. *Τῦβι ιε.*

also: P. Giss. I 8, III 61 (39) A. D. 119; P. Ryl. 168 (201) A. D. 120; P. Oxy. IV 714 (183) A. D. 122; VI 898 (221), P. B. M. III 839 (140) A. D. 123; P. Ryl. 180 (222) A. D. 124; 122 (115) A. D. 127; P. Amh. II 88 (109) A. D. 128; P. Oxy. I 107 (174) A. D. 123; X 1293 (245), XII 1422 (74) A. D. 128; VII 1024 (153), I 75 (138) A. D. 129; B. G. U. II 647 (312) A. D. 130; P. Oxy. I 68 (127) A. D. 131; P. Hamb. 6 (22) A. D. 129; P. Oxy. III 480 (168) A. D. 132; I 100 (163) A. D. 133; IV 715 (184) A. D. 131; I 106

(173), IX 1195 (216), B. G. U. I 73 (87) A. D. 135; P. Ryl. 105 (82) A. D. 136; P. Grenf. II 45 (72) A. D. 137; etc. etc.

A. D. 117 P. Giss. I 6 (ἔτους) β Α. Κ. Τραιανοῦ 'Αδριανοῦ 'Αρίστου Σ. Χοίακ ε.

also: P. Flor. III 326 (61).

A. D. 120 B. G. U. I 69 (83): (ἔτους) δ 'Αδριανοῦ Κ. τ. κ. Παῦνι κη.

also: P. Tebt. II 296 (70) A. D. 123; P. Gen. 56 (37); P. B. M. III 1173 (207) A. D. 125; P. Tebt. II 374 (214) A. D. 131; P. Fay. 107 (258), B. G. U. I 53 (67) A. D. 133; P. Grenf. II 45 (71) A. D. 136.

A. D. 118 P. Giss. II 43 (54): τοῦ β (ἔτους) 'Αδριανοῦ Κ. τ. κ.

also: P. Ryl. 168 (201), B. G. U. I 250 (249); P. Hamb. 32 (140) A. D. 120; P. Oxy. IV 714 (183) A. D. 122; P. Oxy. XII 1547 (270) A. D. 119; VII 1024 (153), P. Hamb. 6 (22) A. D. 129; 7 (24) A. D. 131; P. Amh. II 73 (88) A. D. 129; P. Oxy. IV 715 (184) A. D. 131; P. Oxy. III 515 (250); P Ryl. 103 (79) A. D. 134; 105 (82); P. Grenf. II 45 (71); P. B. M. II 255 (117) A. D. 136; P. Tebt. II 374 (214) A. D. 131; P. Oxy. XII 1472 (209) A. D. 136; etc.

A. D. 125 B. G. U. III 759 (67): τῇ δευτέρᾳ τοῦ ἐνεστῶτος μηνὸς Καισαρείου τοῦ ἐνάτου ἔτους 'Αδριανοῦ Κ. τ. κ.

A. D. 127 P. Tebt. II 323 (131): ια (ἔτους) Τραιανοῦ 'Αδριανοῦ Σ. μηνὸς Καισαρείου κζ.

A. D. 136 P. Ryl. 105 (82): τῷ Θὼθ μηνὶ τοῦ ἐνεστῶτος πρώτου καὶ εἰκοστοῦ (ἔτους) 'Αδριανοῦ τ. κ.

Cp. also P. Strassb. 70 (206) A. D. 138.

A. D. 133 B. G. U. I 53 (67): τοῦ διεληλυθότος ις (ἔτους) Α. Κ. Τραιανοῦ 'Αδριανοῦ Σ.

---

A. D. 138 P. Ryl. 83 (45): (ἔτους) α Α. Κ. Τίτου Αἰλίου 'Αδριανοῦ 'Αντωνείνου Σ. Ε. Φα——.

also: P. Ryl. 97 (65), 163 (190), P. Grenf. II 46 (74), B. G. U. I 111 (128), II 635 (299) A. D. 139; A. D. 141: P. Tebt. II 372 (209); A. D. 142 B. G. U. I 17 (27); A. D. 143: B. G. U. III 741 (46); A. D. 144 B. G. U. III 729 (33); A. D. 145 P. Flor. I 23 (47); A. D. 146 P. Tebt. II 294 (63) ; P. Gen. 30 (5); A. D. 148 B. G. U. I 300 (292); A. D. 150 B. G. U. II 416 (77); P. Oxy. IV 732 (224); IX 1198 (220); P. Fay. 26 (133); A. D. 151 P. Tebt. II 300 (85) ; A. D. 154 P. Oxy. IV 727 (210); C. P. R. 31 (157); A. D. 156 P. Ryl. 88 (52); 115 (100); P. Oxy. III 487 (183); A. D. 157 P. Ryl. 78 (37): P. Oxy. III 479 (167); etc.

A. D. 138 B. G. U. I 257 (259): (ἔτους) β Α. Κ. Τίτου Αἰλίου 'Αδριανοῦ 'Αντωνίνου Ε. 'Αθὺρ τρίτῃ.

A. D. 141 P. Grenf. II 49 (77): (ἔτους) ε 'Αντωνείνου Κ. τ. κ μηνὸς 'Αδριανοῦ κδ.

also: A. D. 142 P. Oxy. IV 728 (212); P. B. M. III 1132 (141); P. Gen. 104 (41); A. D. 143 B. G. U. I 191 (200); A. D. 145

P. Tebt. II 325 (134); A. D. 146 P. Flor. III 358 (82); A. D. 147 P. Amh. II 74 (89); B. G. U. I 95 (114); A. D. 148 P. Gen. 32 (27); P. Meyer 3 (12); P. Grenf. I 47 (79); A. D. 149 P. Tebt. II 394 (253); A. D. 150 P. Giss. I 29 (77); A. D. 154 P. Amh. II 69 (83); A. D. 157 B. G. U. I 166 (176); A. D. 158 P. Fay. 24 (131); P. Gen. 255; P. Ryl. 106 (83); A. D. 159 B. G. U. I 100 (119); 187 (196); P. Fay. 99 (240); P. Amh. II 91 (113); A. D. 160 P. Oxy. III 516 (251).

A. D. 141 P. Tebt. II 372 (209): *ἀπὸ τῆς νεωμηνίας τῆς Θὼθ τοῦ εἰσιόντος πέμπτου ἔτους Ἀντωνείνου τ. κ.*

A. D. 138 B. G. U. I 257 (259): *τοῦ α (ἔτους) Ἀντωνίνου τοῦ κυρίου.*

A. D. 139 P. Amh. II 77 (94): *τοῦ β (ἔτους) Ἀντωνίνου* K. *τ. κ. Ἐπεὶφ ζ.*

also: P. Tebt. II 329 (140); P. Ryl. 83 (45).

A. D. 141 P. Tebt. II 341 (160): *τοῦ (διεληλυθότος) (ἐνεστῶτος) δ (ἔτους) Ἀντωνίνου* K. *τ. κ.*

also: P. Grenf. II 49 (77); A. D. 142 B. G. U. I 17 (27); A. D. 145 P. Gen. 54 (42); A. D. 146 P. Flor. III 358 (82); A. D. 147 P. Tebt. II 321 (128); B. G. U. I 95 (114); A. D. 148 B. G. U. I 340 (332); P. Gen. 32 (27); A. D. 149 P. S. I. III 160 (11); P. Giss. I 29 (77); A. D. 151 B. G. U. I 227 (227); A. D. 154 P. Ryl. 98 (68); C. P. R. 31 (157); A. D. 156 P. Oxy. XII 1550 (272); A. D. 157 P. Oxy. III 479 (167); B. G. U. I 166 (176); A. D. 158 P. Ryl. 106 (83); B. G. U. III 800 (97); P. Oxy. VIII 1123 (215) A. D. 159 P. Amh. II 90, 91 (43); A. D. 160 B. G. U. I 254 (255); A. D. 161 P. Ryl. 111a (91); cp. also P. Fay 28, 35; P. Tebt. II 321, 300; P. Amh. II 69; P. Gen. 21; P. Ryl. 88; P. Good. 19; P. Oxy 516; etc. etc.

A. D. 138-161 B. G. U. I 179 (184): *Μεσορὴ τριακάδος τοῦ εἰσιόντος (ἔτους)* —— A. K. *Τίτου Αἰλίου Ἀδριανοῦ Ἀντωνίνου* Σ. E. *Μεσορὴ ε.*

---

A. D. 161 P. Fay. 34 (145): *ἔτους πρώτου* A. K. *Μάρκου Αὐρηλίου Ἀντωνίνου* Σ. *καὶ* A. K. *Λουκίου Αὐρηλίου Οὐήρου* Σ. *Παῦνι θ.*

also: B. G. U. I 90 (108); 55 (69); 224 (224); P. Grenf. II 55 (89);

A. D. 167 P. Ryl. 104 (81): *(ἔτους) ζ* A. K. *Μάρκου Αὐρηλίου Ἀντωνείνου* Σ. *Ἀρμενιακοῦ Μηδικοῦ Παρθικοῦ* M. *καὶ* A. K. *Λουκίου Αὐρηλίου Οὐήρου* Σ. *Ἀρμενιακοῦ Μηδικοῦ Παρθικοῦ* M. *Ἐπεὶφ κς.*

also: P. Ryl. 120 (111) A. D. 167.

A. D. 159 B. G. U. I 54 (68): *(ἔτους) α Ἀντωνείνου* K. *τ. κ. καὶ Οὐήρου* K. *τ. κ. Ἐπεὶφ γ.*

A. D. 161 P. Meyer 4 (18): (ἔτους) β 'Αντωνίνου καὶ Οὐήρου τῶν κυρίων Σεβαστῶν Φαῶφι κα.

also: P. Gen. 45 (46); P. Fay. 93 (230); A. D. 162 P. Tebt. II 376 (217); A. D. 165 B. G. U. III 708 (10); A. D. 166 P. Tebt. II 318 (123);

A. D. 162 P. B. M. II 168 (190): (ἔτους) β Αὐρηλίου 'Αντωνίνου καὶ Οὐήρου τῶν κυρίων Σεβαστῶν Φαρμοῦθι κε.

A. D. 164 B. G. U. I 237 (234): (ἔτους) ε Αὐρηλίου καὶ Οὐήρου τῶν κυρίων Σεβαστῶν Τῦβι.

A. D. 168 P. B. M. II 470 (212): (ἔτους) η 'Αντωνίνου καὶ Οὐήρου τῶν κυρίων Σῶν 'Αρμενιακῶν Μηδικῶν Παρθικῶν Μων Παχὼν ιγ.

also: B. G. U. II 393 (55); 603 (247); P. Tebt. II 304 (94); P. Grenf. II 57 (92); A. D. 169 P. S. I. III 161 (13);

A. D. 162 P. B. M. II 168 (190): τοῦ ἐνεστῶτος β (ἔτους) Αὐρηλίου 'Αντωνίνου καὶ Οὐήρου τῶν κυρίων Σῶν.

also: P. Grenf. II (90); B. G. U. I 198 (208); P. Tebt. II 376 (217); P. Amh. I 92 (115); A. D. 166 cp. P. Tebt. II 318 (123); A. D. 167 P. Ryl. 104 (82); A. D. 169 P. S. I. III 160 (11).

A. D. 162 P. Oxy. VIII 1132 (229): ταῖς ἐπαγομέναις τοῦ δευτέρου ἔτους 'Αντωνίνου καὶ Οὐήρου τῶν κυρίων Αὐτοκρατόρων.

A. D. 163 P. Fay. 33 (144): πρὸς τὸ ἐνεστὸς γ (ἔτος) 'Αντωνίνου καὶ Οὐήρου τῶν κυρίων 'Αρμενιακῶν Μηδικῶν Παρθικῶν Μεγίστων.

---

A. D. 162 P. Oxy. VII 1037 (169): (ἔτους) α Α. Κ. Μάρκου Αὐρηλίου 'Αντωνίνου Σ. 'Επεὶφ ιδ.

A. D. 170 P. Gen. 201 (47): (ἔτους) ια Α. Κ. Μάρκου Αὐρηλίου 'Αντωνείνου Σ. 'Αρμενιακοῦ Μηδικοῦ Παρθικοῦ Μ. Θὼθ κ.

also: A. D. 171 P. Ryl. 164 (192).

A. D. 174 B. G. U. III 833 (149): (ἔτους) ιε Α Κ. Μάρκου 'Αυρηλίου 'Αντωνίνου Σ. 'Αρμενιακοῦ Μηδικοῦ Παρθικοῦ Γ. Μ. Φαῶφι ζ.

also: cp. A. D. 173 P. Oxy. I 51 (108).

A. D. 174 P. Tebt. II 317 (120): (ἔτους) ιε Α. Κ. Μάρκου Αὐρηλίου 'Αντωνίνου Σ. 'Αρμενιακοῦ Μηδικοῦ Παρθικοῦ Γ. Σαρματικοῦ Μ.

A. D. 173 P. Fay. 30 (139): (ἔτους) ια Αὐρηλίου 'Αντωνίνου Κ. τ. κ. 'Επεὶφ ι.

also: P. Oxy. III 512 (244); A. D. 175 B. G. U. I 127 (146); 55 (69); II 536 (180);

A. D. 172 P. Ryl. 98 (67): (ἔτους) ιγ Μάρκου Αὐρηλίου 'Αντωνίνου Κ. τ. κ. Θὼθ κ.

also: A. D. 176 P. Tebt. II 332 (145);

A. D. 171 B. G. U. I 91 (109): (ἔτους) ια Αὐρηλίου Ἀντωνίνου Κ. τ. κ. Ἀρμενιακοῦ Μηδικοῦ Παρθικοῦ Μεγίστου.

A. D. 175 P. Grenf. II 58 (93): (ἔτους) ιε Φαμενὼθ ιθ Μάρκου Αὐρηλίου Ἀντωνίνου Κ. τ. κ.

A. D. 169 P. Oxy. III 507 (236): τῇ τριακάδι τοῦ Φαμενὼθ τοῦ εἰσιόντος δεκάτου ἔτους Αὐρηλίου Ἀντωνίνου Κ. τ. κ

also: P. Ryl. 98 (67);

A. D. 171 P. Ryl. 164 (192): τοῦ ὄντος μηνὸς Ἀθὺρ τοῦ ἐνεστῶτος ιβ (ἔτους) Αὐρηλίου Ἀντωνίνου τ. κ. ; μεχρὶ τοῦ διεληλυθότος ια (ἔτους) Μάρκου Αὐρηλίου Ἀντωνίνου Κ. τ. κ.

A. D. 177 B. G. U. III 970 (291): τῷ ιδ (ἔτει) τοῦ κυρίου ἡμῶν Α. Αὐρηλίου Ἀντωνείνου.

A. D. 173 Note the following "Latin" formula: B. G. U. IV 1032 (33) epicrisis τῇ πρὸ γ Εἰδῶν Αὐγούστων Σεουήρῳ καὶ Πομπηιανῷ τὸ β ὑπάτοις.

---

A. D. 178 P. Oxy. III 485 (176): (ἔτους) ιθ Αων Κων Μάρκου Αὐρηλίου Ἀντωνίνου καὶ Λουκίου Αὐρηλίου Κομμόδου Σῶν Ἀρμενιακῶν Μηδικῶν Παρθικῶν Γῶν Σαρματικῶν Μων Ἀθὺρ ιθ.

also: P. Amh. II 71 (86); A. D. 179 P. Oxy. I 76 (139);

A. D. 179 P. Oxy. I 88 (151): (ἔτους) εἰκοστοῦ Αων Ἀντωνίνου καὶ Κομμόδου Κων τῶν κυρίων Ἀθὺρ γ.

A. D. 179 P. Hamb. 39 (158): (ἔτους) ιθ Αὐρηλίων Ἀντωνίνου καὶ Κομόδου Κων τῶν κυρίων Σῶν Τῦβι κ.

also: P. B. M. II 339 (200).

A. D. 179 P. Oxy. III 485 (176): (ἔτους) ιθ Αὐρηλίων Ἀντωνίνου καὶ Κομμόδου τῶν κυρίων Σῶν Φαῶφι ζ.

also: P. Gen. 20 (2);

A. D. 178 P. Amh. II 71 (86): εἰς τὸ θ (ἔτος) Αὐρηλίων Ἀντωνίνου καὶ Κομμόδου Κων τῶν κυρίων.

---

A. D. 183 P. B. M. II 341 (213): ἔτους τρίτου καὶ εἰκοστοῦ Αὐρηλίου Κομμόδου Ἀντωνίνου Σ. Φαρμοῦθι πέμπτῃ.

also: P. Fay. 39 (155);

A. D. 181 P. Tebt. II 320 (127): (ἔτους) κα Μάρκου Αὐρηλίου Κομμόδου Ἀντωνίνου Σ. Ἐπεὶφ ζ.

also: A. D. 183 B. G. U. I 28 (42);

A. D. 184 P. Amh. II 78 (97): ἔτους κε Μάρκου Αὐρηλίου Κομμόδου Ἀντωνείνου Σ. Ε. Θὼθ λ.

A. D. 184 P. Oxy. III 513 (245): (ἔτους) κδ Α. Κ. Μάρκου Αὐρηλίου Κομμόδου Ἀντωνίνου Σ. Ε. Ἀρμενιακοῦ Μηδικοῦ Παρθικοῦ Σαρματικοῦ Γ. Μ.

A. D. 182 P. Oxy. III 475 (159): (ἔτους) κγ Α. Κ. Μάρκου Αὐρηλίου Κομμόδου Ἀντωνίνου Σ. Ἀρμενιακοῦ Μηδικοῦ Παρθικοῦ Σαρματικοῦ Γ. Μ. Ἀθὺρ ζ.

A. D. 185 P. Amh. II 107 (134): (ἔτους) κε Λ. Κ. Μάρκου Αὐρηλίου Κομμόδου 'Αντωνίνου Σ. Ε. 'Αρμενιακοῦ Μηδικοῦ Παρθικοῦ Σαρματικοῦ Γ. Βρεταννικοῦ Μ. Παῦνι — — —

A. D. 180-192 P. Strassb. 34 (122): (ἔτους) — Λ. Κ. Μάρκου Αὐρηλίου Κομμόδου 'Αντωνείνου Σ. Ε. Ε. 'Αρμενιακοῦ Μηδικοῦ Παρθικοῦ Σαρματικοῦ Γ. Βρεταννικοῦ Φαῶφι ιθ.

A. D. 189 B. G. U. II 578 (226): (ἔτους) κζ Λ. Κ. Μάρκου Αὐρηλίου Κομμόδου 'Αντωνείνου Σ. Ε. Ε. 'Αρμενιακοῦ Μηδικοῦ Παρθικοῦ Σαρματικοῦ Γ. Μ. Βρεταννικοῦ Τῦβι ια.

A. D. 190 P. Iand. 34 (95): (ἔτους) λα Λ. Κ. Μάρκου Αὐρηλίου Κομμόδου 'Αντωνείνου Ε. Ε. Σ. 'Αρμενιακοῦ Μηδικοῦ Παρθικοῦ Σαρματικοῦ Γ. Μ. Βρεταννικοῦ 'Αθὺρ λ.

also: A. D. 186 P. Oxy. III 716 (186); A. D. 187 P. Oxy. I 91 (153); B. G. U. III 842 (161); I 92 (110); A. D. 190 P. Oxy. I 69 (129);

A. D. 180 P. Oxy. I 96 (158): (ἔτους) κα Μάρκου Αὐρηλίου Κομμόδου 'Αντωνίνου Κ. τ. κ. 'Αθὺρ θ.

also: P. Gen. 4 (26); P. Strasb. 34 (122); A. D. 182 P. Oxy. III 475 (159); A. D. 183 B. G. U I 200 (210); A. D. 186 P. Gen. 103 (49); B. G. U. I 39 (54); A. D. 188 P. B. M. II 343 (213); P. Tebt. II 396 (256); A. D. 189 B. G. U. I 71 (85); II 578 (226); A. D. 191 B. G. U. I 72 (86); A.D. 193 B. G. U. II 515 (162);

A. D. 181 P. Amh. II 93 (117): (ἔτους) κβ Κομόδου 'Αντωνίνου Κ. τ. κ. Τῦβι γ.

A. D. 189 P. Tebt. II 322 (129): (ἔτους) κθ Αὐρηλίου Κομμόδου 'Αντωνίνου Κ. τ. κ. Μεσορὴ ἐπαγομένων δ.

also: B. G. U. I 116 (136); A. D. 190 P. Tebt. II 301 (86);

A. D. 192 B. G. U. II 651 (317): (ἔτους) λβ Λουκίου Αἰλίου Αὐρηλίου Κομμόδου Κ. τ. κ. Παχὼν ιδ.

A. D. 181 P. Amh. II 93 (117): ἀπὸ τοῦ ἐνεστῶτος μηνὸς Τῦβι τοῦ κβ (ἔτους) Κομόδου 'Αντωνίνου τ. κ.

A. D. 181 P. Tebt. II 320 (127): τῷ ἐνεστῶτι κα (ἔτει) Μάρκου Αὐρηλίου Κομμόδου 'Αντωνίνου Κ. τ. κ.

A. D. 184 P. Oxy. III 513 (245): τῷ δευτέρῳ καὶ εἰκοστῷ ἔτι Αὐρηλίου Κομμόδου 'Αντωνίνου Κ. τ. κ. μηνὶ 'Αδριανοῦ.

A. D. 185 P. Amh. II 108 (135): τοῦ ἐνεστῶτος κς (ἔτους) Αὐρηλίου Κομμόδου 'Αντωνίνου Κ. τ. κ.

also: P. Ryl. 85 (48); A. D. 189 P. Tebt. II 322 (129); A. D. 190 P. Tebt. II 301 (86); P. Iand. 34 (95); A. D. 189 B. G. U. I 116 (136);

A. D. 186 P. Fay. 41 (158): Μεχεὶρ, Φαμενὼθ τοῦ ἐνεστῶτος κς (ἔτους) Μάρκου Αὐρηλίου Κομμόδου 'Αντωνείνου Σ.

A. D. 187 B. G. U. I 60 (75): τοῦ διεληλυθότος κη (ἔτους) Αὐρηλίου Κομμόδου Κ. τ. κ.

---

A. D. 193 B. G. U. I 46 (60): (ἔτους) α Λ. Κ. Πουβλίου Ἐλουίου Περτίνακος Σ. Παχὼν κδ.

also: B. G. U. II 646 (311);

A. D. 193 B. G. U. II 454 (113): (ἔτους) α Λ. Κ. Γαίου Πεσκεννίου Νείγερος Ἰούστου Σ. Παῦνι κγ.

A. D. 193 P. Oxy. IV 719 (192): (ἔτους) β Γαίου Πεσκεννίου Νίγερος Ἰούστου Σ. Φαῶφι κη.

A. D. 194 P. Grenf. II 61 (95): (ἔτους)— Λουκίου Σεπτιμίου Σεουήρου Ε. Περτίνακος Σ. Μεχεὶρ s.

A. D. 194 P. Ryl. 116 (102): (ἔτους) β. Α. Κ. Λουκίου Σεπτιμίου Σευήρου Περτίνακος Σ. Παχὼν κ.

A. D. 194-6 P. Tebt. II 388 (154): (ἔτους)— Α. Κ. Λουκίου Σεπτιμίου Σεουήρου Ε. Περτίνακος Σ.——

A. D. 196 P. Fay. 42 (163): (ἔτους) δ Λουκίου Σεπτιμίου Σεουήρου Σ. Μεχεὶρ δ.

A. D. 194 B. G. U. I. 199 (209): (ἔτους) γ Λουκίου Σεπτιμίου Σεουήρου Ε. Περτίνακος Σ. Ἀραβηκοῦ Ἀδιαβηνικοῦ Θὼθ κ.

also: A. D. 197 P. Tebt. II 357 (192); A. D. 195 B. G. U. III 778 (79);

A. D. 195 P. Ryl. 86 (49): (ἔτους) τετάρτου Α. Κ. Λουκίου Σεπτιμίου Σεουήρου Ε. Περτίνακος Σ. Ἀραβικοῦ Ἀδιαβηνικοῦ Ἀθὺρ ἐννακαιδεκάτῃ

also: A. D. 196 B. G. U. IV 1022 (12);

A. D. 195 B. G. U. III 971 (294): τῷ ἐνεστῶτι γ (ἔτει) Λουκίου Σεπτιμίου Σεουήρου.

---

A. D. 196 P. Ryl. 169 (203): (ἔτους) ε Α. Κ. Λουκίου Σεπτιμίου Σεουήρου Ε. Περτίνακος Σ. Ἀραβικοῦ Ἀδιαβηνικοῦ καὶ Μάρκου Αὐρηλίου Ἀντωνίνου Κ. τ. κ.—

A. D. 197-8 B. G. U. III 758 (66): (ἔτους) s Α. Κ. Λουκίου Σεπτιμίου Σεουήρου Ε. Περτίνακος Σ. Ἀραβικοῦ Ἀδιαβηνικοῦ Παρθικοῦ Μ. καὶ Α. Κ. Μάρκου Αὐρηλίου Ἀντωνίνου Σ. Κ— κs.

A. D. 201 P. Oxy. I 54 (111): (ἔτους) θ Αων Κων Λουκίου Σεπτιμίου Σεουήρου Ε. Περτίνακος Ἀραβικοῦ Ἀδιαβηνικοῦ Παρθικοῦ Μ. καὶ Μάρκου Αὐρηλίου Ἀντωνίνου Ε. Σῶν (καὶ Πουβλίου Σεπτιμίου Γέτα Κ. Σ.) Φαρμοῦθι.

also: A. D. 203 P. Oxy. VIII 1113 (189); A. D. 206 P. Tebt. II 340 (158); A. D. 211 P. Oxy. I 56 (114); cp. A.-D. 201 P. Oxy. XII 1473 (212);

A. D. 201 B. G. U. I 156 (169): (ἔτους) θ Αων Κων Λουκίου Σεπτιμίου Σευήρου Περτίνακος Ἀδιαβηνικοῦ Παρθικοῦ Μ. καὶ Μάρκου Αὐρηλίου Ἀντωνείνου Ε. Ἐπεὶφ——

A. D. 210 P. Oxy. VII 1039 (182): (ἔτους) ιθ Αων Κων Λουκίου Σεπτιμίου Σεουήρου Περτίνακος Ἀραβικοῦ Ἀδιαβηνικοῦ Παρθικοῦ Βρεταννικοῦ Μ. καὶ Μάρκου Αὐρηλίου Ἀντωνίνου (καὶ Πουβλίου Σεπτιμίου Γέτα) Βρεταννικῶν Μων Εῶν Σῶν Φαῶφι ιγ.

A. D. 199 B. G. U. I 41 (56): (ἔτους) η Λουκίου Σεπτιμίου Σεουήρου Περτίνακος Ε. Ἀραβικοῦ Παρθικοῦ καὶ Μάρκου Αὐρηλίου Ἀντωνίνου Σῶν Φαῶφι ιβ.

A. D. 200 B. G. U. I 25 (38): (ἔτους) η Λουκίου Σεπτιμίου Σεουήρου Ε. Περτίνακος καὶ Μάρκου Αὐρηλίου Ἀντωνίνου Σῶν Ἐπεὶφ——

A. D. 200-1 P. Tebt. II 334 (147): (ἔτους) θ Λουκίου Σεπτιμίου Σεουήρου Ε. Περτίνακος Ἀραβικοῦ Ἀδιαβηνικοῦ Παρθικοῦ Μ. καὶ Μάρκου Αὐρηλίου Ἀντωνίνου Ε. Σῶν.

A. D. 202 B. G. U. I 45 (59): (ἔτους) ιβ Λουκίου Σεπτιμίου Σεουήρου Ε. Περτίνακος καὶ Μάρκου Αὐρηλίου Ἀντωνείνου Ε. Σῶν καὶ Ποπλίου Σεπτιμίου Γέτα Κ. Σ. Φαῶφι η.

also: A. D. 212 B. G. U. III 990 (319);

A. D. 207 P. Gen. 20 (50): (ἔτους) ιε Λουκίου Σεπτιμίου Σεουήρου Ε. Περτίνακος καὶ Μάρκου Αὐρηλίου Ἀντωνίνου Ε. καὶ Πουβλίου Σεπτιμίου Γέτα Κ. Σ. ——

A. D. 208 P. Ryl. 172 (206): ἔτους ιζ Λουκίου Σεπτιμίου Σευήρου Ε. Περτίνακος Ἀραβικοῦ Ἀδιαβηνικοῦ καὶ Μάρκου Αὐρηλίου Ἀντωνίνου Εῶν Σῶν καὶ Πουπλίου Σεπτιμίου Γέτα Κ. Σ. Θὼθ ιζ.

A. D. 209 P. Oxy. XII 1566 (275): (ἔτους) ιζ Λουκίου Σεπτιμίου Σεουήρου καὶ Μάρκου Αὐρηλίου Ἀντωνίνου Σῶν Φαμενὼθ ιβ.

A. D. 210 P. Tebt. II 377 (210): (ἔτους) ιθ Λουκίου Σεπτιμίου Σεουήρου καὶ Μάρκου Αὐρηλίου Ἀντωνίνου καὶ Πουβλίου Σεπτιμίου Γέτα Εῶν Σῶν Θὼθ ε.

A. D. 211 P. Grenf. II 62 (97): (ἔτους) ιθ Λουκίου Σεπτιμίου Σεουήρου Περτίνακος καὶ Μάρκου Αὐρηλίου Ἀντωνίνου καὶ Πουβλίου Σεπτιμίου Γέτα Βρεταννικῶν Μων Εῶν Σῶν Φαρμοῦθι.

also: B. G. U. I 98 (118);

A. D. 204 P. Oxy. XIV 1719 (165): ἔτους δωδεκάτου τῶν κυρίων Αων Σεουήρου καὶ Ἀντωνίνου Κων Σῶν Παχὼν λ.

A. D. 202-3 P. Oxy. XII 1548 (271): τοῦ διελθόντος ι (ἔτους) Κων τῶν κυρίων Σεουήρου καὶ Ἀντωνίνου.

A. D. 203-4 P. Ryl. 181 (223): ἀπὸ η (ἔτους) τῶν κυρίων Αων Σεουήρου καὶ Ἀντωνίνου.

---

A. D. 210 P. Tebt. II 313 (110): (ἔτους) ιθ Αων Κων Μάρκου

Αὐρηλίου Ἀντωνίνου καὶ Πουβλίου Σεπτιμίου Γέτα Βρεταννικῶν Μων Εῶν Σῶν——

A. D. 212 C. P. R. 239 (263): (ἔτους) κ Μάρκου Αὐρηλίου Ἀντωνίνου Παρθικοῦ Μ. καὶ Πουβλίου Σεπτιμίου Γέτα Βρεταννικοῦ Μ. Εῶν Σῶν Μεχεὶρ ε.

---

A. D. 214 P. Oxy. XII 1432 (191): (ἔτους) κβ Α. Κ. Μάρκου Αὐρηλίου Σεουήρου Ἀντωνίνου.

A. D. 214 P. Ryl. 184 (226): (ἔτους) κβ Μάρκου Αὐρηλίου Σεουήρου Ἀντωνείνου Παρθικοῦ Μ. Βρεταννικοῦ Μ. Γ. Μ. Ε. Σ. Παῦνι λ.

also: A. D. 214-5 P. Hamb. 44 (189); A. D. 215 B. G. U. I 270 (271); A. D. 216 B. G. U. I 322, 321; A. D. 217 B. G. U. III 835 (152);

A. D. 215 P Oxy. XII 1463 (187): (ἔτους) κδ Α. Κ. Μάρκου Αὐρηλίου Σεουήρου Ἀντωνίνου Παρθικοῦ Μ. Βρεταννικοῦ Μ. Γ. Μ. Ε. Σ. Θὼθ ιη.

also: P. Oxy. XII 1553 (273); B. G. U. II 362 (7); A. D. 216 P. Oxy. XII 1474 (220); A. D. 217 B. G. U. II 614 (262); A. D. 216 B. G. U. I 159 (171).

A. D. 214 P. Oxy. XII 1432 (91): —(ἔτους) Μάρκου Αὐρηλίου Σεουήρου Ἀντωνίνου Κ. τ. κ.

A. D. 216 P. Oxy. XII 1474 (220): (ἔτους) κδ Αὐρηλίου Σεουήρου Ἀντωνίνου Κ. τ. κ. Μεχεὶρ ε.

A. D. 216 P. Tebt. 333 (146): (ἔτους) κε Μάρκου Αὐρηλίου Σεουήρου Ἀντωνίνου Κ. τ. κ. Χύακ κς.

also: A. D. 217 B. G. U. II 614 (262);

---

A. D. 218 C. P. R. 32 (159): (ἔτους) β Α. Κ. Μάρκου Αὐρηλίου Ἀντωνίνου Ε. Ε. Σ. Ἀθὺρ ιζ.

also: A. D. 220 P. Leipz. 8 (26); A. D. 221 P. Grenf. I 49 (81).

---

A. D. 221 P. Oxy. I 61 (120): (ἔτους) ε Α. Κ. Μάρκου Αὐρηλίου Ἀντωνίνου Ε. Ε. καὶ Μάρκου Αὐρηλίου Ἀλεξάνδρου Κ. Σῶν Ἀθὺρ κβ.

also: B. G. U. II 633 (298);

A. D. 221 P. B. M. II 353 (112): τοῦ ἐνεστῶτος δ (ἔτους) τῶν [Αων Κων Μά]ρκου Αὐρηλίου Ἀντωνίνου Ε. Ε. καὶ Μάρκου Αὐρηλίου Σεουήρου Ἀλεξάνδρου Κ. Σῶν.

A. D. 222 B. G. U. IV 1015 (4): ἐν τῷ Παῦνι μηνὶ τοῦ ἐνεστῶτος ε (ἔτους) Μάρκου Αὐρηλίου Ἀντωνίνου καὶ Ἀλεξάνδρου Κων τῶν κυρίων.

---

A. D. 222 P. Oxy. XII 1461 (183): (ἔτους) β Α. Κ. Μάρκου Αὐρηλίου Σεουήρου Ἀλεξάνδρου Ε. Ε. Σ. Ἀθὺρ κ.

also: B. G. U. I 35 (51); P. Gen. 41 (56); A. D. 225 C. P. R. 37 (164); P. Hamb. 19 (82); A. D. 223 P. Oxy. I 77 (140); A. D. 226 P. Oxy. XII 1459 (179); A. D. 225 P. Oxy. VI 909 (257); VII 1040 (184); A. D. 228 P. Oxy. VII 1031; A. D. 232 P. Amh. II 80 (100); A. D. 233 P. Leipz. 9 (29).

A. D. 226 P. Oxy. XII 1459 (179): *πρὸς τὸ ἐνεστὸς ε (ἔτος) Μάρκου Αὐρηλίου Σεουήρου Ἀλεξάνδρου Κ. τ. κ.*

---

A. D. 237 P. Grenf. II 67 (101): (*ἔτους*) *γ* Α. Κ. *Γαίου Ἰουλίου Οὐήρου Μαξιμίνου* Ε. Ε. Σ. Γ. Μ. Δ. Μ. *Σαρματικοῦ* Μ. *καὶ Γαίου Ἰουλίου Οὐήρου Μαξίμου* Μ. Γ. Μ. Δ. Μ. *Σαρματικοῦ* Μ. *τοῦ γενναιοτάτου* Κ. *κυρίων αἰωνίων Σῶν Ἐπὶφ*——

A. D. 237 P. Oxy. VIII 1114 (192): *ἔτους τρίτου* Α. Κ. *Γαίου Ἰουλίου Οὐήρου Μαξιμείνου* Ε. Ε. Σ. Γ. Μ. Δ. Μ. *Σαρματικοῦ* Μ. *καὶ Γαίου Ἰουλίου Οὐήρου Μαξίμου* Γ. Μ. Δ. Μ. Σ. Μ. *τοῦ ἱερωτάτου* Κ. Σ. *υἱοῦ τοῦ* Σ. *Ἐπεὶφ ιβ.*

---

A. D. 238 P. Oxy. XII 1433 (92): *μηνὸς Μεσορὴ τοῦ διελθόντος α* (*ἔτους*) *Αων Κων Μάρκου Κλωδίου Μαξίμου καὶ Δεκίμου Καιλίου Καλουίνου Βαλβίνου Εῶν Εῶν Σῶν καὶ Μάρκου Ἀντωνίου Γορδιανοῦ τοῦ ἱερωτάτου Καίσαρος.*

---

A. D. 238 P. Ryl. 100 (71): (*ἔτους*) *β* Α. Κ. *Μάρκου Ἀντωνίνου Γορδιανοῦ* Ε. Ε. Σ. *Φαῶφι ιε.*

also: A. D. 240 P. Oxy. XII 1549 (271); B. G. U. III 942 (271); A. D. 239 P. Flor. 16 (36); 21 (44);

A. D. 238 P. Oxy. XII 1433 (92): *μηνὸς Θὼθ τοῦ ἐνεστῶτος β* (*ἔτους*) *Μάρκου Ἀντωνίνου Γορδιανοῦ* Ε. Ε. Σ.

A. D. 238 P. Ryl. 100 (71): *πρὸς μόνον τὸ ἐνεστὸς β* (*ἔτος*) *Μάρκου Ἀντωνίνου Γορδιανοῦ* Κ. *τ. κ.*

also: A. D. 240 P. Oxy. XII 1549 (271).

A. D. 243 B. G. U. I 141 (157): *τοῦ ἐνεστῶτος s* (*ἔτους*) *τοῦ κυρίου ἡμῶν* Α. Κ. *Μάρκου Ἀντωνίνου Γορδιανοῦ* Ε. Ε. Σ.

---

A. D. 243-4 P. Flor. I 4 (18): (*ἔτους*) *β* Α. Κ. *Μάρκου Ἰουλίου Φιλίππου* Ε. Ε. *καὶ Μάρκου Ἰουλίου Φιλίππου γενναιοτάτου καὶ ἐπιφανεστάτου* Κ. *Σῶν Παχὼν* (A. D. 245);

also: A. D. 246 P. Oxy. XIV 1662 (46); P. Amh. II 72 (87); P. Ryl. 177 (217); cp. also: P. Amh. II 81 (101) A. D. 247.

A. D. 247 P. Oxy. XII 1556 (274): (*ἔτους*) *Αων Κων Μάρκων Ἰουλίων Φιλίππων Εῶν Εῶν Σῶν Τῦβι η.*

also P. Grenf. II 68 (104); A. D. 248 P. Flor. I 19 (41);

A. D. 243-4 P. Flor. I 4 (18): *τοῦ διελθόντος α (ἔτους) Μάρκων Ἰουλίων Φιλίππων τῶν κυρίων Σῶν.*

A. D. 246 P. Ryl. 177 (217): *τοῦ ἐνεστῶτος δ (ἔτους) Μάρκων Ἰουλίων Φιλίππων Κων τῶν κυρίων Σῶν.*

A. D. 248 B. G. U. I 8 (9): *μηνὸς Παῦνι τοῦ ἐνεστῶτος ε (ἔτους) τῶν κυρίων ἡμῶν Αων Κων Μάρκων Ἰουλίων Φιλίππων Εῶν Εῶν Σῶν.*

---

A. D. 249 P. Oxy. XIV 1636 (42): *(ἔτους) α Α. Κ. Γαίου Μεσσίου Κυίντου Δεκίου Τραιανοῦ Ε. Ε. Σ. Χοίακ α.*

also: A. D. 250 C. P. R. I 20 (99); B. G. U. I 287 (282); P. S. I. V 453 (23); P. Oxy. XII 1464 (190); P. Ryl. 112 (94); P. Meyer 15 (77); the Theadelphia libelli, etc.

A. D. 251 C. P. R. 37 (164): *(ἔτους) β Α. Κ. Γαίου [Μεσσίου Κυίντου] Τραιανοῦ Δεκίου Ε [Ε. καὶ Κυίντου] Ἐρεννίου Ἐτρούσκου Μεσσίου Δεκίου καὶ Γαίου Οὐάλεντος Ὀστιλιανοῦ Μεσσίου Κυίντου τῶν Σεβασμιωτάτων Κων Φαμενὼθ η.*

A. D. 251 P. Oxy. XII 1554 (273): *(ἔτους) β Αων Κων Γαίου Οὐιβίου Τρεβωνιανοῦ Γάλλου καὶ Γαίου Οὐιβίου Ἀφινίου Γάλλου Οὐελδουμνιανοῦ Οὐολουσιανοῦ Εῶν Εῶν Σῶν μηνὸς Χοίακ ζ.*

also: P. Gen. 50 (11).

A. D. 255 P. Oxy. XII 1557 (274): *(ἔτους) β Αων Κων Πουπλίου Λικιννίου Οὐαλεριανοῦ καὶ Πουπλίου Λικιννίου Οὐαλεριανοῦ Γαλλιηνοῦ Εῶν Εῶν Σῶν Παχὼν—*

also: P. Flor. I 9 (26);

A. D. 256 P. Leipz. 3 (9): *(ἔτους) δ Αων Κων Πουπλίου Λικιννίου Οὐαλεριανοῦ καὶ Πουπλίου Λικιννίου Οὐαλεριανοῦ Γαλλιηνοῦ Εῶν Εῶν καὶ Πουπλίου Λικιννίου Κορνηλίου Οὐαλεριανοῦ τοῦ ἱερωτάτου Κ. Σῶν Χοίακ κς.*

A. D. 258 P. Oxy. XIV 1717 (164): *(ἔτους) ε Αων Κων Πουπλίου Λικιννίου Οὐαλεριανοῦ καὶ Πουπλίου Λικιννίου Οὐαλεριανοῦ Γαλλιηνοῦ Γῶν Μων Εῶν Εῶν καὶ Πουπλίου Λικιννίου Κορνηλίου Οὐαλεριανοῦ τοῦ ἐπιφανεστάτου Καίσαρος Σῶν Μεχεὶρ κ.*

cp. also: A. D. 255 P. Oxy. X 1277 (217); A. D. 259 P. Ryl. 110 (88).

A. D. 256 P. Flor. II 208 (174): *(ἔτους) ε τῶν κυρίων ἡμῶν Οὐαλεριανῶν καὶ Γαλλιηνοῦ Σῶν Μεσορὴ ἐπαγομένων.*

A. D. 256 P. Leipz. 3 (9): *τὸ ἐνεστὸς δ (ἔτος) τῶν κυρίων Οὐαλεριανοῦ καὶ Γαλλιηνοῦ καὶ Κορνηλίου Οὐαλεριανοῦ Σῶν.*

A. D. 259 P. Ryl. 110 (88): *πρὸς τὸ ἐνεστὸς ζ (ἔτος) τῶν κυρίων ἡμῶν Οὐαλεριανοῦ καὶ Γαλλιηνοῦ Σῶν.*

---

A. D. 260 P. Flor. II 273 (239): (ἔτους) α Αων Κων Τίτου Φουλβίου Ἰουνίου Μακριανοῦ καὶ Τίτου Φουλβίου Ἰουνίου Κυητοῦ Εῶν Εῶν Σῶν Θὼθ α.
also: P. Leipz. 57 (180) A. D. 261;
A. D. 260 P. Flor. II 224 (192): (ἔτους) α τῶν κυρίων ἡμῶν Μακριανοῦ καὶ Κυητοῦ Σεβαστοῦ Χοίακ ιβ.

---

A. D. 263 P. Oxy. VI 964 (318): (ἔτους) ια Α. Κ. Πουπλίου Λικιννίου Γαλλιηνοῦ Γ. Μ. Ε. Ε. Σ. Θὼθ ς.
also: C. P. H. 51-56 II ; A. D. 265 P. Flor. I 2 (5).
A. D. 266 C. P. R. 39 (166): (ἔτους) ιδ Α. Κ. Πουπλίου Λικιννίου Γαλλιηνοῦ Γ. Μ. Περσικοῦ Μ. Ε. Ε. Σ. Χοίακ ς.
also: C. P. H. 119 IV (57), 119 VI, et pluries.
A. D. 267 P. Oxy. XII 1475 (223): (ἔτους) ιδ Α. Κ. Πουπλίου Λικιννίου Γαλλιηνοῦ Γ. Μ. Παρθικοῦ Μ. Ε. Ε. Σ. Ἀθὺρ κγ.
A. D. 263 C. P. R. 38 (165): (ἔτους) ια τοῦ κυρίου ἡμῶν Γαλλιηνοῦ Σ. Φαῶφι β.
also: A D. 265 B. G. U. IV 1093 (154); P. Flor. I 2 (5); P Tebt. II 378 (221);
A. D. 267 P. Oxy. XII 1475 (223): (ἔτους) ιδ Γαλλιηνοῦ Σεβαστοῦ Φαρμοῦθι ιη.
also: A. D. 268-9 P. Oxy. XIV 1646 (77);

---

A. D. 269 P. Ryl 117 (103): (ἔτους) α Α. Κ. Μάρκου Αὐρηλίου Κλαυδίου Ε. Ε. Σ. Παχὼν ιζ.
A. D. 269 P. Oxy. XII 1455 (172): (ἔτους) α τ. κ. ἡμῶν Κλαυδίου Κ. Σ. Παχὼν κ.
A. D. 269 P. Oxy. 1646 (77): αἴτους τρίτου Κλαυδίου Σ. Φαῶφι τρίτη καὶ εἰκάς.
A. D. 271 C. P. R. 9 (28): (ἔτους) β Α. Κ. Λουκίου Δομιτίου Αὐρηλιανοῦ Ε. Ε. Σ. καὶ (ἔτους) ε Ἰουλίου Αὐρηλίου Σεπτιμίου Οὐαβαλλάθου Ἀθηνοδώρου τοῦ λαμπροτάτου βασιλέως Α. στρατηγοῦ Ῥωμαίων.
A. D. 272 P. Oxy. X 1624 (187): (ἔτους) β Α. Κ. Λουκίου Δομιττίου Αὐρηλιανοῦ Ε. Ε. Σ. καὶ ε (ἔτους) Ἰουλίου Αὐρηλίου Σεπτιμίου Οὐαβαλλάθου Ἀθηνοδώρου τοῦ λαμπροτάτου βασιλέως ὑπάτου Α. στρατηγοῦ Ῥωμαίων Φαμενὼθ η.
A. D. 274 B. G. U. IV 1073 (114): (ἔτους) ε τ. κ. ἡμῶν Αὐρηλιανοῦ Σ. Μεχεὶρ—.
A. D. 275 P. Oxy. XIV 1633 (31): (ἔτους) ς Α. Κ. Λουκίου Δομιττίου Αὐρηλιανοῦ Γ. Μ. Περσικοῦ Μ. Γοθθικοῦ Μ. Καρπικοῦ Μ. Ε. Ε. Σ. Μεσορὴ——
also: P. Oxy. XII 1455 (172).

A. D. 275 Note the "Latin" formula: B. G. U. IV 1074 (115): (A. D. 42) Τιβερίῳ Κλαυδίῳ Καίσαρι Σεβαστῷ καὶ Οὐιτελλίῳ τὸ β ὑπάτοις.

---

A. D. 276 B. G. U. II 419 (80): ἔτους δευτέρου τοῦ κυρίου ἡμῶν Πρόβου Σ.

cp. also: A. D. 278 P. Oxy. XII 1409 (17); B. G. U. IV 1064 (102); A. D. 280 P. Oxy. IX 1191 (210).

A. D. 279 P. Oxy. XIV 1713 (162): (ἔτους) ε Α. Κ. Μάρκου Αὐρηλίου Πρόβου Περσικοῦ Μ. Γοττικοῦ Μ. Γ. Μ. Ε. Ε. Σ. Φαῶφι κγ.

cp. also: A. D. 280 P. Oxy. XIV 1631 (15).

A. D. 284 P. Oxy. VIII 1115 (196): (ἔτους) ζ τ. κ. ἡμῶν Α. Κ. Μάρκου Αὐρηλίου Πρόβου Ε. Σ. Τῦβι ἑκκαιδεκάτῃ Τῦβι ις.

A. D. 283 P. Oxy. I 55 (112): (ἔτους) α Α. Κ. Μάρκου Αὐρηλίου Κάρου καὶ Μάρκου Αὐρηλίου Καρείνου Γῶν Μων καὶ Μάρκου Αὐρηλίου Νουμεριανοῦ τῶν ἐπιφανεστάτων Κων Εῶν Εῶν Σῶν Φαρμοῦθι ιβ.

---

A. D. 286 P. S. I. III 162 (15): (ἔτους) β Α. Κ. Γαίου Αὐρηλίου Οὐαλερίου Διοκλητιανοῦ καὶ (ἔτους) α Α. Κ. Μάρκου Αὐρηλίου Μαξιμιανοῦ Εῶν Εῶν Σῶν.

cp. also: A. D. 287 P. S. I. III 164 (17).

A. D. 288-95 P. Oxy. X 1252 (162): (ἔτους) ς Α. Κ. Γαίου Αὐρηλίου Οὐαλερίου Διοκλητιανοῦ καὶ (ἔτους) ε (ἔτους) Α. Κ. Μάρκου Αὐρηλίου Οὐαλερίου Μαξιμιανοῦ Γῶν Μων Εῶν Εῶν Σῶν Θὼθ ιη.

A. D. 289 P. Oxy. XIV 1642 (65): [ἔτους — τοῦ κυρίου] ἡμῶν Διοκλητιανοῦ καὶ (ἔτους) ς τοῦ κυρίου ἡμῶν Μαξιμιανοῦ Σῶν ——κζ.

A. D. 289 B. G. U. I 13 (19): ἔτους πέμπτου τ. κ. ἡμῶν Α. Διοκλητιανοῦ καὶ ἔτους δ Α. Κ. Μάρκου Αὐρηλίου Οὐαλερίου Μαξιμιανοῦ Σῶν Μεσορὴ πέμπτῃ.

A. D. 292 P. Oxy. I 59 (117): (ἔτους) η καὶ (ἔτους) ζ τῶν κυρίων ἡμῶν Διοκλητιανοῦ καὶ Μαξιμιανοῦ Σῶν Μεχεὶρ ις.

A. D. 295 P. Oxy. VIII 1121 (211): ἔτους ια καὶ ἔτους ι τῶν κυρίων ἡμῶν Διοκλητιανοῦ καὶ Μαξιμιανοῦ Σῶν καὶ (ἔτους) γ τῶν κυρίων ἡμῶν Κωνσταντίου καὶ Μαξιμιανοῦ τῶν ἐπιφανεστάτων Κων Μεχεὶρ ιδ.

A. D. 298 P. Oxy. XIV 1643 (70): (ἔτους) ιδ καὶ (ἔτους) ιγ τῶν κυρίων ἡμῶν Διοκλητιανοῦ καὶ Μαξιμιανοῦ Σῶν καὶ (ἔτους) ς τῶν κυρίων ἡμῶν Κωνσταντίου καὶ Μαξιμιανοῦ τῶν ἐπιφανεστάτων Κων Παχὼν ις ὑπατίας Φαύστου καὶ Γάλλου.

cp. also: P. Flor. I 32 (60); P. Oxy. XIV 1705 (159); A. D. 301 C. P. R. 40 (167).

A. D. 292 P. Oxy. XIV 1715 (163): (ἔτους) η (ἔτους) — A. K. Γαίου Αὐρηλίου Οὐαλερίου Διοκλητιανοῦ καὶ (ἔτους) ζ (ἔτους) A. K. Μάρκου Αὐρηλίου Οὐαλερίου Μαξιμιανοῦ Γῶν Μων Εῶν Εῶν Σῶν Ἐπεὶφ α.

A. D. 294 P. Oxy. VI 891 (208): ἐφ' ὑπάτων Οὐαλερίων Κωνσταντίου καὶ Μαξιμιανοῦ τῶν ἐπιφανεστάτων Κων.

A. D. 300 P. Grenf. II 72 (114): ὑπατείας τῶν δεσποτῶν ἡμῶν Διοκλητιανοῦ πατρὸς Αὐγούστων τὸ —— καὶ Γαλερίου Οὐαλερίου Μαξιμιανοῦ Αὐγούστου τὸ — τῇ πρὸ ιζ Καλενδῶν Μαρτίων.

A. D. 306 B. G. U. II 606 (250): (ἔτους) ιδ καὶ β τῶν κυρίων ἡμῶν Κωνσταντίου καὶ Μαξιμιανοῦ Σῶν καὶ Σεουήρου καὶ Μαξιμίνου τῶν ἐπιφανεστάτων Καισάρων Φαμενὼθ ιθ.

A. D. 307 B. G. U. II 408 (70): ὑπατίας τῶν δεσποτῶν ἡμῶν Κωνσταντίνου καὶ Λικιννίου Λικιννιανοῦ Σεβαστῶν Ἀθὺρ κζ.

---

——ἔτους Καίσαρος Θεοῦ——

A. D. 40 P. B. M. II 177 (167): τοῦ λε (ἔτους) Καίσαρος θεοῦ.
also: A. D. 95 P. Oxy. II 257 (217);

A. D. 54-67 P. Ryl. 119 (106): τῶι ιβ (ἔτει) θεοῦ Κλαυδίου Κ. Σ. Γ. Α.

A. D. 86 P. Oxy. VII 1028 (161): τῷ β (ἔτει) θεοῦ Τίτου.

A. D. 94 P. Oxy. II 257 (217): τῷ ε (ἔτει) θεοῦ Οὐεσπασιανοῦ
also: A. D. 134 P. Ryl. 103 (79);

A. D. 97 P. Oxy. IV 713 (180): τῷ δωδεκάτῳ ἔτει θεοῦ Κλαυδίου μηνὶ Σεβαστῷ.

A. D. 109 P. Oxy. III 482 (170): τῷ Τῦβι μηνὶ τοῦ πρώτου ἔτους θεοῦ Νερούα.

A. D. 132 P. Oxy. III 478 (163): —ς (ἔτους) θεοῦ Τραιανοῦ.
also: A. D. 141 P. Grenf. II 49 (77);

A. D. 139 B. G. U. I 111 (128): τοῦ ις (ἔτους) θεοῦ Ἀδριανοῦ.
also: A. D. 141 P. Grenf. II 49 (77); A. D. 162 P. Oxy. VII 1037 (162); A. D. 146 P. Gen. 30 (5); A. D. 148 P. Gen. 32 (27);

A. D. 151 P. Fay. 27 (135): τῷ κ (ἔτει) θεοῦ Αἰλίου Ἀντωνίνου.
also: A. D. 159 B. G. U. I 54 (68); 90 (108); A. D. 161 B. G. U. I 224 (224); P. Grenf. II 55 (89); A. D. 167 P. Ryl. 104 (81); A. D. 162 P. Oxy. VII 1037 (169); A. D. 178 P. Amh. II 71 (86); A. D. 181 P. Gen. 4 (26); A. D. 173 B. G. U. IV 1032 (33); A. D. 177 B. G. U. III 970 (291); A. D. 200 P. Oxy. VI 899 (221); etc. etc.

A. D. 180 P. Gen. 4 (26): τοῦ ιδ (ἔτους) θεοῦ Αὐρηλίου Ἀντωνίνου.
also: A. D. 181 P. Tebt. II 320 (127); 327 (137);

A. D. 258 P. Oxy. XII 1468 (197): πρὸς τὸ θ (ἔτος) τῆς θεοῦ Ἀλεξάνδρου βασιλείας.

A. D. 271 C. P. R. 9 (28): τοῦ ιγ (ἔτους) θεοῦ Γαλλιηνοῦ μηνὸς Χοίακ.

---

A. D. 94 P. Oxy. II 257 (217): πρὸ ς (ἔτους) Νέρωνος.
A. D. 134 P. Ryl. 103 (79): τῶι θ (ἔτει) Δομιτιανου. τῷ η (ἔτει) Οὐεσπασιανοῦ. τῶι ζ (ἔτει) Τραιανοῦ.
A. D. 161 P. Ryl. 111 (91): τοῦ ις (ἔτους) Ἀδριανοῦ.
A. D. 248 P. Tebt. II 319 (125): (ἔτους) ε Φιλίππου Μεχεὶρ θ.
A. D. 254 P. Oxy. VIII 1119 (203): (ἔτους) β Μάρκων Ἰουλίων Ἀθὺρ λ.
A. D. 271 C. P. R. 9 (28): τοῦ α (ἔτους) Κλαυδίου.

---

## *B. COMMENTARY*

In the dating of letters, more easily than in the opening and closing formulas, it is possible to trace the development from the simple form of the earliest documents extant to the elaborate formulas of the late Roman period. At first the date was expressed by a brief formula indicating only the year and the month, sometimes the day. Later the titles of the reigning emperor or emperors were added to the date proper. This custom began with the establishment of the Roman Principate, and continued, increasingly, through the entire Roman period.

The same dating formulas occur in the different kinds of letters. In familiar letters, however, and in other less formal communications, the elaborate—and hence formal—dating formulas in vogue during the later Roman period are found but rarely. If the date is at all given, it is expressed as a rule by means of a shorter formula. The elaborate formulas are employed also in non-epistolary documents, and should be studied in connection with them.

Very frequently the letters are without any date whatsoever. Sometimes the absence of the date may be attributed to the mutilated condition of the papyrus. But much more commonly the date is simply omitted. It is not practicable to give exact figures; but it is approximately correct to say that in private letters the date is missing almost as frequently as it is given; and in official letters the absence of the date is not rare. The reason may be that the need of dating the letters was not so urgent then as it is at present, in view of the fact that the carrier ordinarily was able to supply by word of mouth such information as the written document might lack.

We have no intention to discuss the Egyptian and Macedonian calendars, or their interrelation. This has been ably done by Messrs. Grenfell and Hunt in Hibeh Papyri Appendix I, and by other scholars. We have given a few quotations of dates in which the Egyptian names of the months were used, also a few in which the Macedonian names were employed, and again a few in which both were combined. The Egyptian names occur far more frequently than the Macedonian. In the date formulas of the Empire one may notice the use of the new Roman names for the months. Even during this period the Egyptian names seem to prevail.

The dating formulas occur at the end of the letters. In this respect commercial and legal documents drawn up in epistolary style differ from similar documents drawn up in regular form. In the latter the date is usually placed at the beginning. At times dates are found at the head of epistolary documents also. But these dates are as a rule in a different hand, and occur almost exclusively in official documents. They indicate the time when these documents were received at the respective offices. Cp. B. C. 252 P. P. II 20 (64); B. C. 250 P. P. II 32 (108); B. C. 114 P. Tebt. I 19 (89), 27 (105); P. Gizeh (Archiv II p. 82 no. 10277, 10323); A. D. 104 P. Ryl. 81 (42); A. D. 127 P. Tebt. II 323 (131); A. D. 129-131 P. Fay. 31, 32 (140-2); etc. etc.

The usual formula of a date given at the end of a letter is: year—number of year—month—day. When a date is quoted within the body of the letter, the order is exactly the reverse. The following quotations, taken at random, will illustrate this:

end: A. D. 13 P. Oxy IX 1188 (203):

(ἔτους) μβ Καίσαρος Μεχεὶρ κδ.

within: A. D. 12 B. G. U. III 757 (65):

τῆι ιγ τοῦ Παῦνι τοῦ μα (ἔτους) Καίσαρος.

These quotations are representative of the custom that obtained throughout the Ptolemaic and the Roman periods.

The elaborate dating formulas occurred almost invariably at the end of letters, and seldom within them. When there was need of quoting a date within the body of the letter, a briefer formula was ordinarily employed. However, this briefer formula occurs also at the end of letters, especially,—but not exclusively,—when these letters are of a less formal character.

The later formulas, being more explicit, can be placed in their chronological order without much difficulty. The earlier documents however employ more indefinite formulas, indicating only the year, without the name, of the sovereign; or only a name which several rulers bore. In such documents the chronological order can be determined only by means of internal or of paleographical evidence.

References to deceased emperors in dates regularly contain the title θεός. We have quoted a few of these formulas to show that this practice obtained throughout the later Roman period. At times, however, these deified emperors are quoted unceremoniously by their name only, as the last brief list of references shows.

Numerous though the papyri are of the Roman period, we have not a sufficient number of certain reigns, especially, to warrant decisive conclusions. When future discoveries of papyri have filled up the gaps, it will be possible to study more in detail the development of the dating formulas employed in letters.

# IV. CONVENTIONAL PHRASES IN THE BODY OF THE LETTER.

In this chapter it is our intention to treat of certain set phrases which occur not infrequently in the epistolary papyri of the Ptolemaic-Roman period. These phrases fall into two main groups. To the first group belong those more or less stereotyped wishes found almost exclusively in familiar letters. The second group contains conventional modes of expression which are employed also in documents drawn up in other than epistolary form.

Since the phrases contained in the first group fall directly within the scope of our investigation, we shall take them up first and present them with such a degree of completeness as may be required. The phrases of the latter group, however, we can not pass over in silence. But since they should be studied in connection with non-epistolary documents in which they also occur, we shall not study them to any great extent, but shall satisfy ourselves with the indication of a few of those formulas which occur with greatest frequency.

The first group is divided into two principal parts. In the first part we take up the "initial" phrases which occur at the beginning of the letter proper, and follow immediately upon the opening formula. They are subdivided into three sections: the *ἐρρῶσθαι* wish, the *ὑγιαίνειν* wish without and with the proscynesis, and the *ἀσπάσασθαι* wish. To each section we have added such varying forms as occur during the period covered, yet so infrequently (at least in the papyri now extant) as not to deserve separate treatment. In the second part we have gathered the "final" phrases which occur directly before the closing formula. Here again we have divided the material into three sections, not according to the variation of the formula exactly, but according to the nature of the documents in which they are found. In the first section we have collected the formulas proper to familiar letters. In the second section have been arranged the formulas employed in petitions and similar documents. In the last section we have placed a few miscellaneous phrases. Since a complete survey of this last section would lead us too far afield, we found ourselves obliged to curtail it, and eliminate from it certain phrases occurring rather frequently, but almost exclusively in commercial documents which are really nothing else but contracts and leases with an epistolary beginning.

In the second and third groups two sets of formulas are treated: the illiteracy formula and the oath formula. The former has its place in this investigation, since it curiously reflects upon the ability of the people of those days to employ writing as a means of communication. The oath formula occurs in many official communications, and has much of the phraseology of the date formulas. It forms an interesting means of comparison. In quoting the oath formulas we have used the same abbreviations as above in quoting the dates.

It is obvious that all phrases occurring during the six hundred years covered by our investigation could not be taken up for study at this time. Several other phrases appear to be more or less stereotyped. However, either they do not occur so frequently in the papyri now extant as to warrant separate investigation, or they are not considered quite pertinent to our subject. At a later time, and in connection with other subjects, they may be taken up with profit.

In accordance with our method, we have tried to group the formulas according to their similarity, observing within each group the chronological order. In several cases however this method could not be observed, and there only a chronological arrangement has been retained.

Since it is not feasible to quote all extant texts, only certain representative texts have been given in full; and references have been added to other texts of the same, or very similar, wording. It is hoped that the number of texts quoted will make possible a fairly accurate inference as to the relative importance and frequency of the formulas. Such conclusions as may be deduced therefrom will be added, when the evidence has been submitted.

## *A. I. THE INITIAL PHRASES*

The origin of Greek epistolary formulas is still lost in the great Past, as far as the papyri are concerned. As in the opening and closing formulas, so also in these phrases we find a fully developed form in the earliest papyri extant. It is futile, in lieu of evidence, to advance more or less probable speculations as to the possible source whence these forms have been derived. Inscriptions and other archeological evidence do not furnish sufficient proof for safe conclusions. We can only hope for other fortunate discoveries which will place in our hands the evidence we require.

---

## A. I. INITIAL PHRASES.

### 1. The ἐρρῶσθαι Wish.

B. C. 256-5 P. S. I. IV 342 (70): *εἰ εὐκαιρεῖς καλῶς ποιήσεις.*

B. C. 257 P. S. I. IV 331 (68): *εἰ ἔρρωσαι εὖ ἂν ἔχοι· ἐρρώμεθα δὲ καὶ ἡμεῖς.*

B. C. 258 P. S. I. IV 330 (67): *καλῶς ἂν ἔχοι εἰ ἔρρωσαι· ὑγιαίνομεν δὲ καὶ αὐτοί.*

B. C. 251 P. S. I. IV 361 (92): *εἰ ἔρρωσαι εὖ ἂν ἔχοι· ὑγιαίνομεν δὲ καὶ ἡμεῖς.*

also: B. C. 3dc. P. S. I. IV 417 (142);

B. C. 251 P. S. I. IV 364 (95): *εἰ ἔρρωσαι καλῶς ἂν ἔχοι· ὑγιαίνομεν δὲ καὶ αὐτοί.*

also: B. C. 250 P. S. I. IV 375 (104); B. C. 3dc P. S. I. IV 444 (170);

B. C. 240 P. P. II 40 (135): *εἰ ἔρρωσθε πάντες καλῶς ἂν ἔχοι· ὑγιαίνομεν δὲ καὶ αὐτοί.*

B. C. 3dc. P. P. III 53 (154): *εἰ ἔρρωσαι καὶ ὁ ἀδελφὸς καὶ τὸ θυγατρίον καὶ οἱ ἄλλοι πάντες εὖ ἂν ἔχοι· ὑγίγαινον δὲ καὶ αὐτός.*

B. C. 264 P. P. III 53 (152): *εἰ ἔρρωσαι καὶ τἄλλα σοι κατὰ λόγον ἐστὶν εἴη ἂν ὡς βούλομαι· κἀγὼ δ' ἱκανῶς εἶχον.*

B. C. 257 P. S. I. V 500 (81): *εἰ ἔρρωσαι καὶ τὰ λοιπά σοι κατὰ γνώμην ἐστίν, εἴη ἂν ὡς ἐγὼ θέλω· ὑγίαινον δὲ καὶ αὐτός.*

B. C. 240 P. P. II 11 (27): *εἰ ἔρρωσαι καὶ τὰ λοιπά σοι κατὰ γνώμην ἐστίν, καλῶς ἂν ἔχοι· ἐρρώμεθα δὲ καὶ αὐτοί.*

B. C. 223 P. Eleph. 13 (47): *εἰ ἔρρωσαι καὶ τὰ λοιπά σοι κατὰ λόγον ἐστίν, εἴη ἂν ὡς ἐγὼ θέλω· ὑγίηινον δὲ καὶ αὐτός.*

B. C. 3dc. P. S. I. IV 415 (141): *εἴ ἔρρωσαι καὶ τὰ ἄλλα σοι κατὰ νοῦν ἐστιν, εὖ ἂν ἔχοι· καὶ αὐτοὶ δὲ ὑγιαίνομεν.*

B. C. 2dc. P. Good. 4 (8): *εἰ ἔρρωσαι καὶ τἄλλα σοι κατὰ λόγον ἐστίν, εἴη ἂν ὡς αἱρούμεθα· καὶ αὐτοὶ δ' ὑγιαίνομεν.*

B. C. 3dc. P. P. III 53 (154): *εἰ ἔρρωσαι μεθ' ὧν προαιρῇ καὶ τὰ λοιπά σοι κατὰ γνώμην ἐστίν, ἔχοι ἂν εὖ· ἐρρώμην δὲ καὶ αὐτὸς καὶ οἱ μετ' ἐμοῦ.*

B. C. 264 (227) P. P. III 53 (152): εἰ ἔρρωσαί τε καὶ τἄλλα σοι κατὰ γνώμην ἐστίν, θεῶι πλείστη χάρις· ἔρρωμαι δὲ καὶ αὐτός.

B. C. 260 P. Hib. I 79 (234): εἰ ἔρρωσαι καὶ ὧν πρόνοιαν ποιεῖ καὶ τἄλλα σοι κατὰ λόγον ἐστίν, εἴη ἂν ὡς ἐγὼ θέλω καὶ τοῖς θεοῖς πολλὴ χάρις· ὑγίαινον δὲ καὶ αὐτός.

B. C. 260 P. P. II 2 (4): εἰ ἔρρωσαι καὶ ἐν τοῖς ἄλλοις ἀλύπως ἀπαλλάσσεις, εἴη ἂν ὡς ἐγὼ τοῖς θεοῖς εὐχόμε-[νος διατελῶ· καὶ αὐτὸς δὲ ὑγία]ινον.

B. C. 258 P. P. II 13 (37): εἰ ἔρρωσαι καὶ πάντα σοι κατὰ λόγον ἐστίν, πολλὴ χάρις μοι τοῖς θεοῖς· ἐρρώμεθα καὶ αὐτοί.

B. C. 257 P. S. I. V 502 (83): εἰ ἔρρωσαι καὶ ἐν τοῖς λοιποῖς κατὰ λόγον ἀπαλλάσσεις, εἴη ἂν ὡς ἡμεῖς θέλομεν· ἐρρώμεθα δὲ καὶ αὐτοί.

B. C. 240 P. P. I 30 (80)2: καλῶς ποεῖς εἰ ἔρρωσαι καὶ τὰ λοιπά σοι κατὰ γνώμην ἐστίν· ἐρρώμεθα δὲ καὶ ἡμεῖς.

Cp. also: P. S. I. VI 569 (18) B. C. 253; 577 (25) B. C. 248; B. C. 252 P. P. II 11;

B. C. 242 P. S. I. IV 392 (121): εἰ ἔρρωσαι καὶ τἄλλα σοι κατὰ τρόπον συναντᾶι, εἴη ἂν τὸ δεῖον· ὑγίαινον δὲ καὶ αὐτός.

B. C. 3dc. P. S. I. VI 590 (35): εἰ αὐτός τε ἔρρωσαι καὶ οὓς [αὐτὸς βούλει], τὸ δέον ἂν εἴηι· ὑγίαινον δὲ καὶ ἐγώ.

B. C. 3dc. P. S. I. VI 610 (50): εἰ αὐτός τε ἔρρωσαι καὶ οὓς αὐτὸς βούλει, εἴη ἂν ὡς αὐτὸς [θέλω· ὑγία]ινον δὲ καὶ αὐτός.

B. C. 172 P. B. M. I 42 (29): εἰ ἐρρωμένωι τἄλλα κατὰ λόγον ἀπαντᾶι, εἴηι ἂν ὡς τοῖς θεοῖς εὐχομένη διατελῶ· καὶ αὐτὴ δ' ὑγίαινον καὶ τὸ παιδίον καὶ οἱ μὲν ἐν οἴκωι πάντες σοῦ διὰ παντὸς μνεῖαν ποιούμενοι.

B. C. 168 P. Vat. A (Witk. p. 64): εἰ ἐρρωμένωι σοι τἄλλα κατὰ λόγον ἀπαντᾶι, εἴηι ἂν ὡς βούλομαι· καὶ αὐτὸς δ' ὑγίαινον καὶ Εὐδαιμονὶς καὶ τὰ παιδία καὶ Ἰσιὰς καὶ τὸ παιδίον σου καὶ οἱ ἐν οἴκωι πάντες.

B. C. 153 P. Paris 45 (Witk. p. 83): εἰ ἔρρωσαι καὶ τὰ ἄλλα σοι κατὰ λόγον ἀπαντᾶ, εἴη ἂν ὡς βούλομαι καὶ αὐτὸς δ' ὑγίαινον.

B. C. 153 P. Paris 46 (Witk. p. 85): εἰ ἔρρωσαι καὶ τὰ παρὰ τῶν θεῶν κατὰ λόγον σοι χρηματίζεται, εἴη ἂν ὡς βούλομαι· καὶ αὐτὸς δὲ μετρίως ἐπαρκῶ.

B. C. 165 P. Paris 63 (P. P. III Introd. p. 18): ἔρρωται μὲν βασιλεὺς Πτολεμαῖος καὶ βασιλεὺς Πτολεμαῖος ὁ ἀδελφὸς καὶ βασίλισσα Κλεοπάτρα ἡ ἀδελφὴ καὶ τὰ τέκνα καὶ τὰ πράγματα τ' αὐτοῖς ἔχει κατὰ τρόπον· εἰ δὲ καὶ σὺ ὑγιγαίνις καὶ τἄλλα σοι κατὰ λόγον ἐστίν, εἴη ἂν ὡς βουλόμεθα καὶ τῶι Δὶ ἱκανῶς ἐπανήγομεν.

B. C. 257 P. S. I. IV 333 (70): *συνέβη ἡμῖν ἀγωνιᾶσαι ἀκούσαντας ἐπὶ πλείονα χρόνον ἑλκυσθῆναί σε ἐν ἀρρωστίαι· νυνὶ δὲ ἀκούσαντές σε ὑγιαίνειν καὶ εἶναι ἤδη πρὸς τῶι ἀναλαμβάνειν, ἤσθημεν· ὑγιαίνομεν δὲ καὶ αὐτοί.*

B. C. 240 P. P. I 30 (79): *καλῶς ποεῖς εἰ ὑγιαίνεις· ὑγιαίνω καὶ αὐτός.*

B. C. 3dc. P. P. I 29 (78): *χάρις τοῖς θεοῖς πολλὴ εἰ ὑγιαίνεις· ὑγιαίνει δὲ καὶ Λώκινος.*

B. C. 153 P. Paris 44 (Witk. p. 81): *εἰ ἔρρωσαι, ἔρρωμαι δὲ αὐτός, εἴε ἂν ὡς βούλομαι, καὶ τὰ ἄλλα σοι καιτὰ λόγον ἀπαντᾶ.*

B. C. 102 P. Grenf. I 32 (61): *εἰ ἔρρωσθε —δι —χε ἐρρώμεθα δὲ καὶ αὐτοὶ ὑμῶν τὴν ἀρίστην ——παρὰ τοῖς ἐν Πηλουσίωι θεοῖς.*

---

### Shortened and Elliptic Forms

B. C. 252 P. P. II 20 (63): *εἰ ἔρρωσαι καὶ ὡς προαιρεῖ, καλῶς ἂν ἔχοι.*

B. C. 3dc. P. Grenf. II 14c : *εἰ ἔρρωσαι, εὖ ἂν ἔχοι.*

B. C. 2dc. P. Grenf. I 43 (74): *εἰ ἔρρωσαι, ἐρρώμεθα δὲ καὶ αὐτοὶ καὶ Ἀφροδισία καὶ ἡ θυγάτηρ καὶ ἡ παιδίσκη καὶ ἡ θυγάτηρ αὐτῆς.*

B. C. 162 P. Paris 32 (Witk. p. 66): *εἰ ἔρρωσθε, καὐτὸς δ' ὑγίαινον.*

B. C. 154 P. Paris 43 (Witk. p. 78): *εἰ ἔρρωσθαι, ἔρρωμαι δὲ καὐτοί.* Fragmentary: B. C. 3dc. P. Alex. 3; B. C. 250 III P. P. 42 (113): *εἰ ὑγιαίνεις καὶ τὰ λοιπὰ* ———; P. P. III 42 (114): ——*ἐρρώμεθα δὲ καὶ ἡμεῖς.* Note also the following examples of joining the opening formula with these phrases:

B. C. 2dc. B. G. U. III 1009: ———*τῷ ἀδελφῶι χαίρειν καὶ ἐρρῶσθαι· [καὶ αὐτὸς δ'] ὑγίαινον.*

B. C. 161 P. B. M. I 33 b: *Ἀπολλώνιος Ἱππάλωι κτλ. καὶ τοῖς ἐν οἴκωι πᾶσι χαίρειν καὶ τὰ ἄλλα σοι κατὰ λόγον ἔσται.*

B. C. 103 P. Amh. II 30 (47): *Πόρτεις ἡγεμὼν τῶν ἐν προχειρισμῶι καὶ οἱ ἐκ τοῦ σημείου νεανίσκοι Πατῆτι καὶ Παχράτηι καὶ τοῖς ἄλλοις στρατιώταις πᾶσι χαίρειν καὶ ἐρρωμένωι διὰ παντὸς εὐημερεῖν, ὑγιαίνομεν δὲ καὐτοί.*

B. C. 99 P. Tebt. I 59 (171): *Ποσειδώνιος τοῖς ἐν Τεπτύνει ἱερεῦσι χαίρειν καὶ ἐρρῶσθαι· ὑγίαινον δὲ καὶ αὐτός.*

B. C. 96 P. Lipz. I 104 (300): *Πετεσοῦχος κτλ. καὶ τοῖς παιδίοις χαίρειν καὶ ἐρρῶσθαι· ἔρρωμαι δὲ καὐτὸς καὶ τὰ παιδία καὶ οἱ ἐν οἴκωι πάντες.*

B.C. 95 P. Grenf. II 36 (61): Πετεσοῦχος κτλ. καὶ Ὥρωι Πατῆτος χαίρειν καὶ ἐρρῶσθαι· ἔρρωμαι δὲ καὶ αὐτὸς καὶ Ἐσθλύτις κτλ. καὶ οἱ παρ' ἡμῶν πάντες.

---

## THE ἐρρῶσθαι WISH.

The earliest formula we meet with is the ἐρρῶσθαι wish. Its basic form is εἰ ἔρρωσαι, εὖ ἂν ἔχοι. ἐρρώμεθα (ὑγιαίνομεν) καὶ ἡμεῖς (αὐτοί). It is evident that this formula furnishes little more than a theme which the writer may use and expand as the spirit moves him. All ἐρρῶσθαι wishes express the fundamental idea of concern about the welfare of the correspondent, and the assurance of one's own wellbeing. The variety with which this idea is expressed is almost bewildering. The difference in the wording is not great; yet hardly two forms are quite alike. It has been observed that in this respect the Greek formula differs completely from its later Latin adaptation which became practically invariable. That the Latin phrase, so well known through Cicero's letters, is but a translation and adaptation of this Greek formula, no one now denies.

One must read the quotations given in the preceding pages to realize how slight often, yet how real, the variation between the formulas is. At first it may seem that the one text is but a repetition of the other. But a closer inspection will show that καλῶς is substituted for εὖ; or ἐρρώμεθα for ὑγιαίνομεν; κατὰ λόγον or κατὰ νοῦν for κατὰ γνώμην; τὰ λοιπά for τἄλλα; ἡμεῖς for αὐτοί; βούλομαι for θέλω; and substitution of other verbs occurs. At times words are added, as πάντες, frequently; or invocations of the divinity; and many other expansions. Though these variations seem slight, they have the effect of making the wish more real, more personal, less stereotyped or conventional.

All the texts quoted belong to the Ptolemaic period. According to the extant papyri it would appear that during the latter part of the Ptolemaic period the ἐρρῶσθαι wish joined with the opening formula, thus forming the phrase: A— to B— χαίρειν καὶ ἐρρῶσθαι. It would seem justifiable to infer that this latter phrase is a development, the actual result of the combination of the ἐρρῶσθαι wish and the opening formula. There is no papyrus evidence to the contrary. Yet it may be well to reserve judgment: for a similar inference would not have held in the case of the ὑγιαίνειν wish. There is a gap of about three hundred years between the earliest occurrence of the phrase: *χαίρειν καὶ ὑγιαίνειν* in the letter written on lead by Mnesiergus, and the earliest occurrence of the phrase in epistolary papyri. It may also be observed that in the papyri extant the combined *ὑγιαίνειν* phrase antedates the separate phrasing. If we were to base our judgment only on papyri now extant, we would be compelled to conclude that the opening formula *χαίρειν* combined with the *ἐρρῶσθαί* wish to form the opening formula *χαίρειν καὶ ἐρρῶσθαι*; whereas the opening formula *χαίρειν καὶ ὑγιαίνειν* resolved itself into the opening formula *χαίρειν* and the separate *ὑγιαίνειν* wish. And though such a conclusion may be sound, and may be borne out by the publication of additional papyri, yet it is not impossible that such future publications may necessitate a complete reversal of this theory. Hence it is preferable, in view of the absence of decisive proof, to suspend judgment.

---

## 2. The *ὑγιαίνειν* Wish.

A. D. 25 P. Oxy. II 292 (292) (at the end of the letter!): *πρὸ δὲ πάντων ὑγιαίνειν σε εὔχομαι ἀβασκάντως τὰ ἄριστα πράττων.*

A. D. 2dc. P. Oxy. XII 1581 (282): *πρὸ μὲν πάντων εὔχομαί σε ὑγιαίνειν.*

also: B. G. U. II 602 (246); IV 1040 (45);

A. D. 2dc. P. Oxy. XIV 1757 (180): *πρὸ τῶν ὅλων εὔχομαί σε ὑγιαίνειν.*

A. D. 2dc. P. Flor. III 332 (67): *πρὸ πάντων εὔχομαί σε ὑγιαίνειν μετὰ καὶ τῶν παιδίων μου καὶ τῆς μητρὸς αὐτῶν.*

A. D. 2dc. P. Tebt. II 414 (288): *πρὸ μὲν πάντων εὔχομαί σε ὑγιαίνειν καὶ τὰ παιδία σου καὶ Πᾶσιν τὸν κόρυφον.*

A. D. 2dc. B. G. U. II 632 (297): *πρὸ μὲν πάντων εὔχομαί σε ὑγιαίνειν καὶ 'γὼ γὰρ αὐτὸς ὑγιαίνω.*

A. D. 2dc. P. Giss. III 97 (90): *πρὸ μὲν πάντων εὔχομαί σε ὑγειαίνειν μετὰ τῶν σῶν πάντων καὶ ἐγὸ αὐτὴ μετὰ τῶν τέκνων.*

A. D. 3dc. P. B. M. II 479 (225): *πρὸ μὲν πάντων εὔχομαί σε ὑγιαίνειν πανοικησίᾳ.*

A. D. 3dc. P. Gen. 130 (112): *πρὸ μὲν πάντων εὔχομαί σε ὑγιαίνειν καὶ προκόπτειν.*

A. D. 3dc. P. Oxy XIV 1668 (124): *πρὸ μὲν πάντων εὔχομαι ὑμᾶς ὁλοκληρεῖν.*

A. D. 3dc. P. Oxy. XIV 1678 (137): *πρὸ μὲν πάντων εὔχομαί σε ὁλοκληρεῖν καὶ ὑειένειν παρὰ τῷ κυρίῳ θεῷ.*

also: A. D. 3d-4thc P. Oxy. XII 1493 (250);

A. D. 3dc. P. Oxy. VIII 1158 (260): *πρὸ μὲν πάντων εὐχόμαιθά σαι ὁλοκληρεῖν μετὰ τοῦ οἴκου σου ὅλου.*

A. D. 3dc. P. Oxy. XIV 1773 (186): πρὸ μὲν πάντων εὔχομαι τῷ θεῷ ὁλοκλήρους ὑμᾶς ἀπολαβεῖν.

A. D. 3dc. P. Ryl. 244 (392): πρὸ μὲν πάντων εὔχομαι θεοῖς πᾶσιν ὅπως ὑγιαίνοντας ὑμᾶς ἀπολάβω.

A. D. 117 P. Oxy. X 1293 (245): πρὸ τῶν ὅλων εὔχομαί σε ὑγιαίνειν σὺν τῷ πατρί σου.

A. D. 2d-3dc P. Oxy. III 533 (270): πρὸ τῶν ὅλων εὔχομαι ὑμᾶς ὑγιαίνειν μετὰ τῶν τέκνων καὶ συμβίων.

A. D. 2dc. P. Oxy. XIV 1759 (181): πρὸ τῶν ὅλων εὔχομαί σε ὑγιαίνειν καὶ νικᾶν πάντοτε.

A. D. 3dc. P. Oxy. XII 1586 (283): πρὸ τῶν ὅλων εὔχομαί σε ὑγιαίνειν μετὰ τῶν τέκνων σου καὶ τῶν σῶν πάντων. γράφω δὲ σοὶ καὶ ἐγὼ ἐρρωμένος καὶ εὐχόμενός σοι τὰ κάλλιστα.

A. D. 2dc. B. G. U. III 794 (94): πρὸ τῶν ὅλων εὔχομαί σαι ὑγιένιν παρὰ τῇ τύχῃ Ἀντιωχίας καὶ 'γὼ αὐτὸς καλῶς μοί ἐστιν.

A. D. 2d-3dc. B. G. U. I 164 (175): πρὸ τῶν ὅλων ἐρρῶσθαί σε εὔχομαι μετὰ τῶν σῶν πάντων καὶ διὰ παντός σε εὐτυχεῖν.

A. D. 2dc. P. Giss. 23 (66): πάντων τῶν εὐχῶν μου ἀναγκαιοτάτη — — ἔχω τὴν τῆς ὑγείας σου καὶ τοῦ ἀδελφοῦ σου Ἀπολλωνίου καὶ τῶν ἀβασκάντων ὑμῶν.

A. D. 4thc. P. Oxy. XII 1495 (252): πρὸ μὲν πάντων εὔχομαί σοι ὁλοκληρίαν παρὰ τῷ κυρίῳ θεῷ.

A. D. 4thc. P. Oxy. XIV 1774 (187): προηγουμένως ἀναγκεον (ἀναγκαῖον) ἦν προσαγορεύειν σαι εὐχόμεναι ὑγιένιν σαι ἡμεῖν.

A. D. 2dc. B. G. U. II 423 (84): πρὸ μὲν πάντων εὔχομαί σε ὑγιαίνειν καὶ διὰ παντὸς ἐρωμένον εὐτυχεῖν μετὰ κτλ. εὐχαριστῶ τῷ κυρίῳ Σαράπιδι κτλ.

A. D. 3dc. P. Oxy. XIV 1770 (185): προηγουμένως εὔχομε ὑμᾶς ὑγιαίνειν καὶ εὖ πράττειν. γινώσκειν ὑμᾶς θέλω ὅτι μετὰ πάντων ὁλοκληροῦμεν.

---

A. D. 2dc. B. G. U. II 601 (245): πρὸ μὲν πάντων εὔχομαί σε ὑγιαίνειν καὶ τὸ προσκύνημά σου ποιῶ παρὰ τῷ κυρίῳ Σαράπιδι.

also: A. D. 2d-3dc B. G. U. II 384 (42); 625 (283); P. Strassb. 38 (133); P. Fay. 127 (284); P. Oxy. XIV 1677 (136);

A. D. 3dc. P. Oxy. VI 936 (303): πρὸ μὲν πάντων εὔχομαί σε ὑγιαίνειν καὶ τὸ προσκύνημά σου ποιῶ παρὰ τοῖς ἐπιχωρίοις θεοῖς.

A. D. 2dc. B. G. U. III 775 (76): πρὸ μὲν πάντων εὔχομέ σε ὑγιένιν καὶ τὸ προσκύνημά σου ποιῶ καθ' ἑκάστην ἡμέραν παρὰ τῷ κυρίῳ Σαράπιδι.

Cp. also: P. Iand. 9 (42);

A. D. 2d-3dc. B. G. U. I 276 (272): πρὸ μὲν πάντων εὔχομαί σε ὑγιαίνειν μετὰ τῶν σῶν πάντων καὶ τὸ προσκύνημά σου ποιῶ καθ' ἑκάστην ἡμέραν παρὰ τῷ κυρίῳ Σαράπιδι.

A. D. 3dc. P. S. I. IV 308 (40): πρὸ μὲν πάντων εὔχομαί σε ὑγιαίνειν καὶ διὰ παντὸς εὐτυχεῖν καὶ τὸ προσκύνημά σου ποιῶ καθ' ἑκάστην ἡμέραν παρὰ τῷ κυρίῳ Σαράπιδι.

A. D. 3dc. P. Fay. 130 (286): πρὸ μὲν πάντων εὔχομαί σε ὑγιαίνειν καὶ τὸ προσκύνημά σου ποιῶ κατ' ἑκάστην ἡμέραν παρὰ τοῖς ἐνθάδε θεοῖς.

A. D. 2d-3dc. B. G. U. II 385 (43): πρὸ μὲν πάντων εὔχομαί σαι ὑγιαίνειν καὶ τὸ προσκύνημά σου ποιῶ κατ' ἑκάστην ἡμέραν παρὰ τῷ κυρίῳ Σαράπιδι καὶ τοῖς συννέοις θεοῖς.

A. D. 3dc. P. Meyer 20 (84): πρὸ μὲν πάντων εὔχομαί σε ὑγιαίνειν καὶ τὸ προσκύνημά σου ποιῶ παρὰ οἷς ἐπιξενοῦμαι θεοῖς.

A. D. 2dc. B. G. U. III 845 (160): πρὸ μὲν πάντων εὔχομέ σαι ὑγειαίνιν καὶ τὸ προσκύνημά σου ποιῶ καθ' ἑκάστην ἡμέραν παρὰ τῷ κυρίῳ Σαράπιδι καὶ τοῖς συννάοις θεοῖς εὐχόμενός σαι ὑγειαίνιν.

A. D. 2d-3dc. B. G. U. I 332 (326): πρὸ μὲν πάντων εὔχομαι ὑμᾶς ὑγιαίνιν ὅ μοι πάντων ἐστὶν ἀναγκαιότερον. τὸ προσκύνημα ἡμῶν ποιῶ παρὰ τῷ κυρίῳ Σαράπιδι εὐχομένη ἡμᾶς ὑγιαίνοντες ἀπολαβεῖν ὡς εὔχομαι ἐπιτετευχότας.

A. D. 2dc. P. Giss. 14 (53): πρὸ πάντων σε εὔχομαι ὑγιαίνειν μετὰ τοῦ κυρίου μου Ἡρακλᾶ Ἀπόλλωνος καὶ τῆς κυρίας μου Ἀλίνης ὧν οὐ διαλείπω ποιῶν τὸ προσκύνημα παρὰ τῷ κυρίῳ Ἑρμῇ καὶ παρὰ πᾶσι τοῖς θεοῖς.

A. D. 3dc. P. Oxy. XIV 1670 (126): πρὸ μὲν πάντων εὔχομαί σαι ὁλοκληρεῖν καὶ τὸ προσκύνημά σου ποιῶ καθ' ἑκάστην ἡμαίραν παρὰ τῷ κυρίῳ θεῷ Σαράπιδι.

A. D. 3d-4thc. P. S. I. III 236 (93): προηγουμένως εὔχομαί σε ὁλόκληρον ἀπολαβεῖν καὶ τὸ προσκύνημά σου ποιῶ καθ' ἑκάστην ἡμέραν παρὰ θεοῖς πᾶσι.

A. D. 3dc. P. Oxy. XIV 1769 (184): πρὸ τῶν ὅλων εὔχομαί σαι ὑγιαίνειν καὶ τὸ προσκύνημά σου ποιῶ καθ' ἑκάστην ἡμέραν παρὰ τῷ κυρίῳ Σαράπιδι.

A. D. 3dc. P. S. I. III 206 (16): πρὸ τῶν ὅλων εὔχομαι πᾶσι τοῖς θεοῖς εὐτυχεῖν σαι καὶ τὸ προσκύνημά σου ποιῶ καθ' ἑκάστην ἡμέραν παρ' οἷς ἐπιξενοῦμαι θεοῖς· εὔχομαι δέ σοι τὰ ἐν βίῳ κάλλιστα ἀγαθὰ ὑπαρχθῆναι.

A. D. 1stc. B. G. U. I 38 (53): πρὸ παντὸς εὔχομαι ὑγιαίνειν· τὸ προσκύνημά σου ποιῶ παρὰ πᾶσι τοῖς θεοῖς.

A. D. 2dc. P. Oxy. XIV 1758 (181): πρὸ παντὸς εὔχομαί σε ὑγιαίνειν μετὰ τῶν ἀβασκάντων σου παιδίων καὶ τὸ προσκύνημα ὑμῶν ποιῶ παρὰ τῷ μεγάλῳ Σαράπιδι εὐχομένη σοι τὰ κάλλιστα πανοικεί.

A. D. 2dc. P. Oxy. III 528 (263): πρὸ μὲν παντὸς εὔχομαί σε ὑγιαίνειν καὶ καθ' ἑκάστης ἡμέρας καὶ ὀψίας τὸ προσκύνημά σου πυῶ παρὰ τῇ σε φιλούσῃ Θοήρι.

---

## THE ὑγιαίνειν WISH.

Among the opening formulas we meet the phrase **χαίρειν καὶ διὰ παντὸς ὑγιαίνειν** as early as the latter half of the first century B. C. This formula occurs also in the second century of the Christian era. The ὑγιαίνειν wish makes its first appearance in the papyri in the beginning of the first century A. D. It is interesting to observe, that, late as this formula makes its appearance, its origin can not be traced. For the papyri belonging to the period preceding the first appearance of the ὑγιαίνειν wish are few in number. Here, again, we are dependent on future discoveries of papyri for a solution.

The ὑγιαίνειν wish maintains itself throughout the period under investigation. It appears in its simple form: **πρὸ μὲν πάντων** (or **πρὸ τῶν ὅλων**) εὔχομαί σε ὑγιαίνειν, or in connection with the proscynesis: πρὸ μὲν πάντων εὔχομαί σε ὑγιαίνειν καὶ τὸ προσκύνημά σου ποιῶ παρὰ τῷ κυρίῳ Σαράπιδι. Both forms occur about the same time. Here again it may be said that the basic formulas are little more than the briefest expression of the general theme. The letter-writer could vary, and did vary, the expresssion of this theme in words according to his fancy. Hence the great variety of detail. Usually the formula begins with πρὸ μὲν πάντων or πρὸ **τῶν ὅλων**. The former phrase, at least in the papyri quoted above, is more frequent than the latter. The words εὔχομαί σε ὑγιαίνειν become at times εὔχομαί σε ὁλοκληρεῖν, or an equivalent expression. In the proscynesis the words καθ' ἑκάστην ἡμέραν are often inserted. At times the proscynesis is made to other gods than Serapis. In these formulas the writer frequently associates himself with other members of his household, whom he may mention by name. Thus in these expressions the personal note is not wanting. They are far more than mere stereotyped phrases.

The proscynesis is found occasionally alone, that is, without the ὑγιαίνειν wish preceding it. Scattered examples are found in the first three centuries of the Christian era. We venture no other explanation for it than the whim of the writer.

---

### 3. THE ἀσπάσασθαι WISH AND MISCELLANEOUS PHRASES.

A. D. 98-103 B. G. U. III 811 (126): πρὸ μὲν πάντων ἀναγκαῖον δι' ἐπιστολῆς σε ἀσπάσεσθαι καὶ τὰ ἀβάσκαντα δοῦναι δι' ἃ ἐρωτῶ σε ἵνα δῷς τῷ κομίζοντί σοι τὸ ἐπιστόλιον.

A. D. 2dc. P. Oxy. III 531 (268): ἡδέως σε ἀσπαζόμεθα πάντες οἱ ἐν οἴκωι καὶ τοὺς μετ' ἐσοῦ πάντας.

A. D. 2dc. P. Amh. II 135 (164): ἀσπάζομαί σε πρὸ πάντων καὶ Σαραπίωνα καὶ Σελήνην καὶ Εὐδαιμονίδα.

A. D. 2d-3dc. P. Hamb. 54 (194): ἀσπάζομαί σε ἀδελφέ [πρὸ πάντων?].

A. D. 2dc. P. Giss. III 77 (67): πρὸ πάντων σε ἀσπάζεται Ἡραιδοῦς καὶ ἀσπάζομαι πάντας τοὺς σούς.

A. D. 3d-4thc. P. Oxy. VIII 1160 (263): πρὸ μὲν πάντων πολλά σε ἀσπάζομαι καὶ τὴν σύμβιόν σου κτλ. πάντες κατ' ὄνομα.

A. D. 2dc. P. Giss. 17 (56): πρὸ τῶν ὅλων ἀσπάζομαί σε δεσπότα καὶ εὔχομαι πάντοτε περὶ τῆς ὑγιείας σου.

A. D. 2dc. P. Amh. II 133 (102): πρὸ τῶν ὅλων ἀσπάζομαί σε καὶ εὐχαριστῶ σοι ὅτι ἐδήλωσάς μοι τὴν ὑγείαν σου.

A. D. 2dc. P. Giss. 13 (51): πρὸ μὲν παντὸς ἀσπάζομαί σε καὶ Ἀλινὴν τὴν κυρίαν καὶ τὰ παιδία σου.

A. D. 3dc. P. Grenf. II 73 (115): πρὸ τῶν ὅλων πολλά σε ἀσπάζομαι καὶ τοὺς παρὰ σοὶ πάντας ἀδελφοὺς ἐν Θεῷ.

A. D. 2dc. P. Giss. III 81 (74): ἀσπάζομαί σε πολλὰ καὶ τὸ προσκύνημά σου ποιῶ παρὰ τοῖς θεοῖς πᾶσι.

A. D. 2dc. P. Giss. III 85 (80): —— τοιοῦτό σοι μόνῳ εὐχαριστῶ παρὰ τῷ κυρίῳ Ἑρμῇ καὶ οὐ διαλείπω τὸ προσκύνημά σου ποιῶν καθ' ἑκάστην ἡμέραν.

---

A. D. 1st-2dc. B. G. U. II 451 (110): γενόμενοι εἰς Ἀλεξάνδρειαν τὸ προσκύνημά σου καὶ τῶν παιδίων σου καὶ τῆς ἀδελφῆς σου ἐποιήσαμεν παρὰ τῷ κυρίῳ Σαράπιδι καὶ τ——υτοῦ φίλου ——θεῶν ἐπιτρεπόντων.

A. D. 2d-3dc. B. G. U. II 623 (280): τὸ προσκύνημά σου ποιῶ παρὰ τῷ κυρίῳ Σαράπιδι καὶ τοῖς συννάοις θεοῖς.

A. D. 3dc. P. Ryl. 242 (390): τὸ προσκύνημά σου ποιῶ παρὰ τοῖς ἐνθάδε θεοῖς.

A. D. 3dc. P. Oxy. X 1296 (250): τὸ προσκύνημά σου ποιῶ καθ' ἑκάστην ἡμέραν παρὰ τοῖς ἐνθάδε θεοῖς.

A. D. 2d-3dc. P. Tebt. II 413 (287): τὸ προσκύνημά σου ποιῶ παρὰ τοῖς ἐνθάδε θεοῖς κατ' ἑκάστην ἡμέραν εὐχομένη σοι τὴν ὑγίαν.

A. D. 2dc. P. Tebt. II 412 (287): πρὸ μὲν πάντων τὸ προσκύνημά σου κατ' ἑκάστην ἡμέραν ποιῶ.

A. D. 3dc. P. B. M. III 973 (213): πρὸ μὲν πάντων τὸ προσκύνημά σου ποιῶ καθ' ἑκάστην ἡμέραν πρὸς τοῖς πατρῴοις θεοῖς.

A. D. 3dc. P. Tebt. II 418 (294): πρὸ τῶν ὅλων τὸ προσκύνημά σου ποιῶ παρὰ τῷ κυρίῳ Σαράπιδι καὶ τοῖς συννάοις θεοῖς εὐχόμενός σοι τὰ ἐν βίῳ κάλλιστα ὑπαρχθήσεσθαι.

---

A. D. 2dc. P. Giss. 22 (65): πρὸ πάντων εὔχομαί σε τὸν ἀγαθὸν ἀσπάσασθαι καὶ τὴν γλυκυτάτην σου ὄψιν προσκυνῆσαι —— νῦν ὄντως ἀμοιβὴν —— τῆς εὐσεβείας μου ἀναλαμβανούσης σε ἀπρόσκοπον καὶ ἱλαρώτατον. ταῦτα μοι ἡ πᾶσα εὐχή ἐστι καὶ μέριμνα.

A. D. 3dc. B. G. U. IV 1080 (125): πρὸ τῶν ὅλων ἀσπάζομαί σε συνχαίρων ἐπὶ τῇ ὑπαρχθείσῃ σοι ἀγαθῇ εὐσεβεῖ καὶ εὐτυχῇ συμβιώσι κατὰ τὰς κοινὰς ἡμῶν εὐχὰς καὶ προσευχὰς ἐφ' αἷς οἱ θεοὶ τέλιον ἐπακούσαντες παρέσχον.

A. D. 2dc. P. Giss. 21 (64): λίαν ἐχάρην ἀκούσασα ὅτι ἔρρωσαι καὶ ἡ ἀδελφή σου Σοῆρις.

A. D. 2dc. B. G. U. III 846 (170): 'Αντῶνις Λόνγος Νειλοῦτι τῇ μητρὶ πλεῖστα χαίρειν καὶ διὰ πάντων εὔχομαί σαι ὑγειαίνειν. τὸ προσκύνημά σου ποιῶ κατὰ αἰκάστην ἡμαίραν παρὰ τῷ κυρίῳ Σαράπιδι.

A. D. 2d-3dc. B. G. U. II 449 (108): A— to B— πλεῖστα χαίρειν καὶ τὸ προσκύνημά σου ποιῶ παρὰ τῷ κυρίῳ Σαράπιδι.

A. D. 3d-4thc. P. Oxy. XIV 1680 (140): ——φίλτατε πάτερ καὶ εὔχομαι τῷ θεῷ ὁλοκληρεῖν σε καὶ εὐοδοῦσθαι καὶ ὑγιαίνοντί σε ἀπολαβεῖν ἐν τοῖς ἰδίοις.

---

## The ἀσπάσασθαι Wish and Miscellaneous Phrases.

Sometimes instead of the ὑγιαίνειν wish the ἀσπάσασθαι wish occurs at the beginning of the letter. This salutation, in varying forms, ordinarily occurs at the end of letters, as early as the first century B. C. It has been thought that this form has been transposed from the end of the letter to the beginning; and the view is quite probable. As the other wishes, this formula also is very flexible, admitting various minor changes. The proscynesis is found in connection with it.

In the last section we have placed a few miscellaneous phrases, some of a rather elaborate type, others illustrating the connection of the proscynesis with the opening formula.

It may be added that many letters of a familiar character are without any other introduction than the opening formula.

---

## A. II. THE FINAL PHRASES

### I. In Familiar Letters.

B. C. 240 (252?): P. P. II (27): *ἐπιμέλου δὲ καὶ σαυτοῦ ὅπως ὑγιαίνῃς καὶ πρὸς ἡμᾶς ἐρρωμένος ἔλθῃς.*

B. C. 223 P. P. II 40 (P. P. III p. 149): *καὶ περὶ ὑμῶν ἐντείνεσθε ἕως ἂν ὑγιαίνοντας ὑμᾶς ἴδωμεν.*

B. C. 223 P. Eleph. 13 (47): *εὐχαριστήσεις οὖμ μοι σαυτοῦ τε ἐπιμελόμενος(καὶ μὴ ὀκνῶν γράφειν ἡμῖν καὶ τί ἂν σου ποιοῦντες χαριζοίμην.)*

B. C. 172 P. B. M. I 42 (29): *χαριεῖ δὲ καὶ τοῦ σώματος ἐπιμελόμενος ἵν' ὑγιαίνῃς.*

B. C. 168 P. Vat. A (Witk. p. 64): *συντόμως πειραθεὶς παραγενέσθαι καὶ τοῦ σώματος ἐπιμελόμενος ἵν' ὑγιαίνῃς.*

B. C. 162 P. Par. 32 (Witk. p. 66): *ἐπιμέλου δὲ τοῦ σώματος ὅπως ὑγιαίνοντας ὑμᾶς ἀσπασώμεθα.*

B. C. 153 P. Par. 46 (Witk. p. 85): *ἐπιμέλου με καὶ σαυτοῦ ἵν' ὑγιαίνῃς καὶ περὶ ὧν ἂν βούλῃι γράφε.*

B. C. 2dc. P. Good. 4 (8): *μάλιστα δὲ σαυτοῦ ἐπιμελόμενος ἵν' ὑγιαίνῃς.*

B. C. 2dc. P. Tebt. I 55 (165): *τὰ δὲ ἄλλα ἐπιμέλου σαυτοῦ ἵν' ὑγιαίνῃς.*

B. C. 118 P. Tebt. I 12 (75)a: *τὰ ἄλλα σαυτοῦ ἐπιμελόμενος ἵν' ὑγιαίνῃς.*

B. C. 118 P. Tebt. I 12 (75)b: *τὰ δ' ἄλλα χαιριεῖ σαυτοῦ ἐπιμελόμενος.*

B. C. 114 P. Tebt. I 19 (89): *ἐπιμελόμενος δὲ καὶ σαυτοῦ ἵν' ὑγιαίνῃς.*

also: B. C. 113 P. Tebt. I 20 (90);

B. C. 103 P. Amh. II 39 (P. Grenf. I 30 (59)): *ἐπιμελόμενοι δὲ καὶ ἑαυτῶν ἵν' ὑγιαίνητε.*

also: B. C. 102 P. Grenf. I 32 (61); cp. also B. C. 99 P. Grenf. I 35 (66);

B. C. 95 P. Grenf. II 36 (61): *τὰ δ' ἄλλα χαρίζοισθ' ἑαυτῶν ἐπιμελόμενοι ἵν' ὑγιαίνητε. ἔρρωται Ὧρος καὶ Πετοσῖρις.*

B. C. 1stc. P. Tebt. II 284 (43): *καὶ σεαυτῆς ἐπιμελομένη ἵν' ὑγιαίνῃς.*

B. C. 1stc. P. Oxy. XII 1479 (237): *καὶ σεαυτοῦ ἐπιμέλου ἵν' ὑγιέ(νῃς).*

also: B. C. 23 B. G. U. IV 1209 (351); cp. also: B. C. 29 B. G. U. IV 1203 (315); B. C. 28 B. G. U. IV 1205, 1206 (346); B. C. 22 P. Oxy. VII 1061 (214);

B. C. 25 P. Oxy. IV 805 (256): ἀσπάζου πάντας τοὺς παρ' ἡμῶν καὶ σεαυτῆς ἐπιμέλου ἵν' ὑγιαίνῃς εὐτυχοῦσα.
B. C. 28 B. G. U. IV 1204 (345): καὶ σεατοῦ [ἐπιμέλου ἵν'] ὑγιαίνῃς ὅ δὴ μέγιστόν ἐστι.
B. C. 27 B. G. U. IV 1208 (349): τὰ δ' ἄλλα χαριεῖ τοῦ σώματος ἐπιμελόμενος ἵν' ὑγιένῃς ὃ δὴ μέγιστον ἡγοῦμαι.
B. C. 2 P. Oxy. 743 (242): σεατοῦ ἐπιμέλου ἵν' ὑγιαίνῃς. ἐπισκοποῦ τοὺς σοὺς πάντες.
B. C. 30-A. D. 1: P. Tebt. II 382 (228): γράφομεν ὑμῖν ἵν' ᾖ ἐπιμελές τἄλλα ἐπινοεῖν ὡς καθήκει.
A. D. 1 P. Oxy. IV 745 (244): ἀσπάζου πάντας τοὺς σοὺς καὶ σεαυτοῦ ἐπιμέλου ἵν' ὑγιαίνῃς.
A. D. 3 P. Tebt. II 408 (282): τὰ δ' ἄλλα ἵν' ὑγιαίνῃς.
A. D. 22 P. Oxy. II 294 (294): πρὸ μὲν πάντων σεαυτοῦ ἐπιμέλου εἵν' ὑγιαίνῃς· ἐπισκοποῦ Δημητροῦν καὶ Δωρίωνα τὸν πατέρα.
A. D. 39 B. G. U. IV 1078 (122): τὰ δ' ἄλλα ἐπιμελῶσθε ἀτῶν ἵν' ὑγιαίνητε· ἀσπάζου κτλ.
A. D. 1stc. P. Oxy. VIII 1154 (256): πρὸ πάντων ὡς ἐνετειλάμην σοι κατ' ὄψιν ἐπιμέλου σεαυτῆς ἵνα μοι ὑγιαίνῃς.

---

B. C. 3dc. P. Grenf. II 14 (26)d: χαρίεισαί μοι τοῦτο ποιήσας.
B. C. 130 P. Tebt. I 56 (166): τοῦτο δὲ ποιήσας ἔσῃι μοι κεχαρισμένος εἰς τὸν ἅπαντα χρόνον.
B. C. 131 P. Revill. Mel. p. 295 (Archiv II p. 517): ἐπισκοποῦ καὶ τὰς ἀδελφὰς καὶ Πέλοπα καὶ Στάχυν καὶ Σεναθῦριν.
A. D. 2dc.! P. Giss. I 12 (49): ἐπισκοποῦμαι τὴν σὴν σύνβιον καὶ τοὺς φιλοῦντάς σε πάντας.
A. D. 27 P. Oxy. II 293 (293): ἐπισκοποῦ δὲ ὑμᾶς καὶ πάντας τοὺς ἐν οἴκῳ.
see also: A. D. 22 P. Oxy. II 294 (294);
B. C. 2 P. Oxy. IV 742 (241): μὴ ἀμελήσῃς.
A. D. 3dc. P. Oxy. XIV 1665 (120): ἀλλ' ὅρα μὴ ἀμελήσῃς.
also: A. D. 3d-4thc. P. Oxy. I 112 (177);
B. C. 1 P. Oxy. IV 744: ἐρωτῶ σε οὖν ἵνα μὴ ἀγωνιάσῃς.
A. D. 1stc. P. Fay. 109 (260): μὴ οὖν ἄλλως ποιήσῃς.
also: P. Fay. 110, 111, 112, 119, (261-275) A. D. 94-100; A. D. 3 P. Tebt. II 408 (282); A. D. 40 P. Ryl. 230 (379); A. D. 104 P. Fay. 116 (271); A. D. 110 P. Fay. 118 (277); A. D. 2dc. P. Tebt. II 411 (286); A. D. 2d-3dc. B. G. U. III 884 (200); etc. etc.
A. D. 2d-3dc. P. Oxy. VI 928 (293): τὰ παιδία παρ' ἐμοῦ καὶ Ἰσιδωρίωνος προσαγόρευε.
A. D. 3d-4thc. P. Oxy. XII 1492 (249): πάντας τοὺς ἐν τῷ οἴκῳ σου ἅπαντας προσαγόρευε.

---

B. C. 22 P. Oxy. VII 1061 (214): ἀσπάζου τοὺς σοὺς πάντας. ἀσπάζεται κτλ.

Also supra. B. C. 25 P. Oxy. IV 805 (256);

A. D. 1stc. P. B. M. II 356 (252): ἄσπασαι τοὺς σοὺς πάντας.

also: A. D. 57 P. Oxy. II 269 (250); A. D. 84 B. G. U. II 596 (240) etc. etc. etc.

A. D. 2dc. P. Oxy. XIV 1757 (180): ἄσπασαι Κλαυδίαν τὴν ἀγαθοτάτην καὶ τοὺς φιλοῦντάς σε πάντας.

A. D. 2d-3dc. B. G. U. I 48 (62): ἄσπασαι τὰ παιδία καὶ τὴν σύμβιόν σου.

A. D. 2d-3dc. P. Oxy. I 114 (180): ἄσπασαι πολλὰ 'Αίαν καὶ Εὐτυχίαν.

A. D. 99 P. Fay. 112 (166): ἀσπάζου Ἥρωνα καὶ 'Ορσενοῦφιν καὶ τοὺς ἐν ὕκῳ πάντες.

also 2dc. A. D. P. Tebt. II 314 (113); etc. etc.

A. D. 2dc. P. Tebt. II 412 (287): ἀσπάζου τὴν μητέρα σου καὶ τὸν πατέρα σου.

A. D. 2dc. P. Iand. 9 (42): ἀσπάζου κτλ. καὶ πάντας τοὺς ἐν οἴκῳ κατ' ὄνομα.

also: A. D. 2d-3dc. B. G. U. I 93 (111); A. D. 3dc. P. Oxy. XIV 1769 (184); etc. etc.

A. D. 110 P. Fay. 118 (273): ἀσπάζου τοὺς φιλοῦντές σε πάντες πρὸς ἀλήθιαν.

A. D. 1stc. P. Oxy. II 300 (301): ἀσπάζεται ὑμᾶς Λογγεῖνος. ἀσπάζου κτλ.

A. D. 2d-3dc P. Oxy. I 114 (180): ἀσπάζεται 'Αίαν Ξάνθιλλα καὶ πάντας τοὺς αὐτῆς.

A. D. 2dc. P. Iand. 9 (42): πλεῖστα κτλ. ἀσπάζεται ὑμᾶς πάντας κατ' ὄνομα Λοπεινᾶς.

A. D. 2d-3dc. P. Oxy. VI 930 (295): ἀσπάζονται κτλ· κατ' ὄνομα.

also: A. D. 2d-3dc. B. G. U. I 261 (261); II 449 (108); etc. etc.

A. D. 2dc. P. Tebt. II 415 (291): ἀσπάζομαι πολλὰ τὸν πατέρα σου καὶ τοὺς ἐνοίκους πάντας.

.A. D. 2d-3dc. B. G. U. I. 276 (273): ἀσπάζομαι ὑμᾶς πάντες κατ' ὄνομα.

cp. also: B. G. U. II 384 (42); A. D. 2dc. B. G. U. I 602 (246); P. Oxy. XIV 1758 (181); A. D. 3dc. P. Oxy. XIV 1767 (184); 1770 (185); etc. etc.

A. D. 2d-3dc. B. G. U. I 27 (41): ἀσπάζομαι κτλ. πολλὰ κτλ. κατ' ὄνομα.

A. D. 3dc. P. Oxy. VII 1067 (221): ἀσπάζομαι ὑμᾶς πολλά.

A. D. 3d-4thc. P. Oxy. I 123 (100): ἀσπάζομαι τὴν γλυκυτάτην μου θυγατέρα Μακαρίαν καὶ τὴν δεσποίνην μου μητέραν ὑμῶν καὶ ὅλους τοὺς ἡμῶν κατ' ὄνομα.

---

## 1. In Familiar Letters.

The basic formula at the end of familiar letters during the Ptolemaic period is: ἐπιμέλου δὲ σεαυτοῦ ἵν' ὑγιαίνῃς. This formula also admits many variations, either by way of substitution, as ὅπως for ἵνα, or σώματος for σεαυτοῦ; or by way of addition, as the adding of the words τὰ δὲ ἄλλα, and other phrases. The verb ἐπιμέλου is at times converted into the participle ἐπιμελόμενος, which then is dependent on another verb, χαρίζοισθε, χαριεῖ, etc., or even on the closing formula ἔρρωσο.

There is a close connection between this final phrase and the ἐρρῶσθαι wish. Many texts, quoted to support the former, will be found with the latter also. Both phrases make their first appearance about the same time; and when the combined ἐρρῶσθαι wish ceases to be used, the ἐπιμέλου final phrase also disappears, that is, during the first hundred years of the Christian era.

During the Roman period, especially from the beginning of Augustus' reign, the ἀσπάσασθαι phrase is mainly employed. Its basic form is: ἀσπάζου (ἄσπασαι) τοὺς σοὺς πάντας. In this form it occurs during the first century B. C. P. Par. 32, dated B. C. 162, combines the salutation with the older form: ἐπιμέλου δὲ τοῦ σώματος ὅπως ὑγιαίνοντας ὑμᾶς ἀσπασώμεθα. The ἀσπάσασθαι phrase is of very frequent occurrence in familiar letters. The briefest form consists of the verb only and the name of the person saluted. Frequently the writer commissions the recipient of the letter to convey his greetings to others mentioned. Hence one meets not rarely with letters in which there is an accumulation of greetings, the verbs employed being: ἀσπάζου ——, ἄσπασαι——, ἀσπάζομαι——. The writer himself frequently transmits the greetings of others: —— ἀσπάζεται ——. We have quoted a few examples of each, by way of illustration, selecting as a rule the more developed forms. It has already been pointed out by Deissmann and others that the frequent greetings in the Pauline epistles reflect the custom of the times. The ἀσπάσασθαι formula was still in use at the end of the Roman period.

---

## 2. In Petitions.

B. C. 254 P. S. I. IV 352 (86): δέομαι οὖν σου εἰ σοὶ δοκεῖ βοήθησόμ μοι.

B. C. 248 P. S. I. IV 383 (110): δέομαί σου βασιλεῦ ἀποσταλῆναί μου ἔντευξιν κτλ. ἵνα καταπεφευγὼς ἐπὶ σὲ τὸμ πάντων σωτῆρα μὴ ἀδικηθῶ ἀλλὰ τῶν δικαίων τύχω.

B. C. 222 P. Lille II 2 (65): δέομαι οὖν βασιλεῦ προστάξαι κτλ. γράψαι κτλ. ἵνα ἐπὶ σὲ καταφυγοῦσα βασιλεῦ τοῦ δικαίου τύχω.

B. C. 221 P. Lille II 9 (90): δέομαι οὖν σου βασιλεῦ εἰ σοὶ δοκεῖ προστάξαι κτλ. γράψαι κτλ.
also B. C. 222 P. Lille II 11 (95): προστάξαι κτλ. ἐπισκέψασθαι κτλ.
B. C. 141 P. Rein. 7 (54): ἠνάγκασμαι τὴν ἐφ' ὑμᾶς καταφυγὴν ποιήσασθαι. δέομαι οὖν ἵνα τύχω βοηθείας.
B. C. 99 P. Leid. G (41)b; (also H 47 b): καὶ ἀξιῶ δεόμενος ἐὰν ὑμῖν δοκῇ προστάξαι κτλ. ἵνα τυχὼν τῆς παρ' ὑμῶν φιλανθρωπίας ἐπιτελῶ τὰς τῶν θεῶν λειτουργίας.
B. C. Ptol. P. P. III 27 (57): δέομαι κτλ. ἵνα ἐπὶ σὲ καταφυγοῦσα καὶ τοῦ δικαίου τύχω.
B. C. 250 P. P. III 32 (69): ἀξιοῦμεν κτλ. γράψαι κτλ. ἐπιστεῖλαι κτλ.
B. C. 240 P. P. III 29 (62): ἀξιῶ κτλ. ἀνακαλέσασθαι κτλ. ἵνα τύχω τῆς παρὰ σοῦ φιλανθρωπίας.
B. C. 223 P. Eleph. 19 (62): ἀξιῶ σε ἀνακαλέσασθαι Μίλωνι καὶ ἐπιτάξαι αὐτῶι ὅπως πλεῖον γίνηται τῶι βασιλεῖ.
B. C. 161 P. B. M. I 44 (33): ἀξιῶ οὖν σε ἐὰν φαίνηται συντάξαι μεταστῆσαι αὐτοὺς ἐπὶ σὲ ὅπως περὶ ἁπάντων τούτων τύχωσι τῆς προσηκούσης μισοπονηρίας.
B. C. 118 P. S. I. III 168 (23): ἀξιῶ ἐὰν φαίνηται ἀναγαγόντα αὐτοὺς ἐνδεχομένην ἔμσκεψιν ποήσασθαι ἵν' ἐὰν ἐνσχεθῶσι τύχωσι τῶν ἐξακολουθούντων.
B. C. 2dc. P. Ryl. 66 (8): ἀξιῶ κτλ. ἐὰν φαίνηται κτλ. συντάξαι κτλ. γράψαι κτλ.
B. C. 116-111 P. B. M. II 401 (12): διὸ καταπεφευγυῖαι ἐπὶ σὲ ἀξιοῦμεν ἐὰν φαίνηται κτλ. etc. etc.
B. C. 3dc. P. S. I. IV 399 (128): ἵνα μὴ τῷ ῥίγει καὶ τῆι λιμῶι ἀπόλωμαι καὶ οὕτως διὰ σὲ βασιλεῦ τετευχὼς ὦ τοῦ δικαίου.
B. C. 3dc. P. S. I. IV 442 (168): ὅπως ἂν μηθείς σε παρακρούηται καὶ ἐγὼ πολυωρίας τύχω.
B. C. 240 P. P. III 32 (66): ἵνα καὶ αὐτὸς δύνωμαι τὰ δίκαια ποιῆσαι.
B. C. 3dc. B. G. U. III 1006 (345): ἵνα διὰ σοῦ τοῦ δικαίου τύχω.
B. C. 3dc. P. P. III 36 (74): ἵνα τῆς σωτηρίας τύχω.
B. C. 221 P. Lille II 23 (136): ὅπως ἂν τύχωμεν τῆς παρὰ σοῦ φιλανθρωπίας.
B. C. 221 P. Lille II 18 (124): ἵνα ὦ βασιλεῦ διὰ σοῦ τοῦ δικαίου καὶ ἐλέου τετευχὼς εἰς τὸ λοιπὸν τοῦ βίου.
B. C. 221 P. Lille II 25 (143): ἵνα μὴ ἀδικηθῶ ἀλλ' ἐπὶ σὲ καταφυγὼν βασιλεῦ τῶν πάντων εὐεργέτην τοῦ δικαίου τύχω.
B. C. 221 P. Lille II 34 (182): ἵνα τοῦ δικαίου τύχω διὰ σὲ βασιλεῦ.
B. C. 218 P. Lille II 26 (146): ἵνα ἐπὶ σὲ καταφυγόντες βασιλεῦ τύχωμεν τοῦ δικαίου.

B. C. 218 P. Lille II 13 (107): ἵνα ἐπὶ σὲ προσφυγόντες βασιλεῦ τὸν πάντων βοηθὸν καὶ εὐεργέτην τοῦ δικαίου τύχωμεν.

B. C. 160 P. B. M. I 45 (35): ἵν' ὦ καὶ αὐτὸς μετελειψὼς τῆς παρ' ὑμῶν εἰς τὸν βίον ἀντιλήψεως.

B. C. 116 P. B. M. II 401 (12): ἵνα ὦμεν ἀντειλημένοι.

B. C. 2dc. B. G. U. III 1012 (352): ἵνα τύχω τῶν δικαίων.

B. C. 260 P. P. II 2 (3): φρόντισαι ὅπως τῶν δικαίων τύχηι.

B. C. 3dc. P. P. III 36 (73)a: δυνατὸς γὰρ εἶ καὶ ἔσει με σεσωικώς.

B. C. 161 P. B. M. I 44 (33) within the document: ἐπὶ σὲ τὴν καταφυγὴν ποιοῦμαι νομίζων μάλισθ' οὕτως τεύξεσθαι τῶν δικαίων.

B. C. 246 P. P. III 20 (39): ἐφ' ὑμᾶς καταπεφευγὼς οὕτως δικαίου τετευχώς.

B. C. 250 P. S. I. IV 372 (101): καλῶς ἂμ ποιήσαις γράψας Λέοντι περὶ τούτων ὡς σοὶ δοκεῖ.

B. C. 248 P. S. I. IV 383 (112): καλῶς ἂν οὖμ ποιήσαις εἰ σοὶ φαίνεται γράψας κτλ. καὶ μὴ ἀδικῶμαι ὑπ' αὐτῶν.

B. C. 2dc. P. Ryl. 66 (8): τύχων τῆς παρὰ σοῦ ἀντιλήψεως.

B. C. 89 P. Ryl. 68 (9): ἵνα λάβω παρ' αὐτῆς τὸ δίκαιον ὡς καθήκει.

B. C. 34 P. Ryl. 69 (10): πρὸς τὸ μηθὲν τῶν ἐκφορίων διαπεσεῖν αὐτὸς δὲ τύχηι ὧν προσήκει.

B. C. 241 P. P. II 12 (31): ἀλλὰ διὰ σὲ τοῦ δικαίου τύχω.

B. C. 250 P. P. II 32 (108): τούτου δὲ γενομένου ἔσομαι τετευχὼς τῶν παρὰ σοῦ φιλανθρώπων.

B. C. 250 P. P. III 32 (69): τούτου δὲ γενομένου ἐσόμεθα τῆς παρὰ σοῦ βοηθείας τετευχότες.

B. C. 241 P. P. II 12 (31): τούτου γὰρ γενομένου οὐ τὸν πλείω χρόνον καταφθαρησόμεθα ἀλλὰ διὰ σὲ τῆς πάσης φιλανθρωπίας τευξόμεθα.

B. C. 225 P. Eleph. 27 (75): τούτου δὲ γενομένου ἐσόμεθα οὐκ ἠδικημένοι.

B. C. 222 P. Lille II 12 (102): τούτου δὲ γενομένου ἔσομαι βασιλεῦ τῆς παρὰ σοῦ βοηθείας τετευχώς.

B. C. 231 P. Lille II 14 (112): τούτου γὰρ γενομένου βασιλεῦ οὐ ἀδικηθήσομαι χρείας καὶ σοὶ καὶ τῶι σῶι πατρὶ ἀμέμπτως παρεσχημένος.

B. C. 221 P. Lille II 21 (130): τούτου γὰρ γενομένου βασιλεῦ ἐπὶ σὲ καταφυγὼν τὸγ κοινὸν εὐεργέτην καὶ βοηθὸν τεύξομαι τῆς παρὰ σοῦ βοηθείας.

B. C. 222 P. Lille II 4 (74): τούτου γὰρ γενομένου ἐπὶ σὲ καταφυγὼν τῶν πάντων κοινὸν εὐεργέτην ἔσομαι τοῦ δικαίου τετευχώς.

also P. Lille II 5 (at the end: τεύξομαι τοῦ δικαίου).

---

B. C. 222 P. Lille II 6: τούτου γὰρ γενομένου [——σω]τῆρα τοῦ δικαίου καὶ βοηθείας τεύξομαι.

B. C. 222 P. Lille II 3 (69): τούτου δὲ γενομένου ἐσόμεθα τοῦ δικαίου τετευχότες.

B. C. 221 P. Lille 22 (133): τούτου γὰρ γενομένου ἔσομαι διὰ σὲ βασιλεῦ τετευχὼς ὢν [τοῦ δικαίου].

B. C. 218 P. Lille II 27 (151): τούτου γὰρ γενομένου ἐπὶ σὲ καταφυγοῦσα βασιλεῦ τεύξομαι τῆς πάσης βοηθείας.

B. C. 218 P. Lille II 7 (82): τούτου [———] τὸν πάντων βοηθὸν τῶν δικαίων τεύξομαι.

B. C. 218 P. Lille II 31 (167): ——— τῶν εὐγνωμόνων τύχω.

B. C. 218 P. Lille II 28 (153): τούτου γὰρ γενομένου ἐπὶ σὲ καταφυγὼν βασιλεῦ κτλ. ἐγώ τε ἔσομαι τῆς παρὰ σοῦ φιλανθρωπίας τετευχώς.

B. C. Ptol. P. Leid. A (1): τούτου δὲ γενομένου ἔσομαι τετευχὼς τῆς παρὰ σοῦ ἀντιλήψεως.

also: P. Vat. D. vs. 21; B. C. 93-60 P. Tebt. II 283 (41); B. C. 141 P. Rein 7 (54);

B. C. 164 P. Leid. B (9): τούτου δὲ γενομένου δυνησόμεθα τὴν καθ' ἡμᾶς λειτουργίαν ἀμέμπτως τῶι μεγίστωι θεῶι Σαράπει ἐπιτελεῖν ὃς διδοίη σοι μετὰ τῆς Ἴσιος νίκην κράτος τῆς οἰκουμένης ἁπάσης.

B. C. 164 P. B. M. I 22 (7): τούτου δὲ γενομένου ἐσόμεθα τετευχυῖαι τῆς παρὰ σοῦ βοηθείας καὶ διὰ σὲ τὰς χρείας ἐπιτελοῦσαι τῶι θεῶι.

B. C. 163 P. B. M. I 44 (31): τούτου δὲ γενομένου τεύξομαι βοηθείας.

B. C. 158 P. B. M. I 23 (37): τούτου δὲ γενομένου ἔσομαι δι' ὑμᾶς ἐσχηκὼς τὸν βίον τὸν ἀέναον χρόνον.

B. C. 144 P. Meyer 1 (3): τούτου δὲ γενομένου τευξόμεθα τῆς παρ' ὑμῶν εἰς τὸν βίον βοηθείας.

B. C. 135 P. Grenf. I 15 (35): τούτου γὰρ γενομένου ἐσόμεθα βεβοηθημέναι.

cp. also: B. C. 115 P. Fay. 11 (100);

B. C. 108 P. Grenf. I 37 (68): τούτων γὰρ γενομένων ἐσόμεθα βεβοηθημένοι ὑφ' ὑμῶν.

B. C. 108 P. Rein. 18 (95): τούτου δὲ γενομένου οὐδὲν τῶν τῶι βασιλεῖ χρησίμων διαπεσεῖται ἐγώ τε ἔσομαι ἀντειλημμένος.

B. C. 103 P. Fay. 12 (103): τούτων δὲ γενομένων ἔσομαι ἀντειλημμένος.

cp. also: B. C. 1stc. P. Oxy. XII 1465 (191).

B. C. 157 P. Amh. II 34 (41): τούτων δὲ γενομένων ἐσόμεθα τετευχότες τῆς παρ' ὑμῶν βοηθείας.

---

B. C. 13 B. G. U. IV 1197 (338): ἵνα ὦμεν εὐεργετημένοι.

also: A. D. 71 P. Tebt. II 302 (88); A. D. 140 P. Fay. 106 (257); A. D. 2dc P. Strassb. I 57 (191); A. D. 266 P. Tebt. II 326 (136);

A. D. 14 P. B. M. II 357 (165): ἵνα ὦ ὑπὸ σοῦ εὐεργετημένος.

A. D. 40 P. B. M. II 177 (167): διὸ ἀξιῶ σὲ τὸν πάντων σωτῆρα καὶ εὐεργέτην ἐὰν φαίνηται διαλαβεῖν ὅπως τύχω τῶν δικαίων ἵν' ὦ εὖ ἐνευεργετημένος.

A. D. 54 P. Ryl. 119 (106): ὧν χάριν ἀξιοῦμεν περὶ πάντων τούτων διαλαβεῖν ὅπως τύχωμεν τῶν παρὰ σοῦ δικαίων καὶ ὦμεν εὐεργετημένοι.

A. D. 140 P. B. M. III 846 (131): διὸ ἀξιῶ σε τὸν κύριον βοηθῆσαί μοι ἵνα τύχω τῆς ἀπὸ σοῦ εὐεργεσίας.

A. D. 145 P. Gen. 54 (42): ἀξιῶ σε τὸν εὐεργέτην ἐάν σοι δόξῃ ποιῆσαι τὰ δέοντα πρὸς αὐτὸν καὶ πέρας ἐπιθεῖναι τοῖς κακουργήμασι κτλ. ἵνα ὦ εὐεργετημένη.

A. D. 139 P. Amh. II 77 (94): ὅθεν κατὰ τὸ ἀναγκαῖον ἐπιδίδωμι καὶ ἀξιῶ ἐὰν δόξῃ σοι κτλ. ἵνα δυνηθῶ τὴν ἀπόδιξιν ἐπ' αὐτοὺς ποιησάμενος τυχεῖν καὶ τῆς ἀπὸ σοῦ εὐεργεσίας.

A. D. 169 B. G. U. I 168 (177): ὅθεν ἀξιῶ ἐὰν σαυτῇ τύχῃ δόξῃ διακοῦσαί μου πρὸς αὐτοὺς ὅπως δήποτε ἐκ τῆς σῆς εὐεργεσίας δυνηθῶσι οἱ ἀφήλικες τῶν ἰδίων ἀντιλαμβάνεσθαι ἵν' ὦ σὺν αὐτοῖς ὑπὸ σοῦ εὐεργετημένος.

A. D. 193 B. G. U. I 46 (60): διὸ ἐπιδίδωμι τόδε τὸ βιβλίδιον ἀξιῶν κτλ. ἵν' ὦ ὑπὸ σοῦ τοῦ κυρίου εὐεργετημένος καὶ βεβοηθημένος.

B. C. 1 B. G. U. IV 1189 (327): ἀξιῶ ἐὰν φαίνηται ἐπιτάξαι κτλ. ἵνα ὦι τῆς σῆς βοηθείας τετυχηκώς.

A. D. 136 P. Gen. 18 (39): διὸ ἀξιοῦμεν μένειν παρὰ σοὶ κτλ. καὶ ἀχθῆναι κτλ ἵν' ὦμεν ὑπὸ σοῦ βεβοιηθημένοι.

A. D. 176 P. Tebt. II 332 (145): ὅθεν ἐπιδίδωμι καὶ ἀξιῶ τὴν δέουσαν ἐξέτασιν γενέσθαι ἐξ ὧν δέον ἐστὶν ἵν' ὦ ὑπὸ σοῦ βεβοηθημένος.

A. D. 193 B. G. U. II 454 (113): διὸ ἐπιδίδωμι καὶ ἀξιῶ τὴν δέουσαν ἐξέτασιν γενέσθαι κτλ. καὶ ὦμεν ὑπὸ σοῦ βεβοηθημένοι.

A. D. 217 P. Oxy. IX 1202 (230): κατὰ τὸ ἀναγκαῖον προσφεύγω σοι ἀξιῶν ἐνταγῆναι κτλ. καὶ ὦ βεβοηθημένος.

A. D. 28 P. Ryl. 125 (120): διὸ ἀξιῶ ἐὰν φαίνηται ἀχθῆναι τὸν ἐνκαλούμενον ἐπὶ σὲ πρὸς τὴν ἐσομένην ἐπέξοδον.

also: P. Ryl. 126 (122); 128 (125); 131 (127) A. D. 31;

A. D. 29 P. Ryl. 127 (123): διὸ ἀξιῶ συντάξαι τῷ τῆς Εὐημερίας ἀρχεφόδωι ἀναζητῆσαι ὑπὲρ τοῦ μέρους καὶ τοὺς αἰτίους ἐξαποστεῖλαι ἐπὶ σὲ πρὸς τὴν ἐσομένην ἐπέξοδον.

A. D. 31 P. Ryl. 130 (127): διὸ ἀξιῶι ἐὰν φαίνηται συντάξαι γράψαι ἀναζητῆσαι ὑπὲρ τοῦ μέρους πρὸς τὴν ἐσομένην ἐπέξοδον.

Cp. also: P. Ryl 137 (134) A. D. 34; also P. Ryl. 134, 140, 142;

A. D. 34 P. Ryl. 139 (136): *διὸ ἀξιῶ γράψαι τῷ τῆς κώιμης ἀρχεφόδῳ ὅπως τὴν ἀναζήτησιν ποιήσηται καὶ τοὺς τὸ τοιοῦτο διαπράξαντες ἀχθῆναι ἐπὶ σὲ πρὸς τὴν ἐσομένην ἐπέξοδον.*

A. D. 34 P. Ryl. 136 (133): *ἀξιῶι γραφῆναι τῶι τῆς κώμης ἀρχεφόδῳ καταστῆσαι ἐπὶ σὲ πρὸς τὴν ἐσομένην ἐπέξοδον.*

A. D. 34 P. Ryl. 135 (132): *διὸ δίδυμε (— δίδομαι) τὸ ὑπόμνημα ὕπος (— ὅπως) ἀναζητήσῃ ὁ τῆς κώμης ἀρχήφοδος καὶ ἀκθῆναι τοὺς αἰδίους ἐπὶ σὲ ἔκξοδον.*

A. D. 38 P. Ryl. 143 (140): *διὸ ἀξιῶ γράψαι ἀκθῆναι τὸν ἐνκαλούμενον ἐπὶ σὲ πρὸς τὴν δέουσαν ἐπέξοδον.*

also: P. Ryl. 144 (141); A. D. 39 P. Ryl. 147 (144); cp. B. G. U. I 22 (36) A. D. 114.

A. D. 39 P. Ryl. 146 (143): *διὸ ἀξιῶ γράψαι ἀναζητῆσαι ὑπὲρ τοῦ μέρους πρὸς τὴν δέουσαν ἐπέξοδον.*

A. D. 39 P. Ryl. 149 (146): *ἀξιῶ καταστῆσαι αὐτοὺς ἐπὶ σὲ πρὸς τὴν ἐσομένην ἐπέξοδον.*

A. D. 2d-3dc. B. G. U. I 39 (51): *ἀξιῶ ἀχθῆναι αὐτοὺς ἐπὶ σὲ πρὸς τὴν δέουσαν ἐπέξοδον.*

---

A. D. 20-50 P. Oxy. II 281 (271): *διὸ ἀξιῶ συντάξαι καταστῆσαι αὐτὸν ἐπὶ σὲ ὅπως ἐπαναγκασθῇ κτλ.*

A. D. 30-35 P. Oxy. II 282 (273): *διὸ ἀξιῶ ἀχθῆναι ταύτην ἐπὶ σὲ ὅπως τύχῃ ὧν προσήκει καὶ ἀποδῷ μοι τὰ ἡμέτερα.*

A. D. 108 B. G. U. IV 1036 (38): *διὸ ἀξιῶ ἀχθῆναι αὐτοὺς ἐπὶ σὲ ὅπως τύχω τῆς ἀπὸ σοῦ δικαιωδωσίας.*

A. D. 131 P. Tebt. II 371 (143): *ἀξιῶ ἀχθῆναι αὐτοὺς ἐπὶ σέ.*

A. D. 185 P. B. M. II 342 (173): *ὅθεν ἐπιδίδωμι καὶ ἀξιῶ ἀχθῆναι αὐτοὺς ἐπὶ σέ.*

A. D. 167 P. Tebt. II 304 (94): *ἀξιῶ καιλεύσεται ἀχθῆναι αὐτὸν ἐπὶ σὲ πρὸς τὸ ἀκόλουθον γείνεσθαι καὶ τυχεῖν με τῆς δεούσης ἐγδικίας.*

A. D. 193 B. G. U. II 515 (162): *ἀξιῶ [ἀχθῆναι] αὐτοὺς ἐπὶ σὲ ὅπως τῶν ἀπὸ σοῦ δικαίων τύχω.*

A. D. 195 B. G. U. III 778 (79): *περὶ πάντα ἐπιμέλεαν κελεῦσαι αὐτὸν ἀχθῆναι ἐπὶ σὲ λόγον ἀποδώσοντα περὶ τῶν ὑπ' αὐτοῦ τετολμημένων.*

A. D. 207 P. Gen. 10 (22): *ἐπιδίδομεν ἀξιοῦντες ἐὰν σοὶ δόξῃ κελεῦσαι αὐτοὺς ἀχθῆναι ἐπὶ σὲ λόγον ἀποδώσοντας περὶ τούτου.*

A. D. 2d-3dc. B. G. U. I 157 (170): *ὅθεν ἐπιδίδωμι καὶ ἀξιῶ ἀχθῆναι αὐτὸν ἐπὶ σὲ καὶ τυχεῖν τῶν ἀπὸ σοῦ δικαίων.*

---

A. D. 30 P. Ryl. 129 (126): *διὸ ἀξιῶι τὴν ἀναζήτησιν ποιήσασθαι καὶ τοὺς τὸ τοιοῦτο διαπράξαντας τυχεῖν ὧν προσῆκόν ἐστιν.*

A. D. 33 P. Ryl. 133 (129): διὸ ἀξιῶι διαλαβεῖν ὑπὲρ τοῦ μέρους.

A. D. 37 P. Ryl. 141 (138): διὸ ἀξιῶι ἀντιλήμψεως τυχεῖν ἵνα μηδὲν τῶν δημοσίων διαπέσῃ.

A. D. 50 P. Oxy. II 284 (275): διὸ ἀξιῶι διαλαβεῖν κατ' αὐτοῦ ὡς ἐὰν σοὶ δοκῇ.

A. D. 50 P. Oxy. II 285 (276): διὸ ἀξιῶ διαλαβεῖν κατ' αὐτοῦ ὡς ἐάν σοι φαίνηται.

A. D. 1st c. P. Amh. II 68 (75): ὅπως οὖν τὸ ἀκόλουθον τούτῳ γίνηται ὡς καθήκει.

A. D. 133 P. Ryl. 113 (96): τοῦ οὖν πράγματος δεομένου τῆς σῆς μειζοπονηρίας ἀξιῶ σε τὸν κύριον καὶ δικαιοκρίτην ἀκοῦσαί μου πρὸς αὐτούς.

A. D. 135 B. G. U. I 19 (30): γράφω σε ἵνα τὸ δόξαν κελεύσῃς γενέσθαι.

A. D. 144 B. G. U. III 729 (33): καθάπερ ἐγ δίκης ἀξιο.

A. D. 145 P. Tebt. II 325 (134): διὸ ἐπιδίδωμί σοι ἵνα τὸ ἀκόλουθον γένηται ὡς ἐπὶ τῶν ὁμοίων.

A. D. 184 P. Amh. II 78 (97): ἐπιδίδωμι καὶ ἀξιῶ αὐτὸν εἰς τὸ διακουσθῆναι.

A. D. 191 B. G. U. I 72 (86): διὸ ἀξιῶ τούτου τὸ ἴσον ἐν καταχωρισμῷ γενέσθαι πρὸς τὸν ἔτιόν μοι φανησόμενον.

A. D. 210 P. Flor. I 6 (22): ὅθεν ἀξιῶ τὸ παρὸν συνχωρηθῆναι.

A. D. 211 B. G. U. I 98 (118): περὶ τούτου ἀναγκαίως ἐπιδίδωμι καὶ ἀξιῶ ἐάν σοι δόξῃ κελεῦσαι αὐτὸν ἀχθῆναι ἐπὶ σὲ λόγον ἀποδώσοντα περὶ τούτου.

A. D. 216 B. G. U. I 159 (171): ἐπιδίδωμι καὶ ἀξιῶ ἀκοῦσαί μου πρὸς αὐτοὺς καὶ τὸ δοκοῦν σοι κελεύσῃς γενέσθαι.

A. D. 222 B. G. U. I 35 (51): ὅθεν ἐπιδίδωμι τάδε τὰ βιβλίδια καὶ ἀξιῶ ἐν καταχωρισμῷ γενέσθαι πρὸς τὸ μένιν μοι τὸν λόγον πρὸς τοὺς φανησομένους αἰτίους.

---

## 2. In Petitions.

The final phrase in petitions is frequently very extensive. It usually consists of a request that something be done, so that the petitioner may obtain justice. Among the opening formulas we have pointed out two phrases usually employed in petitions and in related documents, such as complaints and applications, namely: To B— χαίρειν A—; and: To B— from A—. The former is found during the Ptolemaic period only, the latter during both the Ptolemaic and the Roman periods. The former is addressed to the king or to high officials; and the final form corresponding to it frequently begins with δέομαι. The latter, addressed to minor officials at first, regularly begins with the verb ἀξιῶ. This custom is not always strictly observed.

The δέομαι or ἀξιῶ formula contains the request, either for direct action, or for the summoning of the persons interested. The anticipated outcome of the request is expressed either by a purpose clause: ἵνα μὴ ἀδικηθῶ ἀλλὰ τοῦ δικαίου τύχω, and similar phrasing; or by a conditional construction with the protasis expressed by a participle: τούτου δὲ γενομένου ἐσόμεθα τῆς παρὰ σοῦ βοηθείας τετευχότες. Like the other formulas, these also are subject to many changes, the theme remaining substantially the same.

The purpose clause continues in use throughout both the Ptolemaic and the Roman periods, though during the latter period an infinitive construction practically replaces it. The τούτου δὲ γενομένου phrase is found only during the Ptolemaic period, as far as we have observed. A common phrase during the Roman period is: (ἀχθῆναι) ἐπὶ σὲ πρὸς τὴν ἐσομένην ἐπέξοδον (τὴν δέουσαν ἐπέξοδον). In general there is a great freedom of phraseology, the writer evidently not feeling himself restricted to any set phrase.

---

### 3. Miscellaneous

A. D. 13 P. Oxy. IX 1188 (203): ὡς πρὸς σὲ τοῦ περὶ τῶν ἀγνοηθέντων ζητήματος ἐσομένου.

A. D. 13 ibidem: ὡς πρὸς ὑμᾶς τοῦ περὶ τῶν ἀγνοηθέντων λόγου συσταθησομένου.

A. D. 13 P. Oxy. IX 1188 (203): ὡς πρὸς σὲ τοῦ λόγου ἐσομένου.

A. D. 131 P. Tebt. II 374 (214): ὡς πρὸς σὲ τοῦ λόγου ὄντος.

A. D. 136 P. Ryl. 105 (82): ὡς πρὸς σὲ τοῦ λόγου ἐσομένου ἐάν τι παρὰ τὸ δέον γένηται.

A. D. 145 P. Tebt. II 325 (134): ὡς πρὸς σὲ τοῦ λόγου ἐσομένου ἐάν τι παράνομον γένηται.

A. D. 37 P. Fay. 29 (138): διὸ ἐπιδίδωμί σοι τὸ ὑπόμνημα ὅπως ταγῆι τούτου ὄνομα ἐν τῆι τῶν τετελευτηκότων τάξει κατὰ τὸ ἔθος.

A. D. 66 P. B. M. II 281 (65): διὸ ἐπιδίδωμι τὸ ὑπόμνημα ὅπως ἀνενεχθῇ ἐν [τοῖς] τετελευτηκόσι.

A. D. 138 P. B. M. II 208a: διὸ ἐπιδίδωμι ὅπως ταχθῇ ἐν τῇ τῶν τετελευτηκότων.

A. D. 138 B. G. U. I 111 (128): διὸ ἐπιδίδομεν τὸ τῆς ἐπιγενήσεως ὑπόμνημα.

also: A. D. 150 P. Fay. 28 (137); A. D. 156 P. Gen. 21 (44);

A. D. 158 P. Ryl. 106 (83): διὸ ἐπιδίδωμι ὅπως ταγῇ αὐτοῦ τὸ ὄνομα ἐν τῇ τῶν τετελευτηκότων τάξει.

A. D. 173 P. Fay. 30 (139): διὸ ἀξιῶ ταγῆναι αὐτοῦ τὸ ὄνομα ἐν τῇ τῶν τετελευτηκότων τάξει.

A. D. 170 P. B. M. II 338 (88): διὸ ἐπιδίδωμει καὶ ἀξιῶ ταγῆναι αὐτοῦ τὸ ὄνομα ἐν τῇ τῶν τετελευτηκότων τάξει.
A. D. 292 P. S. I. III 184 (41): διὸ τοῦτο ἀναγκαίως ἐπιδίδωμι τάδε τὰ βιβλίδια σημαίνων τὸ γεγονώς.

---

### 3. Miscellaneous Phrases.

Under this head we have arranged a few phrases which are found not infrequently in official letters. The first six phrases are used by officials in writing to their subordinates, placing on them the responsibility for the execution of certain tasks. The remaining phrases are employed by people informing the officials of the death of members of their household. The last quotation is used in an official report. Several other phrases might have been included under this head; but we have thought it best to confine ourselves to these few.

---

## B. THE ILLITERACY FORMULA.

B. C. Ptol. P. P. III 68 (194): Ἄμωτος τοῦ προγεγραμμένου συντάξαντος διὰ τὸ μὴ ἐπίστασθαι αὐτὸν γράμματα.
B. C. 136 P. Grenf. II 17 (34): ἔγραψεν Δρύτων Παμφίλου ὑπὲρ αὐτῶν διὰ τὸ φάσκειν αὐτοὺς μὴ εἰδέναι γράμματα.
B. C. 111 P. Rein. 11 (75): Θοᾶς Ἀπολλωνίου γέγραφα ὑπὲρ Ἐμσιγήσις τῆς προγεγραμμένης αὐτῆς μοι συνταξάσης διὰ τὸ μὴ εἰδέναι αὐτὴν γράμματα.
B. C. 74-44 P. Oxy. XIV 1639 (56): Ἀμμώνιος Σωσιπάτρου γέγραφα ὑπὲρ αὐτῶν ἀξιωθεὶς διὰ τὸ μὴ ἐπίστασθαι αὐτοὺς γράμματα.
B. C. 33 P. Ryl. 73 (21): ἔγραψεν ὑπὲρ αὐτῶν Δίδυμος κοινὸς γραμματεὺς ἀξιωθεὶς διὰ τὸ ἡμεῖν μὴ ἐπίστασθαι γράμματα.
A. D. 7 B. G. U. I 189 (198): ἔγραψεν ὑπὲρ αὐτοῦ Πανεφρύμις Στοθῆτος διὰ τὸ μὴ εἰδέναι αὐτὸν γράμματα.
A. D. 14-37 P. Ryl. 94 (62): Ἀφροδίσιος ὁ προγεγραμμένος ἔγραψα ὑπὲρ αὐτοῦ Ἡρακλήου διὰ τὸ μὴ εἰδέναι αὐτὸν γράμματα.

A. D. 15 P. B. M. II 256 (95); A. D. 16 P. Ryl. 183 (225); cp. also: A. D. 36 P. Oxy. II 267 (243); A. D. 127 P. Ryl. 122 (115);

A. D. 36 P. Oxy. II 267 (243): Θέων Παάητος γέγραφα ὑπὲρ αὐτοῦ μὴ εἰδότος γράμματα. (A. D. 45 P. Oxy. II 251 (203): γέγραφα ὑπὲρ αὐτῆς μὴ εἰδυίης γράμματα.)

cp. also: A. D. 54 P. Oxy. II 264 (234); A. D. 57 P. Oxy. II 269 (250); A. D. 90 P. Oxy. I 72 (135); A. D. 91 P. Flor. I 85 (168); A. D. 99 P. Fay. 100 (241); P. Oxy. III 481 (169); A. D. 98 cp. P. Iand. 26 (80); A. D. 102 P. Rein. 43 (139); A. D. 116 P. Tebt. II 309 (103); A. D. 120 P. Ryl. 168 (201); A. D. 124 P. Gen. 300 (36); A. D. 125 P. Amh. II 104 (132); A. D. 132 P. Oxy. III 478 (163); A. D. 135 P. Oxy. I 106 (173); A. D. 141 P. Tebt. II 372 (209); A. D. 142 P. Gen. 104 (41); A. D. 154 B. G. U. II 453 (112); A. D. 159 B. G. U. I 187 (196); A. D. 162 P. B. M. II 168 (190); A. D. 164 (196) B. G. U. II 648 (314); A. D. 167 P. Ryl. 120 (111); A. D. 178 P. Amh. II 71 (86); A. D. 179 P. Oxy. I 76 (139); A. D. 186 P. Oxy. III 716 (186); A. D. 187 P. Oxy. I 91 (153); B. G. U. III 842 (161); A. D. 190 P. Oxy. I 69 (129); A. D. 193 B. G. U. I 515 (162); A. D. 196 B. G. U. IV 1022 (12); P. Ryl. 169 (203); A. D. 215 P. Oxy. XII 1463 (187); A. D. 220 P. Leipz. 8 (26); A. D. 223 P. Oxy. I 77 (146); A. D. 238 P. Ryl. 100 (71); A. D. 246 P. Ryl. 177 (217); A .D. 249 P. Oxy. XIV. 1636 (42); A. D. 251 P. Gen. 50 (11); A. D. 255 P. Oxy. X 1277 (217); A. D. 265 P. Flor. 2 (5); A. D. 269 P. Ryl. 117 (103); A. D. 276 B. G. U. II 419 (80); A. D. 287 P. S. I. III 164 (17); C. P. H. 96, 9; A. D. 290 P. Grenf. II 72 (114); A. D. 3dc. P. Grenf. II 79 (125);

A. D. 187 B. G. U. I 92 (110): *ἔγραψα ὑπὲρ αὐτοῦ Νεικίας Ἰσιδώρου μὴ εἰδότος γράμματα.*

A. D. 289 B. G. U. I 13 (19) Spelling!: *Αὐρήλιος Ἀμμῶνις ἀπὸ χώρας Νεθειτῶν ἀξειοθεὶς ὑπαὶρ ἀτῶν γράματα μεὶ εἰδώτων ἔγραψα ὑπαὶρ ἀτῶν.*

A. D. 87 P. Hamb. 4 (16): *ἔγραψεν ὑπὲρ αὐτοῦ φαμένου μὴ εἰδέναι γράμματα (Ἰσίδωρος νομογράφος).*

cp. also: A. D. 129 P. Hamb. 6 (22);

A. D. 111 P. Fay. 36 (149): *Κάστωρ νομογράφος εἰκόνικα φαμένου μὴ εἰδέναι γράμματα.*

cp. also: A. D. 131 P. Hamb. 7 (24);

A. D. 156 P. Ryl. 88 (52): *ἐγράφη διὰ Ἀμμωνίου νομογράφου καί ἐστιν ὁ Διογᾶς φάμενος μὴ εἰδέναι γράμματα.*

A. D. 158 P. Fay. 24 (131): *ἐγράφη διὰ Σα—— νομογράφου ἐπακολοῦντος Διοδώρου ὑπηρέτου φαμένου μὴ εἰδέναι γράμματα.*

A. D. 187 B. G. U. III 842 (161): *Λούκιος Ἰσιδώρου ἔγραψα ὑπὲρ αὐτῶν φαμένων μὴ εἰδέναι γράμματα.*

A. D. 225 P. Oxy. VII 1040 (184): *Αὐρήλιος Πετρώνιος Μάρκου ἔγραψα ὑπὲρ αὐτῶν φαμένων μὴ εἰδέναι γράμματα.*

A. D. 297 P. Oxy. XII 1469 (200): *Αὐρήλιος Πλούτων ἔγραψα ὑπὲρ αὐτῶν ἀξιωθεὶς ὑπ' αὐτῶν φαμένων μὴ εἰδέναι γράμματα.*

also: A. D. 295 P. Oxy. VIII 1121 (211);

A. D. 3dc. C. P. H. 119 III, VI : ἔγραψα ὑπὲρ αὐτοῦ φάσκοντος μὴ εἰδέναι γράμματα.

A. D. 2dc. P. B. M. II 475 (102): Ὧρος ἔγραψα ὑπὲρ αὐτοῦ ἀγραμμάτου.

A. D. 156 B. G. U. I 171 (179): Ὡρίων ὁ καὶ Χαιρήμων ἔγραψα ὑπὲρ αὐτοῦ ἀγραμμάτου.

A. D. 186 B. G. U. I 39 (54): ἔγραψα ὑπὲρ αὐτοῦ ἀγραμμάτου.

also A. D. 265 P. Tebt. II 378 (221);

A. D. 189 B. G. U. I 118 (140): ἔγραψα καὶ ὑπὲρ αὐτῆς ἀγραμμάτου.

also: A. D. 2d-3dc. P. Iand. 35 (96);

A. D. 212 P. B. M. III 915 (26): Στοτοῆτις ἔγραψα καὶ ὑπὲρ τοῦ Ὥρου ἀγραμμάτου.

A. D. 239 P. Flor. I 21 (44): Αὐρήλιος Πρωτᾶς ἔγραψα ὑπὲρ αὐτῶν ἀγραμμάτων.

A. D. 306 B. G. U. II 606 (205): Αὐρήλιος Πωλίων ἔγραψα ὑπὲρ αὐτοῦ ἀγραμάτου (sic).

B. C. 27 B. G. U. II 543 (188): ἔγραψεν ὑπὲρ αὐτοῦ Ζήνων Ζήνωνος ἀξιωθεὶς διὰ τὸ βραδύτερα αὐτὸν γράφειν.

A. D. 16 P. Ryl. 183a (226): ἔγραψεν ὑπὲρ αὐτοῦ Μάρων γραμματεὺς αὐτοῦ διὰ τὸ βραδύτερον αὐτὸν γράφιν.

A. D. 2dc. P. Giss. I 29 (77): ἔγραψα ὑπὲρ τῆς Διδύμης τῆς καὶ Ματρώνας βραδέα γραφούσης.

A. D. 120 B. G. U. I 69 (83): ἔγραψα ὑπὲρ αὐτοῦ ἐρωτηθεὶς διὰ τὸ μὴ δύνασθαι ἐπέταξα αὐτὸν γράφιν αὐτοῦ γράφοντος τὸ ὄνομα.

A. D. 142 P. B. M. III 1132b (141): ἔγραψα τὸ σῶμα[αὐτοῦ τὸ ὄ]νομα ὑπογράφοντος.

A. D. 150 P. Fay. 28 (137): ἔγραψεν ὑπὲρ αὐτῶν Ἀμμώνιος νομογράφος.

A. D. 247 P. Grenf. II 68 (104): ἔγραψα ὑπὲρ αὐτοῦ Αὐρήλιος Φιλεῖνος ὁ καὶ Θεόγνωστος ἐρωτηθείς.

---

## B. The Illiteracy Formula.

The papyri discovered in Egypt have shown that the art of writing was more widely, and more popularly, known in the past, than some scholars had been inclined to think. It is remarkable, also, how well most letters are written. Though there are many peculiarities of spelling, these are to be attributed,—not to the individual writer as a rule, but to the custom prevailing at the time. For the Greek employed in these papyri, though in many respects very much like the Greek of the best period, had as a matter of course to admit many words and phrases which had come into use during the period; and the spelling also began to show a tendency toward certain changes which became incorporated in what is now known as modern Greek.

One of the reasons for this remarkable correctness of expression and spelling may be the employment of professional scribes. Not a few papyri have been found which were written in the same hand yet addressed by and to entirely different persons. In purely private letters the scribe or whoever wrote the letter did not need to declare that he, and not the person whose name was found on the document, was the writer. In official communications, however, and in contractual and business letters, such a declaration seems to have been required. As a consequence we have several documents, drawn up in epistolary style, containing this declaration.

In some instances this declaration is drawn up in the third person. More frequently, however, after giving his name, the scribe added in the first person the statement that he had written the document because of the unfamiliarity with, or the total ignorance of, writing on the part of the person for whom he wrote. The earlier forms use a prepositional infinitive construction: *διὰ τὸ μὴ εἰδέναι (ἐπίστασθαι) αὐτὸν γράμματα*. This formula remained in use as late as the second century A. D. But from the beginning of the Christian era the participial construction became far more common: *ἔγραψα ὑπὲρ αὐτοῦ μὴ εἰδότος γράμματα*. A combination of the two constructions is seen in the formula: *ἔγραψα ὑπὲρ αὐτοῦ φαμένου (φάσκοντος) μὴ εἰδέναι γράμματα*. To our knowledge, its first occurrence in the epistolary papyri is in P. Hamb. 4 (16) A. D. 87. During the second and the third centuries there occurs also the formula: *ἔγραψα ὑπὲρ αὐτοῦ ἀγραμμάτου*.

---

## C. THE OATH FORMULA.

B. C. 251 P. S. I. IV 361 (92): *ὀμνύω δὲ σοὶ τὸν βασιλέως δαίμονα καὶ τὸν Ἀρσινόης ἦ μὴν κτλ.*

B. C. Ptol. P. P. III 104 (249): *κεχειρογραφήκασι τὸν εἰθισμένον ὅρκον.*

B. C. 157 P. Grenf. I 11 (27)b: *ὀμόσαι ἐπὶ τοῦ κρονείου.*

B. C. 132 P. Amh. II 35 (42): *ὑπὲρ ὧν κεχειρογράφηκεν τὸν βασιλικὸν ὅρκον.*

B. C. 112 P. Tebt. I 22 (92): *ὀμνύομεν τοὺς Θεούς.*

B. C. 30-A. D. 1 P. Tebt. II 382 (228)a: *ὀμνύο (—ω) Καίσαραν Θεοῦ υἱὸν Αὐτοκράτορα εἶ μὴν κτλ.*

B. C. 27 B. G. U. II 543 (188): ὄμνυμι K. A. Θεοῦ υἱὸν εἶ μὴν κτλ. εὐορκοῦντι ἔστω μοι εὖ, ἐφιορκοῦντι δὲ ἐναντία.

A. D. 19 P. Oxy. II 253 (206): καὶ ὀμνύω Τιβέριον K. Σ. A. Θεοῦ Διὸς Ἐλευθερίου Σεβαστοῦ υἱὸν ἀληθῆ εἶναι τὰ προγεγραμμένα κτλ. εὐορκοῦντι μέμ μοι εὖ εἴη, ἐπιορκοῦντι δὲ τὰ ἐναντία.

A. D. 23 P. Oxy. II 259 (227): ὀμνύω Τιβέριον K. Νέον Σ. A. εἶ μὴν κτήσεσθαι κτλ., εὐορκοῦντι μέν μοι εὖ εἴη, ἐπιορκοῦντι δὲ τὰ ἐναντία.

A. D. 37 P. Oxy. II 240 (184): ὀμνύω Τιβέριον K. Νέον Σ. A. Θεοῦ Διὸς Ἐλευθερίου Σεβαστοῦ υἱὸν κτλ. εὐορκοῦντι κτλ.

A. D. 44 P. Oxy. II 251 (203): καὶ ὀμνύω Τιβέριον Κλαύδιον K. Σ. Γ. A. ἀληθῆ εἶναι τὰ προγεγραμμένα κτλ. εὐορκούσῃ μέν μοι εὖ εἴη, ἐπιορκούσῃ δὲ τὰ ἐναντία. (ὀμώμεκα τὸν προγεγραμμένον ὅρκον.)

cp. also A. D. 45 P. Oxy. X 1258 (178); A. D. 48 P. Oxy. II 255 (215);

A. D. 59 P. Oxy. II 260 (229): ὀμνύω Νέρωνα Κλαύδιον K. Σ. Γ. A. εἶ μὴν κτλ. εὐορκοῦντι μέν μοι κτλ.

A. D. 54-68 P. Amh. II 68 (75): ὑπὲρ ὧν καὶ ὀμνύομεν Νέρωνα Κλαύδιον K. Σ. Γ. A. εἶ μὴν ἐξ ὑγειοῦς καὶ ἐπὶ ἀληθείας κτλ. εὐορκοῦντι κτλ.

A. D. 61 P. Oxy. II 262 (232): καὶ ὀμνύωι Νέρωνα Κλαύδιον K. Σ. Γ. A. ἀληθῆ εἶναι.

also: A. D. 66 P. Oxy. II 246 (195)——μή ὑπεστάλθαι; 239 (183)——μηδεμίαν λογείαν γεγονέναι κτλ.

A. D. 77 P. Oxy. II 263 (232): ὀμνύω A. K. Οὐεσπασιανὸν Σ κτλ. εὐορκούσῃ κτλ.

A. D. 86 P. Oxy. II 258 (225): καὶ ὀμνύω A. K. Δομιτιανὸν Σ. Γ. ἀληθῆ εἶναι τὰ προγεγραμμένα.

A. D. 86 P. Oxy. VII 1028 (161): ὀμνύω A. K. Δομιτιανὸν Σ. Γ. μὴ ψεύσασθαι.

A. D. 87 P. Hamb. 4 (6): ὀμνύω A. K. Δομιτιανὸν Σ. Γ. εἶ μὴν κτλ. ———εἰ ἔνοχος εἴην τῷ ὅρκῳ.

cp. also A. D. 94-5 P. Oxy. II 257 (217);

A. D. 100 B. G. U. IV 1068 (106): Σωτελὴς Ἰωσήπου ὁ πρωγεγραμένος ὠμνύω A. K. Νετούα Τραιανὸν Σ.———

A. D. 105 P. Iand. 30 (89): ὀμνύομεν A. K. Νερούαν Τραιανὸν Σ. Γ. Δ. ἑκουσίως καὶ αὐθαιρέτως ἐγγυᾶσθαι κτλ.

A. D. 107 P. Oxy. VII 1029 (163): καὶ ὀμνύομεν A. K. Νερούαν Τραιανὸν Σ. Γ. Δ. ἐξ ὑγιοῦς καὶ ἐπ' ἀληθείας ἐπιδεδωκέναι κτλ. ——ἢ ἔνοχοι εἴημεν τῷ ὅρκῳ.

A. D. 108 P. Oxy. III 483 (172): καὶ ὀμνύω θεοὺς Σεβαστοὺς καὶ τὴν A. K. Νερούα Τραιανοῦ Σ. Γ. Δ. τύχην καὶ τοὺς πατρῴους θεούς.

A. D. 109 P. Oxy. III 482 (170): ὀμνύω Α. Κ. Νερούαν Τραιανὸν Σ. Γ. Δ. μὴ ἐψεῦσθαι.
A. D. 110-111 P. Ryl. 108 (85): ὀμνύομεν τὴν Α. Κ. Νερούα Τραιανοῦ Σ. Γ. Δ. τύχην ἀληθῶς ἐπιδεδωκέναι καὶ μὴ ἐψεῦσθαι. εὐορκοῦσι μὲν ἡμεῖν εὖ εἴη ἐπιορκοῦσι δὲ τὰ ἐναντία.
A. D. 113 P. Ryl. 82 (43): ὀμνύωμεν τὴν Α. Κ. Νερούα Τραιανοῦ Σ. Γ. Δ. τύχην κτλ. ἢ ἔνωχοι εἴημεν τῶι ὅρκωι.
A. D. 116 P. Oxy. I 74 (137): καὶ ὀμνύω Α. Κ. Νερούαν Τραιανὸν Ἄριστον Σ. Γ. Δ. μὴ ἐψεῦσθαι.
A. D. 118 P. Giss. II 43 (54): καὶ ὀμνύω τὴν Α. Κ. Τραιανοῦ Ἁδριανοῦ Σ. τύχην ἐξ ὑγίους καὶ ἐπ' ἀληθείας ἐπιδεδωκέναι κτλ. ἢ ἔνοχος εἴην τῶι ὅρκωι.
A. D. 117 P. Flor. III 326 (61): ὀμνύομεν τὴν Α. Κ. Τραιανοῦ Ἁδριανοῦ Ἀρίστου Σ. Γ. Δ. Παρθικοῦ τύχην κτλ. ἢ ἔνοχοι εἴημεν τῷ ὅρκωι.
A. D. 119 P. Oxy. XII 1547 (279): ὀμνύω Α. Κ. Τραιανὸν Ἁδριανὸν Σ. ἐξ ὑγιοῦς καὶ ἀληθείας ἐπιδεδωκέναι.
A. D. 123 B. G. U. I 250 (249): προσεφώνησα ὀμνύων τὴν Α. Σ. Τραιανοῦ Ἁδριανοῦ Σ. τύχην.
A. D.' 129 P. Oxy. I 75 (138): καὶ ὀμνύω Α. Κ. Τραιανὸν Ἁδριανὸν Σ. μὴ ἐψεῦσθαι.
A. D. 130 B. G. U. II 647 (312): ὀμνύντες τὴν Α. Κ. Τραιανοῦ Ἁδριανοῦ Σ. τύχην κτλ. ἢ ἔνοχοι εἴημεν τῷ ὅρκῳ.
A. D. 131 P. Hamb. 7 (24): καὶ ὀμνύω μὲν τὴν Α. Κ. Τραιανοῦ Ἁδριανοῦ Σ. τύχην ἀληθῆ εἶναι τὰ προγεγραμμένα.
A. D. 132 P. Oxy. III 478 (163): καὶ ὀμνύω Α. Κ. Τραιανὸν Ἁδριανὸν Σ. ἀληθῆ εἶναι τὰ προγεγραμμένα.
A. D. 132 P. Oxy. III 480 (168): καὶ ὀμνύο Α. Κ. Τραιανὸν Ἁδριανὸν Σ. κτλ. ἢ ἔνοχος εἴην τῷ ὅρκῳ.
cp. also: A. D. 135 P. Oxy. IX 1195 (216);
A. D. 131 P. Oxy. IV 715 (184): καὶ ὀμνύομεν τὴν Α. Κ. Τραιανοῦ Ἁδριανοῦ τύχην καὶ τοὺς πατρῴους θεοὺς ἐξ ὑγείας καὶ ἐπ' ἀληθείας ἐπιδεδωκέναι τὴν προκιμένην ἀπογραφὴν καὶ μηδὲν διεψεῦσθαι ἢ ἔνοχοι εἴημεν τῶι ὅρκωι.
A. D. 133 P. Oxy. I 100 (163): ὀμνύω τὸν Ῥωμαίοις ἔθιμον ὅρκον κτλ.
A. D. 142 B. G. U. I 17 (27): καὶ ὀμνύω τὴν Α. Κ. Τίτου Αἰλίου Ἁδριανοῦ Ἀντωνίνου Σ. Ε. τύχην ἀληθῆ εἶναι τὰ προγεγραμμένα.
A. D. 150 P. Oxy. IX 1198 (220): καὶ ὀμνύω Α. Κ. Τίτον Αἴλιον Ἁδριανὸν Ἀντωνεῖνον Σ. Ε. ἀληθῆ εἶναι τὰ προγεγραμμένα καὶ μηδὲν διεψεῦσθαι ἢ ἔνοχος εἴην τῷ ὅρκῳ.
A. D. 151 P. Tebt. II 300 (85): καὶ ὀμνοίω τὴν Ἀντωνίνου Κ. τ. κ. τύχην.

A. D. 156 P. Ryl. 88 (52): *καὶ ὀμνύω τὴν Ἀντωνίνου Κ. τ. κ. τύχην κτλ. ἦ ἔνοχος εἴην τῷ ὅρκῳ.*

A. D. 158 P. Fay. 24 (131): *ὀμνύω τὴν Α. Κ. Ἀδριανοῦ Ἀντωνίνου Σ. τύχην.*

A. D. 160 P. B. M. III 915 (26): *καὶ ὀμνύω τὴν τ. κ. Α. Κ. Τίτου Αἰλίου Ἀδριανοῦ Ἀντωνίνου Σ. Ε. τύχην ἀληθῆ εἶναι τὰ προ[κείμενα.]*

A. D. 160 B. G. U. I 16 (27): *προσφωνοῦμεν ὀμνύοντες τὴν Α. Κ. Τίτου Αἰλίου Ἀδριανοῦ Ἀντωνείνου Σ. Ε. τύχην*

A. D. 161 P. Meyer 4 (18): *ὀμνύοντες τὴν Α. Κ. Μάρκου Αὐρηλίου Ἀντωνίνου Σ. τύχην καὶ τὴν Α. Κ. Λουκίου Αὐρηλίου Οὐήρου Σ. τύχην κτλ. ἦ ἔνοχοι εἴημεν τῷ ὅρκωι.*

A. D. 178 P. Amh. II 71 (86): *ὀμνύω τὴν Αὐρηλίων Ἀντωνίνου καὶ Κομμόδου Κων τῶν κυρίων τύχην οὕτως ἔχειν.*

A. D. 180-192 P. Strassb. 34 (122): *καὶ ὀμνύω τὴν Αὐρηλίου Κομμόδου Ἀντωνίνου Κ. τ. κ. τύχην καὶ τὸν θεὸν μέγιστον Ὀσειραντίνοον ἀληθῆ εἶναι τὰ προγεγραμμένα.*

A. D. 181-192 P. Oxy. I 79 (142): *ὀμνύω Α. Κ. Μάρκον Αὐρήλιον Κόμοδον Ἀντωνῖνον Σ. ἀληθῆ εἶναι τὰ προγεγραμμένα.*

A. D. 187 B. G. U. II 649 (314): *ὀμνύω τὴν Μάρκου Αὐρηλίου Κομμόδου Ἀντωνίνου Κ. τ.κ. τύχην κτλ.*

A. D. 187 P. Tebt. II 293 (61): *προσφωνοῦμεν ὀμνύοντες τὴν Μάρκου Αὐρηλίου Κομμόδου Ἀντωνίνου Σ. τύχην κτλ. ἦ ἔνοχοι εἴημεν τῷ ὅρκῳ. ὤμοσα τὸν προκείμενον ὅρκον καθῶς πρόκειται.*

A. D. 187 B. G. U. I 92 (110): *προσφωνῶ ὀμνύων τὴν Μάρκου Αὐρηλίου Κομμόδου Ἀντωνίνου Κ. τ. κ. τύχην κτλ. παραστήσω ἤνοχος εἶναι τῷ ὅρκῳ.*

A. D. 3dc. P. Grenf. II 79 (125): *ὀμνὺς τὴν τῶν δεσποτῶν ἡμῶν Αων Σῶν τύχην.*

A. D. 202 P. Oxy. XII 1548 (271): *καὶ ὀμνύω τὴν Λουκίου Σεπτιμίου Σεουήρου Ε. Περτίνακος καὶ Μάρκου Αὐρηλίου Ἀντωνίνου Ε. Σῶν καὶ Πουβλίου* ——.

A. D. 203 P. Oxy. VIII 1113 (189): *καὶ ὀμνύω τὴν Λουκίου Σεπτιμίου Σεουήρου Ε. Περτίνακος καὶ Μάρκου Αὐρηλίου Ἀντωνίνου Ε. Σῶν τύχην καὶ Πουβλίου Σεπτιμίου Γέτα Κ. Σ. μὴ ἐψεῦσθαι.*

A. D. 210-12 P. Oxy. IX 1196 (217): *ὀμνύω τὴν τ. κ. Α. Μάρκου Αὐρηλίου Σεουήρου Ἀντωνίνου Ε. Σ. τύχην κτλ.*

A. D. 3dc. P. Hawara (Archiv V p. 399): *ὀμνύω τὴν Μάρκου Αὐρηλίου Σεουήρου Ἀντωνίνου Παρθικοῦ Μ. Βρεταννικοῦ Μ. Ε. Σ. τύχην ἑκουσίως καὶ αὐθαιρέτως ἐγγυᾶσθαι.*

A. D. 211 P. Grenf. II 62 (97): *ὀμνύω τὴν Λουκίου Σεπτιμίου Σεουήρου Περτίνακος καὶ Μάρκου Αὐρηλίου Ἀντωνίνου καὶ Πουβλίου Σεπτιμίου Γέτα Βρεντανικῶν Μων Εῶν Σῶν τύχην κτλ. ἶ(— εἶ —ῇ) ἔνοχος ἴην τῷ ὅρκῳ.*
A. D. 212 P. Oxy. VII 1030 (165): *καὶ ὀμνύω τὴν τ. κ. Μάρκου Αὐρηλίου Σεουήρου Ἀντωνίνου τύχην μὴ ἐψεῦσθαι.*
A. D. 216 P. B. M. III 935 (29): *καὶ ὀμνύω τὴν Αὐρηλίου Σεουήρου Ἀντωνίνου Κ. τ. κ. τύχην οὕτως ἔχειν.*
A. D. 220 P. Leipz. 8 (20): *καὶ ὀμνύω τὴν Μάρκου Ἀντωνίνου Κ. τ. κ. τύχην οὕτως ἔχειν.*
A. D. 223 P. Oxy. I 77 (140): *ὀμνύω τὴν Μάρκου Αὐρηλίου Σεουήρου Ἀλεξάνδρου Κ. τ. κ. τύχην κτλ. καὶ μηδὲν διεψεῦσθαι.*
A. D. 225 P. Hamb. 19 (82): *καὶ ὀμνύω τὴν Μάρκου Αὐρηλίου Σεουήρου Ἀλεξάνδρου Ε. Ε. Σ. τύχην μὴ ἐψεῦσθαι.*
A. D. 228 P. Oxy. VII 1031 (167): *καὶ ὀμνύω τὴν Μάρκου Αὐρηλίου Σεουήρου Ἀλεξάνδρου Κ. τ. κ. τύχην μὴ ἐψεῦσθαι.*
A. D. 235 P. Ryl. 109 (87): *ὀμνύομεν τὴν τ. κ. ἡμῶν Α. Κ. Γαίου Ἰουλίου Οὐήρου Μαξιμείνου Ε. Ε. Σ. τύχην κτλ.*
A. D. 238-244 P. Oxy. I 80 (143): *ὀμνύω τὴν Μάρκου Ἀντωνίου Γορδειανοῦ Κ. τ. κ. τύχην κτλ.*
A. D. 243 P. Flor. I 4 (18): *καὶ ὀμνύομεν τὸν ἔθιμον Ῥωμαίοις ὅρκον μὴ ἐψεῦσθαι.*
A. D. 244 P. Oxy. I 81 (144): *ὀμνύω τὴν Μάρκου Ἰουλίου Φιλίππου Κ. τ. κ. τύχην κτλ.*
A. D. 246 P. Amh. II 72 (87): *καὶ ὀμνύω τὴν Μάρκων Ἰουλίων Φιλίππων Κων τῶν κυρίων Σῶν τύχην οὕτως ἔχειν.*
A. D. 256 P. Leipz. 3 (9): *καὶ ὀμνύω τὴν τῶν κυρίων Οὐαλεριανοῦ καὶ Γαλλιηνοῦ καὶ Κορνηλίου Οὐαλεριανοῦ Σῶν τύχην οὕτως ἔχειν.*
A. D. 259 P. Ryl. 110 (88): *καὶ ὀμνύω τὴν τῶν κυρίων ἡμῶν Οὐαλεριανῶν καὶ Γαλλιηνοῦ Σῶν τύχην μηδὲν καταλελοιπέναι.*
A. D. 260 P. Oxy. XII 1555 (273): *ὀμνύω τὴν τῶν μυρίων ἡμῶν Μακριανοῦ καὶ Κυήτου Σῶν τύχην. κτλ.*
A. D. 272 P. Oxy. X 1264 (187): *καὶ ὀμνύω τὸν ἔθιμον Ῥωμαίοις ὅρκον μὴ ἐψεῦσθαι.*
also: A. D. 287 P. S. I. III 164 (17);
A. D. 275 P. Oxy. XII 1455 (172): *ὀμνύω τὴν τοῦ κυρίου ἡμῶν Αὐρηλιανοῦ Σ. τύχην κτλ. ἢ ἔνοχος εἴην τῷ ὅρκῳ.*
A. D. 275 P. Oxy. XII 1456 (173): *ὀμνύω τὴν τ. κ. ἡμῶν Γαίου Οὐαλερίου Διοκλητιανοῦ Κ. Σ. τύχην.*
A. D. 286 P. S. I. III 162 (15): *ὀμνύω τὴν τῶν κυρίων ἡμῶν Γαίου Αὐρηλίου Οὐαλερίου Διοκλητιανοῦ καὶ Μάρκου Αὐρηλίου Οὐαλερίου Μαξιμιανοῦ Κων Σῶν τύχην κτλ. ἢ ἔνοχος εἴην τῷ ὅρκῳ.*

A. D. 292 P. Oxy. X 1255 (172): *κατὰ τοῦτο ὁμολογοῦμεν ὀμνύντες τὴν τῶν κυρίων ἡμῶν Διοκλητιανοῦ καὶ Μαξιμιανοῦ Σῶν τύχην κτλ.*

A. D. 298 P. Flor. I 32 (60): *καὶ ἐξόμνυμι τὴν τῶν κυρίων ἡμῶν Διοκλητιανοῦ καὶ Μαξιμιανοῦ Σῶν καὶ Κωνσταντίου καὶ Μαξιμιανοῦ τῶν ἐπιφανεστάτων Κων τύχην κτλ. εἰ δὲ μὴ ἔσομαι ὑπεύθυνος τῷ σεβασμιῷ ὅρκῳ.*

---

## C. The Oath Formula.

Many of the official letters are sworn declarations. These declarations were needed for certain official statements, especially in apographai, surety cases, and others. These oath formulas we thought it well to quote somewhat extensively, since they employ the same titular formulas which we have seen in the dates. It is not our intention to discuss these formulas in detail. They remain the same in substance throughout, the oath being sworn either by the name of the emperor himself, or by his *τύχην*. We have noticed no striking differences in the titles applied to the rulers. These oath formulas ought to be read in connection with the date formulas quoted above.

# V. CONCLUSION.

In the preceding pages we have gathered various formulas employed in Greek epistolography, and have discussed them briefly. It may be well before closing this monograph, to sum up in a few words the principal conclusions which we have reached.

The numerous papyri now extant do not furnish us with proof regarding the origin, and the early development, of practically any of the formulas employed. The earliest papyri we have exhibit these formulas in fully developed form. On account of the small number of papyri belonging to the first century B. C. we are unable, at least now, to trace the history of several formulas which were in use at the beginning of the Christian era.

Throughout the entire period covered by our investigation there is a remarkable similarity in the formulas employed. Their phraseology remains substantially the same. Yet so great is the variety in detail, that hardly any two forms are quite alike.

The opening formulas of the Greek letters have been grouped according to the nature of the letters in which they are found. In familiar letters, as well as in business letters and in official communications, the formula A— to B— *χαίρειν* prevails. In petitions addressed to the rulers of Egypt in Ptolemaic days, and to the higher officials, the formula To B— *χαίρειν* A— is employed. In other petitions, in applications, and in similar documents, the regular formula is To B— from A—.

The formula A— to B— *χαίρειν* is used not only by superiors when writing to their inferiors, but also by the latter when addressing their superiors. Children use it when writing to their parents, and servants in writing to their masters. A later formula in which the relative position of the names is reversed: To B— A— *χαίρειν* is used in the same way. This later formula did not succeed in supplanting the former.

The familiar relationship existing between the writer and his correspondent was frequently expressed by the addition of appropriate words to the opening formula. This practice is not confined to familiar letters, but is observed also in official letters, though less frequently. Not all these additions occur with the same frequency; and in many familiar letters they are not found at all.

Many business letters are not letters in the strict sense of the word, but are in reality commercial documents drawn up in epistolary form. These letters frequently introduce into the opening formula much detail for the purpose of identifying both the writer and his correspondent. For this reason the various names are given by which the writer and his correspondent are known, as well as the names of parents, husband, guardians, etc.

The basic formula A— to B— *χαίρειν* at times unites with the *ἐρρῶσθαι* wish or the *ὑγιαίνειν* wish to form the extended formula A— to B— *χαίρειν καὶ ἐρρῶσθαι, χαίρειν καὶ (διὰ παντὸς) ὑγιαίνειν*. The former occurs during the Ptolemaic period, the latter during the Roman period.

The formula To B— from A—, whether used in petitions or in business letters, also admits much detail for the purpose of closer identification. The word *ὑπόμνημα*, occasionally found prefixed to this formula, may, or may not, be part of it. If it did belong to the formula, its primary meaning was mostly lost sight of.

There is no need of confining the formula To B— *χαίρειν* A— to petitions belonging to the early part of the third century B. C. Its correct punctuation, namely after the nominative, can no longer be questioned. In many cases it would be impossible to construe the first sentence of the petition, if the period were placed after *χαίρειν*.

Several abbreviations of the main opening formulas occur. Various reasons have been assigned for their occurrence. They may be due to the influence of the ostraca, or to the fancy of the writer. For hurried and less important messages such brief forms may have been quite satisfactory.

The apostrophic formulas **Χαίροις**, **Χαῖρε**, were not necessarily employed by the uneducated. While we do not vouch for any explanation in their regard, we bear in mind that the writer was at liberty to use a less formal mode of address if he chose to do so.

Familiar letters having the opening formula A— to B— *χαίρειν* are followed by the closing formula *ἔρρωσο* or one of its modifications. Most official letters use the same final salutation. Business letters also use it, but less frequently; they are often without any special closing formula.

The opening formula To B— *χαίνειν* A— is always followed by the closing formula *εὐτύχει*. The formula To B— from A—, when used in petitions and similar documents, is followed by εὐτύχει, which during the Christian era is gradually supplanted by διευτύχει. In other documents this opening phrase is without final salutation.

The form ἔρρωσο is used throughout the period under discussion; but its expanded form ἐρρῶσθαί σε εὔχομαι is used much more commonly during the second and third centuries A. D.

The reversed formula To B— A—, lacks the closing phrase. When the greeting is attached to this opening formula, thus giving: To B— A— χαίρειν, the closing phrase is also expressed: ἐρρῶσθαί σε εὔχομαι. The final greeting is frequently lacking in the abbreviated formulas.

The closing phrases are greatly varied by the addition of terms of familiarity. Practically all of these extended closing phrases belong to the second and third centuries A. D.

In the dating formulas the development from the simple form to the more elaborate expressions can be traced with comparative ease. During the Ptolemaic period the dating formulas were rather vague, indicating year and month, sometimes day, of a certain reign without properly qualifying the king so that he might easily be identified. Both the Macedonian and the Egyptian calendars were in use, the names of the months being taken from either one, at times from both in the same formula. In Roman days the names of the months were those of certain emperors. But the Egyptian names prevailed throughout the period under discussion.

During the Ptolemaic period, and down to the accession of Augustus, the dating formulas remain very much the same. Henceforth the titles of the reigning emperors are added, making the formulas at times quite elaborate and formal.

The different kinds of letters employ the same dating formulas. In familiar letters, however, and in letters of a similar type, the elaborate dating formulas occur but rarely.

The dating formulas are given ordinarily at the end of the letters . If dates are quoted within the body of a letter, the formulas are practically reversed. To the names of deceased emperors the title θεός is added; but at times they are mentioned unceremoniously by name only.

Of the two groups of conventional phrases within the body of the letter one belongs almost exclusively to familiar letters. It comprises the ἐρρῶσθαι wish, the ὑγιαίνειν wish, and the ἀσπάσασθαι wish, with a few miscellaneous phrases. Their origin is lost in the past. They, too, are fully developed in the earliest papyri now extant and admit of so great a variety of detail that hardly any two forms are quite alike. The ἐρρῶσθαι wish belongs to the Ptolemaic period. During the later part of this period it is found in conjunction with the opening formula. The ὑγιαίνειν wish, according to papyrological evidence, belongs to the Roman period; but its history can not be traced. The combination of the opening formula and the ὑγιαίνειν wish antedates in the papyri the simple form. The ὑγιαίνειν wish frequently appears in connection with the proscynesis. In it, also, there is great variety of detail. The ἀσπάσασθαι wish seems to be the final phrase transposed to the beginning of the letter. The proscynesis is found with it also.

The ἐπιμέλου clause at the end of letters belongs to the Ptolemaic period. It is frequently found in letters that have the ἐρρῶσθαι wish at the beginning. The verb is changed at times to the participial form, which then depends on another expressed verb, or on the closing formula.

During the Roman period it was a common custom to add greetings at the end of letters. These ἀσπάσασθαι phrases appear in various forms. At times an accumulation of such phrases is found in one and the same letter. This custom was noted before in the Pauline epistles.

The final phrase in petitions is frequently very extensive. In petitions beginning with the formula To B— χαίνειν A— the final phrase usually begins with δέομαι. In other petitions the verb ἀξιῶ is used. The anticipated effect of the petition is expressed by a purpose clause, or by a conditional clause, with the protasis expressed by a genitive absolute. Like the other phrases, they too are subject to many minor changes, the general theme remaining the same.

The purpose clause in these final phrases continues in use during the entire period under discussion, though during the latter part an infinitive construction practically replaces it. The conditional clause is found only during the Ptolemaic period. A common phrase during the Roman period is: (ἀχθῆναι) ἐπὶ σὲ πρὸς τὴν ἐσομένην (δέουσαν) ἐπέξοδον.

The illiteracy formula curiously reflects on the ability of the common people to practice the art of writing. The remarkable correctness of spelling and expression in most letters may be due to the professional scribes employed. In other than familiar letters a declaration was attached regarding the identity of the scribe. This declaration is drawn up at times in the third person, at times in the first person. The earlier forms use a prepositional infinitive construction in the illiteracy formula, which remained in use as late as the second century A. D. From the beginning of the Christian era the participial construction became much more common. A combination of the two constructions is seen in the formula: *ἔγραψα ὑπὲρ αὐτοῦ φαμένου (φάσκοντος) μὴ εἰδέναι γράμματα*. During the second and the third centuries there occurred also the formula: *ἔγραψα ὑπὲρ αὐτοῦ ἀγραμμάτου*.

The oath formulas furnish interesting material for a comparison with the dating formulas. They ,too, remain in substance the same, the oath being sworn by the name of the emperor or by his *τύχην*.

# GENERAL INDEX

## VITA

Francis Xavier J. Exler was born at Winssen, Netherlands, November 30, 1891. He received his elementary education in the parish schools, and his classical training in the preparatory seminary of the archdiocese of Utrecht and in the Latin School of Gemert. He entered the Order of the Canons Regular of Premontré at St. Norbert's Priory, West Depere, Wis., on August 28, 1909. He took his simple vows on August 28, 1911, and made his solemn profession on August 28, 1914. He was raised to the priesthood on October 17, 1914. Until June 1918 he was instructor in Greek and Latin at St. Norbert's College. He entered the United States Army and was commissioned a Chaplain with station in the Philippine Islands. Upon his discharge from the army in July 1919 he resumed his teaching at St. Norbert's College. In September 1920 he entered the Catholic University of America, where, in June 1921, he received the degree of M.A. During his course at the University he attended the lectures of Roy Joseph Deferrari, M.A., Ph.D., in Greek, Latin, and Sanskrit Languages and Literature; of the Rev. J. P. Christopher, M.A., in Latin; of J. M. Campbell, M.A., in Greek; of the Rev. A. A. Vaschalde, S.T.L., Ph. D., in Arabic; and of the Rev. R. Butin, S.M., S.T.L., Ph.D., in Hebrew and in Aramaic.

www.ingramcontent.com/pod-product-compliance
Lightning Source LLC
LaVergne TN
LVHW020635100826
845148LV00012B/2187
* 9 7 8 1 5 9 2 4 4 2 1 5 7 *